Inclusive Commons Sustainability of Peas Communities in the N Low Countries

Is inclusiveness in the commons and sustainability a paradox? Late medieval and Early Modern rural societies encountered ever-growing challenges because of growing population pressure, urbanisation and commercialisation. While some regions went along this path and commercialised and intensified production, others sailed a different course, maintaining communal property and managing resources via common pool resource institutions. To prevent overexploitation and free riding, it was generally believed that strong formalised institutions, strict access regimes and restricted use rights were essential.

By looking at the late medieval Campine area, a sandy, infertile and fragile region, dominated by communal property and located at the core of the densely populated and commercialised Low Countries, it has become clear that sustainability, economic success and inclusiveness can be compatible. Because of a balanced distribution of power between smallholders and elites, strong property claims, a predominance of long-term agricultural strategies and the vitality of informal institutions and conflict resolution mechanisms, the Campine peasant communities were able to avert ecological distress while maintaining a positive economic climate.

Maïka De Keyzer is a historian affiliated with the Department of History and Art History at Utrecht University, working within the ERC project "Coordinating for Life."

Rural Worlds: Economic, Social and Cultural Histories of Agricultures and Rural Societies

Series Editor: Richard W. Hoyle *(University of Reading, UK)*

Series Advisory Board: Paul Brassley *(University of Exeter, UK)*, R. Douglas Hurt *(Purdue University, USA)*, Leen Van Molle *(KU Leuven, Belgium)*, Mats Morell *(Stockholm University, Sweden)*, Phillipp Schofield *(Aberystwyth University, UK)*, Nicola Verdon *(Sheffield Hallam University, UK)*, and Paul Warde *(University of East Anglia, UK)*

We like to forget that agriculture is one of the core human activities. In historic societies most people lived in the countryside: a high, if falling proportion of the population were engaged in the production and processing of foodstuffs. The possession of land was a key form of wealth: It brought not only income from tenants but prestige, access to a rural lifestyle and often political power. Nor could government ever be disinterested in the countryside, whether to maintain urban food supply, as a source of taxation, or to maintain social peace. Increasingly it managed every aspect of the countryside. Agriculture itself and the social relations within the countryside were in constant flux as farmers reacted to new or changing opportunities, and landlords sought to maintain or increase their incomes. Moreover, urban attitudes to the landscape and its inhabitants were constantly shifting.

These questions of competition and change, production, power and perception are the primary themes of the series. It looks at change and competition in the countryside: social relations within it and between urban and rural societies. The series offers a forum for the publication of the best work on all of these issues, straddling the economic, social and cultural, concentrating on the rural history of Britain and Ireland, Europe and its colonial empires, and North America over the past millennium.

Transforming the Countryside
The Electrification of Rural Britain
Edited by Paul Brassley, Jeremy Burchardt, and Karen Sayer

Rockites, Magistrates and Parliamentarians
Governance and Disturbances in Pre-Famine Rural Munster
Shunsuke Katsuta

Inclusive Commons and the Sustainability of Peasant
Communities in the Medieval Low Countries
Maïka De Keyzer

For more information about this series, please visit: www.routledge.com/history/series/RW

Inclusive Commons and the Sustainability of Peasant Communities in the Medieval Low Countries

Maïka De Keyzer

Routledge
Taylor & Francis Group

NEW YORK AND LONDON

First published 2018
by Routledge
605 Third Avenue, New York, NY 10017

and by Routledge
2 Park Square, Milton Park, Abingdon, Oxon OX14 4RN

First issued in paperback 2022

Routledge is an imprint of the Taylor & Francis Group, an informa business

© 2018 Taylor & Francis

Publisher's Note
The publisher has gone to great lengths to ensure the quality of this
reprint but points out that some imperfections in the original copies
may be apparent.

Library of Congress Cataloging-in-Publication Data
A catalog record for this book has been requested

ISBN 13: 978-1-03-240193-5 (pbk)
ISBN 13: 978-1-138-05404-2 (hbk)
ISBN 13: 978-1-315-16706-0 (ebk)

DOI: 10.4324/9781315167060

Typeset in Sabon
by Apex CoVantage, LLC

To my parents and grandmother

Contents

Figures

Tables

Abbreviations

BP   Before Present
CPI   Common Pool institution
CPR   Common Pool Resource
Ha   Hectare
Kg   Kilogramme
OSL   Optically Stimulated Luminescence

Measurements

1 hectare = 2.47 acre
1 square kilometre = 247 acre
1 kg = 2.2 pound
1 viertel = 79.6 litre of rye

Money
1 pond = 20 schellingen
1 schelling = 12 denier/penningen
1 gulden = 20 stuiver
1 stuiver = 2 groten
In the 1550s one viertel (or 79.6 litre) of rye could be bought for 71 groten.

Acknowledgements

I have a lot of people to thank. First, I want to thank Tim Soens for giving me the opportunity to start my academic career and guiding me through the process of writing this book. The history department of the University of Antwerp, with its environmental and rural history group, was the most supportive and fruitful place to explore the success and sustainability of pre-modern commons. I want to thank Eline Van Onacker in particular as my companion de route, who has explored the Campine past with me and has read and improved all of my work for the last couple of years. Many thanks to Bas van Bavel, for providing the stimulating environment for my postdoc position, which has greatly influenced this book in the revision stage. For this entire endeavour, I have to gratefully acknowledge the financial support offered by the FWO and ERC (Coordinating for Life Project). My gratitude also goes to the editors of Routledge and the Rural World series and the anonymous reviewers. Their instructive comments have greatly improved this book and made the publication possible. Finally, I want to thank my parents, grandmother and husband for their endless support.

Parts of this book were originally published as Maïka De Keyzer, "All we are is dust in the wind: 'The social causes of a "subculture of coping' in the late medieval coversand belt", *Journal for the History of Environment and Society*, vol. 1 (2016), pp. 1–35.

1 The Dominance of Exclusive Commons
An Exploration and Re-evaluation

Is it ever possible to reconcile inclusive access to commons and their long-term sustainability? Inclusive access to commons is not to be confused with open access, a situation that has been considered to be destructive of commons wherever it occurs, regardless of the size of the communal resources. In this book inclusive access refers to common pool institutions (CPI) that were open to all or most members of the society in which the institution operated. The danger that every pre-industrial society faced was the overexploitation of the ecosystem through its mismanagement, whereby vital resources were ruined for future generations. All societies have had to devise and adopt management strategies which would avoid scenarios leading to overexploitation. Overexploitation was a particular danger in late medieval and early modern northwestern Europe, one of the most densely populated and developed regions in the world.

While many early modern societies opted for private property as the means to avoid overexploitation, others chose to manage their natural resources in a communal way. Communal property, however, had to confront the problem of overexploitation and free riding: it is difficult, but not impossible, to exclude users from taking resources to which they are not entitled especially because of population growth and increasing commercialisation during the late medieval and early modern period. Excessive pressure on the commons, and especially the heathland commons studied in this book, could lead to what Garrett Hardin has called 'a tragedy of the commons'. This would involve the loss of plant cover, the appearance of purple heather fields in place of diverse green heathlands and ultimately exposed soil, drifting sand and the formation of sand dunes. A growing exclusivity of access to communal resources has often been put forward as the most efficient response to growing pressure on the scarce resources. Nevertheless, not all societies have followed the path of excluding groups such as immigrants and landless households from the commons. Where the choice was made to be inclusive, were these societies able to manage their natural resources sustainably in the long run, or was a degradation of the soil and depletion of resources inevitable? And if sustainability was possible, how did a society that managed its resources collectively have to be designed, in order to prevent 'a tragedy of the commons'?

Historiography

During the last two decades commons have conquered the academic world. As our quest for a more sustainable economy has developed, and traditional prescriptions based on private property and/or state intervention have been found wanting, sociologists, economists, anthropologists and (even) historians have turned their attention towards the commons.[1] After all, it is now some 50 years since Hardin's pessimistic paper on the 'Tragedy of the Commons', was published and we are now able to look at commons without accepting his suppositions.[2] Hardin's thesis was that freedom of access to the commons would bring ruin to all. When extractors were not restricted either in terms of their numbers, or in the way in which they could exploit a common, the degradation of the commons would inevitably follow. This doomsday scenario immediately stirred the academic community to formulate an alternative model which demonstrated that both local, as well as large-scale communities, were able to manage collective resources in such a way as to avert a tragedy. Guided by the work of Nobel prize–winner Elinor Ostrom, who argued that communal management of natural resources is as efficient as, and, in certain circumstances, might even outshine private or public arrangements, scholars have undertaken countless studies devoted to discovering which types of societies or institutions were best able to cope with a scarcity of resources and external pressures.[3] Ostrom discovered that most societies created common pool institutions (CPIs) to regulate and monitor the use of common pool resources, therefore preventing 'freedom in the commons'. Common Pool institutions were

> the sets of working rules that are used to determine who is eligible to make decisions in some area, what actions are allowed or constrained, what rules will be used, what procedures must be followed, what information must or must not be provided, and what payoffs will be assigned to individuals dependent on their actions.[4]

Most CPIs employed a set of design principles in order to avoid the main problems of free riding, trespassing and overexploitation.[5]

According to the scientific community, Hardin fundamentally misjudged commons, since the aim of almost all design principles which govern commons is to prevent freedom of access—or more accurately—free riding. Two design principles have been almost unanimously accepted as key to the success of commons. The first is that commons differ from public goods both because of a clear demarcation between the users entitled to access and outsiders who were excluded from the common pool resources and the actual, physical boundaries of the common pool resource itself.[6] According to Ostrom, it was vital that the limits were defined through an agreement between the members of the community who used the commons. Later, McKean added the precondition that rules must be constructed in such a manner that a rapid growth of the community of users was impossible.[7] A second key principle, according to Elinor Ostrom, is congruence between the natural environment and the rules governing the appropriation of the resource.[8] This implies that limits, in the form of maximum amounts of resource a user was allowed to harvest or consume and the time of the year at which they could draw on it, have to be defined in order to remain within the carrying capacity of the ecosystem. Although it has been stated that collective action in itself was a strong incentive to reduce the total pressure that appropriators exert,[9] most scholars have stressed the necessity of additional regulation and management.

Historians contribute to the debate over common pool institutions by looking at societies in the past which have engaged in collective action to manage their natural resources (and their success in doing so) as well as attempting to explain them. Because of the Collective Action Network based at Utrecht, the number of historical studies of commons and institutions for collective action in the past has exploded the past few years.[10] Many of these studies have questioned the 'design' of the institutions that were required to bring about the sustainable management of natural resources. They have asked which forces and conditions were required to allow and stimulate successful and enduring collective action.[11] Rules regulating access and measures to avoid overexploitation figure prominently within the historical debates. Within pre-modern northwestern Europe, inclusive regimes, granting access to all the inhabitants of the surrounding area or village community, are considered an anomaly and are therefore held to exist mostly in areas of extensive commons, such as Scandinavian forests.[12] Most historical European commons not only demarcated the community of users and excluded outsiders, but restricted access to defined groups within village communities as well.

We can identify four main types of communally-managed resources, ranging from closed access regimes, in which access was limited to certain privileged households, to relatively open institutions, which conferred access on all members of a community or geographical area.[13] In the first, the rights could be linked with tenancy or ownership of a particular building, farmstead or plot of land. Second, membership of a community or municipality gave access to common rights which were owned collectively by members of the commune. The land could be owned by the community itself, or it could remain in the hands of a lord who retained a certain degree of authority or claim over the commons. Third, a cooperative or association of members (in German a 'Genossenschaft' or in Dutch a 'markgenootschap') owned the rights to a material resource. The right to membership could be inherited, but could also be attached to a certain building or property. Finally, we find arrangements in which all the residents of an extended area, or the subjects of a particular landlord or ruler, could use the common resources.

Despite this institutional diversity, a tendency towards more exclusive and restrictive regimes has been noticed. According to most scholars, this manifested itself via two strategic sets of rules. First of all, progressively smaller sections of pre-modern communities had access to common pool resources. For the majority of European regions, growing population pressure, rising urbanisation and commercial opportunities forced local CPIs to implement more exclusive measures. Marco Casari, for example, discovered that several late medieval mountain communities in the Italian Alps changed from egalitarian inheritance systems in which access rights were inherited by all heirs, to semi- or fully patrilineal inheritance systems which served to discourage immigration and the mixed marriages which would lead to a large influx of new appropriators.[14] More fundamental steps to limit access were possible as well. In Schleswig-Holstein the '*Hüfner*', farmers who owned a full farmstead and claimed descent from the colonising settlers, formally excluded all other community members from using the commons when the population rose after the late medieval crisis.[15] A similar pattern is found in the Brecklands in East Anglia where landlords excluded tenants from obtaining grazing rights after the Black Death since sheep breeding was reserved for a very small group of manorial leaseholders who intensively exploited the open fields and wastelands in order to produce the much sought-after wool.[16]

Next to limiting the number of entitled users, pre-modern communities increasingly tried to limit the benefits that each entitled user could take from the common in order to lower the pressure on the landscape. In most CPIs households could only obtain resources for their own subsistence needs. Several scholars studying early modern CPIs have stated that the commercialised sale of resources obtained from the commons was prohibited.[17] Resources were scarce and their depletion a reality. Since the workings of the market would lead communities dependent on resources to increase production at the cost of sustainability, most common pool institutions have been believed to have banned the marketing of products derived from the commons. De Moor, for example, has referred to 'forbidding the sale of direct (for example, wood and berries) or indirect (for example milk from a cow that had spent some time on the commons) produce from the commons'.[18]

These bans on the commercialisation of products taken from the commons were complemented by strict rules to prevent an extensive interpretation of subsistence needs. The most invasive and exploitative agricultural practices, such as grazing cattle, harvesting peat or felling wood were limited in time and extent. Most scholars have focussed on the restrictions placed on grazing. Commons in densely populated areas or valuable pieces of land would be the first to be regulated as an unlimited system presupposes a sufficiency of common land.[19] Joan Thirsk underlined this point. She demonstrated long ago that predominantly upland communities were able to maintain a common pool institution without strict grazing delimitations.[20] Two principles were employed to control and limit the number of livestock on any common pasture. First, commoners were only allowed to put as many animals on the commons as they could keep alive during the winter on their own private property or thanks to their own fodder reserves. Second, a numerical limitation of grazing rights could be applied. The first rule was more focussed on equitable access, while the second actively responded to the carrying capacity of the common field. Winchester, who elaborated on regulations introduced by common pool institutions in England, has described stinting as a common practice that became increasingly prevalent after the Middle Ages.[21]

Exclusiveness Reviewed. A Reflection on the Historiography

Despite the countless micro studies which have revealed hundreds of different common pool institutions and communities of users in Europe, barely any attention has been given to regional variations in the access regime or the causal factors behind these variations. Some have claimed that if the extent of the commons determined how rights to them were allocated, the allocation was part of a wider constellation of tenure and income opportunities.[22] The ecological factor is, however, the most dominant explanation and often held to be the most logical one. The dominant paradigm is that vast commons with almost limitless resources tend to have had an open character. On the other hand, precious resources in densely inhabited regions were strictly regulated and the access to these commons had to be monitored tightly, in order to prevent an unstoppable inward migration and the inevitable degradation of the material resources.[23]

As plausible as this may sound, most of the scholars who have focussed on ecological factors have overlooked two aspects. First of all, similar regions could and did develop quite different rules concerning access to the commons. Similar push and pull factors, such as urbanisation levels, market incentives and population pressure, did not always result in the same or even similar institutional choices.[24] This becomes immediately clear when we look at the distribution of communal property and CPIs in Europe. While some societies opted for collective action to limit the negative effects of commercialisation, others fully embraced private property and market incentives.[25] The same goes for the institutional framework of CPIs themselves. For example, within the Low Countries, a densely populated, urbanised and commercialised region of western Europe, two remarkably similar ecosystems existed, 'het Gooi' near Hilversum and the Campine. Yet the first region developed a system of 'markgenootschappen', while the other had 'gemeindes'. 'Marken' or 'markengenootschappen' are common pool institutions that are independent organisations (water boards for instance) whose members are drawn from a section of a village, several villages or even regions. 'Gemeindes' on the other hand are common pool institutions that coincide with the local village government.[26] Moreover, in 'het Gooi', the common rights were reserved for a selection of farms or families which had to be inherited from father to son, whereas in the Campine the rights of access were conferred on all the members of the community, regardless of their lineage or socioeconomic status.[27] Given the fact that both were located in the European coversand belt and had almost identical resource availability and fragility, these institutional differences cannot be explained by the type of resource or any ecological factor. The two societies, did however differ on the basis of their socioeconomic and political blueprint. Whilst the Campine remained highly egalitarian and no one social group within the community was able to become dominant, the farmers in het Gooi who were descended from the original colonisers of the region had a much stronger power base and were able to implement rules that excluded others from becoming members of the community of users.

Second, it is often not appreciated that the choice made between the exclusive and inclusive regimes might serve several purposes. Ecological restrictions are an important factor underpinning the design of an access regime but are definitely not the only one. Power relations are equally important. As Sheilagh Ogilvie and Jean Ensminger have shown, institutions are first and foremost the instruments whereby the dominant group within a community secures their interests, rather than being the most efficient tool to tackle contemporary challenges.[28] Some institutions and access rules survived although they had utterly failed to prevent overexploitation. Despite the exclusion of the majority of tenants and the introduction of strict stints in the pre-modern Breckland in England, the landscape was fundamentally degraded from the seventeenth century onwards. A real tragedy of the commons even occurred here in 1668 when the sandy soils drifted and entirely destroyed the village of Santon Downham.[29] Apart from an attempt to lower the pressure on the landscape, exclusion measures are also a way to distribute the benefits from the commons among the different interest groups within the community. As José Miguel Lana Berasain discovered, the type of access regime and management of commons can be understood as the point of equilibrium between the natural restrictions of a region on the one hand, and the interests of the elites who were able to detract benefits and resources on the other. An access regime was not designed to repair injustices or protect the natural resources, but rather to maintain a balance in a vulnerable and socially diverse society.[30] Therefore, it is important to look more closely at the diversity in access regimes within northwestern Europe and analyse how and why divergent institutions developed.

Next to the lack of attention which has been paid to the causal factors unpinning exclusiveness, the existence of inclusive CPIs is a further blind spot in the current literature. While every pre-modern society wanted to prevent free riding and overexploitation to avoid a tragedy of the commons, not all of them, even within northwestern Europe, opted for exclusive or increasingly restrictive CPIs. Whilst the strategy of excluding parts of society from obtaining access may be said to be generally dominant, some regions opted to implement and retain an inclusive access regime. As we noted earlier, 'inclusive' does not mean a free for all or an open access situation. All CPIs in one way or another defined the community of users and therefore excluded a group of outsiders. Some deliberately defined that group in a very broad sense, so as to distribute the benefits from the commons among all the inhabitants or members of a community. In this book 'inclusive' refers to an access regime in which all or most of the members of the community were granted access to the commons, although not necessarily in an absolutely equal manner. It is therefore time to move beyond the majority of exclusive CPIs and look at the different strategies and institutions that were developed to prevent a tragedy of the commons.

A limited—although important—proportion of northwest European common pool institutions implemented and maintained inclusive commons despite similar growing pressures on the landscape. For example Winchester had to acknowledge that as much as 46 per cent of England and Wales remained stint-free, despite his claim that there was a general tendency to introduce more restrictive rules. England was not alone however. Alpine pastures, French garrigues, fish stocks and open fields throughout pre-modern Europe were often managed more inclusively.[31] While livestock, timber and grazing land in lowland and urbanised regions became more exclusive, a large proportion of common pool resources were managed in a less restricted way, despite the value of the resources for the communities. Even today, commons exist or reappear and provide resources for growing populations and communities. Will they be able to do this without giving up on sustainability? Is exclusivity the only path towards sustainability? If not, how does a common pool institution have to be designed if the community of users is not strictly delimitated and growing numbers of entitled users are allowed?

Research Approach

This book will show that inclusive access to the commons and the long-term sustainable management of the landscape is not a paradox. This will be shown by an illustrative case study of the Campine in the southern Low Countries, in modern Belgium. Here neither stinting, nor restrictions on the use rights of the commoners, nor the exclusion of community members from the commons took place before the abolition of the commons during the eighteenth century. Even when the population grew during the later Middle Ages and beyond, new members of the community were not banned from the commons. In fact, all members of the communities were allowed access and we can show that 98 per cent of households actively used the commons during the sixteenth century.

Despite the apparent paradox of inclusiveness in a limited and fragile natural world, Campine communities were able to manage the landscape in a sustainable manner. Between 1200 and 1750 the Campine CPIs retained a remarkable stability and prevented the region's main hazard, drifting sand, from turning into a disaster. The landscape retained the same level of eco-diversity for successive generations. The Campine developed what could be called a culture of coping, as its communities were able to handle the constant threat of sand posed by the ecosystem and the challenges imposed by human society in the form of immigration, population growth and market incentives.[32] They succeeded because of the inclusiveness of their collective action.

This book will deal with the questions of how and why Campine communities developed inclusive access to the commons during the late medieval and pre-modern periods and why the commons remained successful. Here we offer a new definition of success. Successful commons have three characteristics. First, they achieve a degree of ecological resilience. Second, they prevent other allocation strategies developing which might transfer common property into private hands, public management or other allocation mechanisms. Third, they distribute benefits of the commons equitably.

The research questions posed here will be solved by using an interdisciplinary, regional and source-based approach. First of all, the geographical scope of the book will not be either national or European, but will have a regional focus. If we start with the idea that both immediate surroundings and local circumstances (in the sphere of soil, landscape, environment, economy, social relations, politics and administration, institutions, religion and culture) influence or perhaps even determine human actions and behaviour, then the region is a relevant point of departure for historical research. This is all the more important because the organisation of society is often determined on a regional or local level.[33] Thanks to the work of Erik Thoen, Bas van Bavel, Tim Soens and other rural historians working in their tradition, it has become clear that even within the relatively restricted area of the Low Countries, rural societies could diverge quite fundamentally. In the view of these scholars, regional divergences are influenced by but not determined by the soil. Due to social differences, as defined by property, the environmental context, as well as different market dynamics, even neighbouring regions with similar characteristics began to diverge significantly from the later Middle Ages onwards.[34] Thoen labelled these different regions 'social agrosystems'.[35] The choice between private and common property, inclusive and exclusive access regimes, is therefore never the pure result of infertile ecological conditions, but rather of a complex interplay of ecological, social and political factors.

Therefore, instead of focussing on a grand model to explain the appearance and survival of common pool institutions within a wider geographical context,[36] this book has concentrated on the forces that generated regional or chronological differences. So far, few historical case studies have been undertaken which approach the commons from this evolving regional context.[37] As a result of this lacuna, I have selected the late medieval Campine,[38] a region often described as a traditional peasant society, with extensive areas of commons (mostly common waste or heathlands, but also common pastures along rivers) which lies at the heart of the Low Countries to the northeast of Antwerp.

Apart from the detailed study of one region over a period of two centuries, a more comparative approach is needed to pinpoint the real causes and mechanisms behind the evolution of the Campine. Until now either broad studies on a European level or micro studies have dominated the field of commons' studies. As Curtis has stated, a comparative approach is needed to go beyond a descriptive approach.[39] Only in this way can the characteristics of the Campine and success of its Common Pool Institutions be measured and assessed. Consequently, an additional region will be frequently drawn on as a comparative case study, namely the East Anglian Breckland. Both regions were located in the coversand belt stretching from Breckland through continental western Europe to Russia (Figure 1.1).[40]

Both regions have been called 'marginal economies'. Both of them experienced challenging ecological circumstances due to the subsoil being largely made up of barren, acid and loose sandy soils.[41] Both regions therefore adopted a mixed farming system, combining intensive arable production on the infields near village centres with extensive grazing and the collecting of resources on the infertile wastelands. Both managed the majority of their territories as communal property until the late eighteenth century.[42] Despite their ecological similarities, these societies evolved in divergent directions. While before the late medieval crises the majority of smallholders in both the Campine and Breckland were able to enjoy the benefits of communal property and steer the institutions that managed them, the Breckland

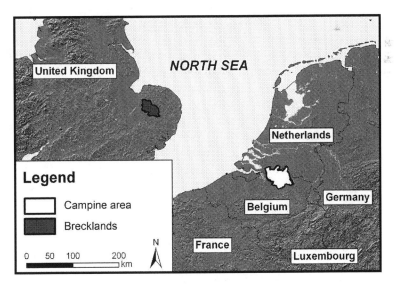

Figure 1.1 The Location of the Campine in Relation to the Breckland in East Anglia

Map drawn by Iason Jongepier, GIStorical Antwerp (Uantwerpen/Hercules Foundation).

subsequently underwent a fundamental transformation which saw the emergence of exclusive and restricted institutions, which gave access to only a minority of the village community.[43] So whilst the Campine and Breckland are quite similar in ecology, they came to differ in their socioeconomic constellation. In this way they are appropriate case studies to assess the impact of socioeconomic and institutional factors on the success of commons.

Second, a wide range of original source material forms the basis of this study. Until now, most historical commons' studies have relied predominantly on normative sources, namely the villages' or institutions' by-laws or regulations. Following Ostrom, historians have been interested in the design of common pool institutions. Missing the opportunities that oral history and anthropological research offered Ostrom, they have turned towards the one source that provides an insight into the design of historical CPIs: by-laws. These contain the rules for the collective management of the commons, but also rules concerning the village as a whole. Consequently, these normative sources provide the possibility of tracing the origins of formal common pool institutions and investigating how the commons were managed and controlled in theory. Nevertheless, it has become generally accepted that normative sources tend to conceal more than they reveal regarding actual day-to-day management and practices. The usefulness of by-laws and regulations as source material has been discussed by both medievalists and early modernists.[44]

In order to go beyond a standard institutional approach, and get a grasp of both the formal access rules and actual day-to-day practices, in this work we have supplemented an analysis of the normative sources with a study of socioeconomic and legal sources. In the tradition of the regional and social approach to rural societies, we have tried to gain an understanding of the social differences in terms of property, agricultural practices and income strategies. Only by looking into the socioeconomic background of the different rural interest groups can the importance of the common property regime for the different rural subgroups be properly evaluated and its importance for each of them established. Consequently, sources regarding social differences and the distribution of power are necessary to complement the picture painted by these normative sources. Court records comprise a third body of material employed in this study. We use them to supplement our knowledge of the different social subgroups with a perspective on their interests and bargaining power.[45] Since legal records reveal both the tensions that arose as well as the way they were settled, they allow the different interests of all social subgroups to be assessed in addition to establishing why some could prevail while others could not. In this way discrepancies between the normative or theoretical management and employment of the commons and the actual practices and interests come to the surface.

Finally, an interdisciplinary approach is used. Understanding ecological conditions in the past is a real challenge for historians. Nevertheless, archaeologists, geologists and climatologists have contributed greatly to our understanding of evolving landscapes. Throughout the coversand belt, the main goal of rural communities has been to prevent the overexploitation of the sandy soils, which would lead to a degradation of the heather vegetation cover, and lead to drifting sand. Sand mobility is therefore a good proxy to measure the success of the historical communities in managing the landscape and preventing unsustainable policies. Our insights into sandy landscapes have recently been increased thanks to the development of Optically Stimulated Luminescence dating (OSL).[46] Because of the new technique, accurate datings of sand mobility and dune formation have become available. Extensive use of these reports and findings are used in this book to complement the traditional historical sources and to provide an insight into evolving landscapes and the impact of management on sandy soils.

The Structure of the Book

This book proceeds as follows. In Chapter 2 a short introduction to the Campine is provided. The basic social, economic, political and institutional characteristics of the region in pre-modern times are described. In Chapter 3 the evidence for inclusive common pool institutions is discussed. The unique administrative sources for the common pool institution of the village of Zandhoven are discussed in greater detail. The pressures pushing towards the establishment of a more exclusive regime are examined. In Chapter 4, the success of the inclusive Campine commons is assessed employing the three criteria we outlined earlier: ecological resilience, a fair distribution of benefits and the resilience of communal property over other allocation strategies. The final chapter looks into the causes of the Campine's success. What made the Campine sustainable, when they refrained from exclusiveness? Informal institutions, strong communal ties and efficient conflict resolution mechanisms are put forward as the main ingredients of the success of the Campine in overcoming the apparent paradox. We end with a conclusion.

Notes

1 Tobias Haller, Greg Acciaioli, and Stephan Rist, 'Constitutionality: Conditions for crafting local ownership of institution-building processes', *Society and Natural Resources* 28, no. 9 (2015); Tobias Haller and Harry N. Chabwela, 'Managing common pool resources in the Kafue flats, Zambia: From common property to open access and privatisation', *Development Southern Africa* 26, no. 4 (2009); Menno Hurenkamp, Evelien Tonkens, and Jan Willem Duyvendak, *Wat burgers bezielt: Een onderzoek naar burgerinitiatieven* (The Hague: University of Amsterdam/NICIS Kenniscentrum Grote Steden, 2006). For the Vincent and Elinor Ostrom workshop in political theory and policy analysis, see www.indiana.edu/~workshop/

2 Garrett Hardin, 'The tragedy of the commons', *Science* 162, no. 3859 (1968).

3 Elinor Ostrom, *Governing the commons: The evolution of institutions for collective action* (Cambridge: Cambridge University Press, 1997).

4 Ibid., 51.

5 Ibid., 15.

6 Ibid., 90.
7 Margaret A. Mckean, *People and forests: Communities, institutions, and governance* (Cambridge, MA: MIT Press, 2000).
8 Ostrom, *Governing the commons.*
9 Nancy Mccarthy, Abdul B. Kamara, and Michael Kirk, 'Co-operation in risky environments: Evidence from southern Ethiopia', *Journal of African Economies* 12, no. 2 (2003).
10 For the Collective Action Network: www.collective-action.info/
11 José Miguel Lana Berasain, 'From equilibrium to equity: The survival of the commons in the Ebro basin: Navarra from the 15th to the 20th centuries', *International Journal of the commons* 2, no. 2 (2008); Jan Luiten Van Zanden, 'The paradox of the marks: The exploitation of commons in the eastern Netherlands, 1250–1850', *Agricultural History Review* 47 (1999); Paul Warde, 'Common rights and common lands in south-west Germany, 1500–1800', and Angus Winchester, 'Upland commons in northern England', both in *The management of common land in north west Europe, c. 1500–1850*, eds Martina De Moor, Leigh Shaw-Taylor and Paul Warde (Turnhout: Brepols, 2002); Tine De Moor, ' "Tot proffijt van de ghemeensaemheijt": Gebruik, gebruikers en beheer van gemene gronden in zandig vlaanderen, 18de en 19de eeuw' (Unpublished thesis, University of Ghent, 2003).
12 De Moor, Shaw-Taylor, and Warde (eds), *Management of common land.*
13 Ibid.
14 Marco Casari, 'Gender-biased inheritance systems are evolutionary stable: A case study in northern Italy in the xii–xix century' (unpublished seminar paper, Utrecht, 2010).
15 Bjørn Poulsen, 'Landesausbau und umwelt in schleswig 1450–1550j', in *Dünger und dynamit: Beitrage zur umweltgeschichte schleswig holsteins und dänemarks,* eds Manfred Jakubowski-Tiessen and Klaus-J. Lorenzen-Schmidt (Neumünster: Wachholtz Verlag Neumünster, 1999).
16 K. J. Allison, 'The sheep-corn husbandry of Norfolk in the sixteenth and seventeenth centuries', *Agricultural History Review* 5 (1957).
17 De Moor, Shaw-Taylor, and Warde (eds), *Management of common lands*; Van Zanden, 'Paradox of the marks'.
18 De Moor, Shaw-Taylor, and Warde (eds), *Management of common lands,* 9.
19 Angus J. L. Winchester and Eleanor A. Straughton, 'Stints and sustainability: Managing stock levels on common land in England, c.1600–2006', *Agricultural History Review* 58 (2010).
20 Joan Thirsk, *The agrarian history of England and Wales, IV, 1500–1640* (Cambridge: Cambridge University Press, 1967), 22.
21 Winchester and Straughton, 'Stints and sustainability'.
22 Warde, 'Common rights', 205.
23 Ibid.
24 Daniel R. Curtis, 'Tine de Moor's "Silent Revolution": Reconsidering her theoretical framework for explaining the emergence of institutions for collective management of resources', *International Journal of the Commons* 7, no. 1 (2013).
25 Ibid.
26 Peter Hoppenbrouwers, 'The use and management of commons in the Netherlands: An overview', in *Management of common lands,* eds De Moor, Shaw-Taylor, and Warde; Anton Kos, *Van meenten tot marken. Een onderzoek naar de oorsprong en ontwikkeling van de gooise marken en de gebruiksrechten op de gemene gronden van de gooise markegenoten (1280–1568)* (Hilversum: Verloren, 2010).
27 Kos, *Van meenten tot marken.*

28 Sheilagh Ogilvie, ' "Whatever is, is right"? Economic institutions in pre-industrial Europe', *Economic History Review* 60, no. 4 (2007); Jean Ensminger, *Making a market: The institutional transformation of an African society* (Cambridge: Cambridge University Press, 1996).

29 Mark Bailey, *A marginal economy? East Anglian Breckland in the later middle ages* (Cambridge: Cambridge University Press, 1989); Mark D. Bateman and Steven P. Godby, 'Late-holocene inland dune activity in the UK: A case study from Breckland, East Anglia', *The Holocene* 14, no. 4 (2004).

30 Lana Berasain, 'From equilibrium to equity'.

31 Nadine Vivier, *Proprieté collective et identité communale: Les biens communaux en France, 1750–1914* (Paris: Publications de la Sorbonne, 1998); Stefan Brakensiek, 'Les biens communaux en Allemagne: Attaques, disparition et survivance (1750–1900)', in *Les propriétés collectives face aux attaques libérales (1750–1914)*, eds M-D. Demélas and Nadine Vivier (Rennes: Presses Universitaires de Rennes, 2003); R. Netting and R. Mcguire, 'Leveling peasants? The maintenance of equality in a Swiss alpine community', *American Ethnologist* 9 (1982); Aleksander Panjek, 'Reclamation of commons in an integrated rural economy: Pre-industrial western Slovenia (an Alpine area)' (unpublished paper given to the World Economic History Congress, Stellenbosch, 2012); Gerardus Hubertus Antonius Venner, 'De meinweg, onderzoek naar de rechten op gemene gronden in het voormalig gelders- guliks grensgebied circa 1400–1822' (Unpublished thesis, University of Nijmegen, 1985).

32 Greg Bankoff, 'Cultures of disaster, cultures of coping: hazard as a frequent life experience in the Philippines', in *Natural disasters, cultural responses: Case studies toward a global environmental history*, eds Christof Mauch and C. Pfister (Lanham: Lexington Books, 2009).

33 Tim Soens, 'Threatened by the sea, condemned by man? Flood risk, environmental justice and environmental inequalities along the North Sea coast, 1200–1800', in *Environmental and social justice in the city: Historical perspectives*, eds Geneviève Massard-Guilbaud and Richard Rodger (Cambridge: The White Horse Press, 2011); Erik Thoen, ' "Social agrosystems" as an economic concept to explain regional differences: An essay taking the former county of Flanders as an example (Middle Ages-19th century)', in *Landholding and land transfer in the North Sea area (late middle ages- 19th century)*, eds Bas Van Bavel and Peter Hoppenbrouwers (Turnhout: Brepols, 2004).

34 Tim Soens, *De spade in de dijk? Waterbeheer en rurale samenleving in de vlaamse kustvlakte (1280–1580)* (Ghent: Academia Press, 2009); Tim Soens, 'Capitalisme, institutions et conflits hydrauliques autour de la mer du nord (xiiie–xviii siècles)', in *Eaux et conflits dans l'europe médiévale et moderne: Actes des xxxiies journées internationales d'histoire de l'abbaye de flaran, 8 et 9 octobre 2010*, ed. P. Fournier (Toulouse: Presses Universitaires du Mirail, 2012); Tim Soens and Erik Thoen, 'The origins of leasehold in the former county of Flanders', in *The development of leasehold in northwestern Europe, c.1200–1600*, eds Bas Van Bavel and Phillipp Schofield (Turnhout: Brepols, 2008); Erik Thoen, 'A "commercial survival economy" in evolution. The Flemish countryside and the transition to capitalism (Middle Ages—19th century)', in *Peasants into farmers? The transformation of rural economy and society in the Low Countries (middle ages-19th century) in the light of the Brenner debate*, eds Peter Hoppenbrouwers and Jan Luiten Van Zanden (Turnhout: Brepols, 2001); Thoen, ' "Social agrosystems" '; Erik Thoen, 'The rural history of Belgium in the Middle Ages and the Ancien Régime: Sources, results and future avenues for research', in *Rural history of the North Sea area: An overview of recent research (middle ages- twentieth century)*, eds Erik Thoen and Leen Van Molle (Turnhout: Brepols, 2006); Bas

Van Bavel, *Transitie en continuïteit: De bezitsverhoudingen en de plattelandsec-onomie in het westelijke gedeelte van het gelderse rivierengebied, ca. 1300–ca. 1570* (Hilversum: Verloren, 1999); Bas Van Bavel, *Manors and markets: Econ-omy and society in the low countries, 500–1600* (Oxford: Oxford University Press, 2010); Bas Van Bavel and Erik Thoen, 'Rural history and the environ-ment: A survey of the relationship between property rights, social structures and sustainability of land use', in *Rural societies and environments at risk: Ecology, property rights and social organisation in fragile areas (middle ages- twentieth century)*, eds Bas Van Bavel and Erik Thoen (Turnhout: Brepols, 2013).

35 Thoen defines a social-agrosystem as a 'rural production system based on region-specific social relations involved in the economic reproduction of a given geo-graphical area' Thoen, ' "Social agrosystems" ', 47.

36 Such an approach is becoming more popular in commons studies: Tine De Moor, 'The Silent Revolution: A new perspective on the emergence of commons, guilds, and other forms of corporate collective action in Western Europe', *International Review of Social History* 52, suppl. 16 (2008); Miguel Laborda Peman and Tine De Moor, 'A tale of two commons. Some preliminary hypotheses on the long-term development of the commons in Western and Eastern Europe, 11th–19th centuries', *International Journal of the Commons* 7, no. 1 (2013).

37 As mentioned previously, either large-scale projects or micro studies are cur-rently popular. For regional studies, see Lana Berasain, 'From equilibrium to equity'. See also the 'Contested Common Land Project' under the direction of Angus Winchester. www.collective-action.info/affiliated-projects.

38 The exact delimitation of the case study is given in Chapter 2.

39 Daniel R. Curtis, *Coping with crisis: The resilience and vulnerability of pre-industrial settlements* (Farnham: Ashgate, 2014), 18.

40 Eduard Koster, 'Aeolian environments', in *The physical geography of Western Europe*, ed. Eduard Koster (Oxford: Oxford University Press, 2007).

41 Bailey, *Marginal economy*.

42 Bailey, *Marginal economy*; Malcolm Robert Postgate, 'Historical geography of Breckland, 1600 to 1850' (Unpublished MA thesis, University of London, 1961); John Sheail, 'Documentary evidence of the changes in the use, management and appreciation of the grass-heaths of Breckland', *Journal of Biogeography* 6, no. 3 (1979); Allison, 'Sheep-corn husbandry'.

43 Allison, 'Sheep-corn husbandry'; Mark Bailey, 'Sand into gold: The evolution of the fold-course system in west Suffolk, 1200–1600', *Agricultural History Review* 38 (1990); Nicola Whyte, 'Contested pasts: Custom, conflict and land-scape change in west Norfolk, c.1550–1650', in *Custom, improvement and the landscape in early modern Britain*, ed. R. W. Hoyle (Farnham: Ashgate, 2011).

44 Jean-Pierre Sosson, 'Les métiers, normes et réalité. L'exemple des anciens pays-bas méridionaux aux xive et xve siècles', in *Le travail au moyen âge: Une approche interdisciplaire*, eds Jacqueline Hamesse and Colette Muraille-Samaran (Louvain-La-Neuve: Publications de l'Institut d'études médiévales, 1990); Marc Boone, 'Les métiers dans les villes flamandes au bas moyen âge (xive–xvie siè-cles): Images normatives, réalités socio-politiques et économiques', in *Les métiers au moyen âge: Aspects économiques et sociaux*, eds Pascale Lambrechts and Jean-Pierre Sosson (Louvain-La-Neuve: Publications de L'Institut d'Études Médiévales, 1994); Peter Stabel, 'Guilds in late medieval Flanders: Myths and realities of guild life in an export-oriented environment', *Journal of Medieval History* 30 (2004).

45 The utility of legal records for research into peasant communities and village life has been demonstrated most convincingly by a number of authors includ-ing Rodney Hilton, *Bond men made free: Medieval peasant movements and*

the English rising of 1381 (London: Methuen, 1973); Christopher Dyer, 'The English medieval village community and its decline', *Journal of British Studies* 33, no. 4 (1994); Christopher Dyer, *Everyday life in medieval England* (London: Hambledon and London, 2000); Christopher Dyer, 'The political life of the fifteenth-century', in *Political culture in late medieval Britain*, eds Linda Clark and Christine Carpenter (Woodbridge: The Boydell Press, 2004); Miriam Müller, 'Conflict, strife and cooperation; aspects of the late medieval family and household', in *Marriage, love and family ties in the middle ages*, eds Isabel Davies, Miriam Müller, and Sarah Rees Jones (Turnhout: Brepols, 2003); Miriam Müller, 'Social control and the hue and cry in two fourteenth-century villages', *Journal of Medieval History* 31, no. 1 (2005); Miriam Müller, 'Arson, communities and social conflict in later medieval England', *Viator* 43, no. 2 (2012).

46 Cilia Derese et al., 'A medieval settlement caught in the sand: Optical dating of sand-drifting at Pulle (N. Belgium)', *Quaternary Geochronology* 5 (2010); M. Ballarini et al., 'Optical dating of young coastal dunes on a decadal time scale', *Quaternary Science Reviews* 22, no. 10–13 (2003); Koster, 'Aeolian environments'; H. A. Heidinga, 'The birth of a desert: The kootwijkerzand', in *Inland drift sand landscapes*, eds Josef Fanta and Henk Siepel (Zeist: KNNV Publishing, 2010); Ilona Castel, 'Late holocene aeolian drift sands in Drenthe (the Netherlands)' (Unpublished thesis, University of Utrecht, 1991); A. A. Sommerville et al., 'Optically Stimulated Luminescence (OSL) dating of coastal aeolian sand accumulation in Sanday, Orkney Islands, Scotland', *The Holocene* 17, no. 5 (2007).

2 The Campine

An Overview

De Kempen or the Campine as an entity is difficult to grasp: It has been described and defined in a multitude of ways. First of all, it can be delineated through its geographical features. The Campine is the area between the Scheldt, Meuse, Demer and Nethe valleys, stretching across the Belgian provinces of Antwerp and Limburg, together with northern Brabant in the Netherlands. This entire area falls within the coversand belt of Aeolian deposits, which resulted in an extremely infertile and challenging ecosystem. Some areas are extremely dry where others incline to being waterlogged. The Campine was originally dominated by woodland but, from the medieval period onwards, heathland.[1] Arable cultivation was difficult to undertake, which has led the entire region to adopt strategies of intensively using the arable infields and extensively using the heathland for grazing.[2] Second, historical jurisdictions can also be used to demarcate the area. By the eighth century, the 'pagus Taxandria' had been founded. Although its exact borders are difficult to determine, it is supposed to have stretched between the axis of Antwerp and the river Dijle to the Meuse valley and Peel swamps. Within Taxandria, two distinct regions developed: Rijen and Strijen, of which Rijen largely corresponds to the contemporary province of Antwerp.[3]

Depending on the definition employed, the Campine can be large or small. It is not our aim to introduce a new or definite definition, but rather to demarcate a research area, which we will present as being located within the Campine. For our purposes, we have chosen the area delimited by the Nethe in the south and west, the border between the polder region and sandy interior in the east and the present-day Belgian-Dutch border in the North (see Figure 2.1). This subjective and ahistorical boundary in the North was chosen entirely for practical considerations.[4]

Dominated by Sand: The Campine Ecosystem and Landscape

One prominent feature of the Campine is the predominance of sandy soils. During the last Ice Age, and especially in the Younger Dryas period, also known as the Loch Lomond stadial (11400–11560 BP), wind-borne sand

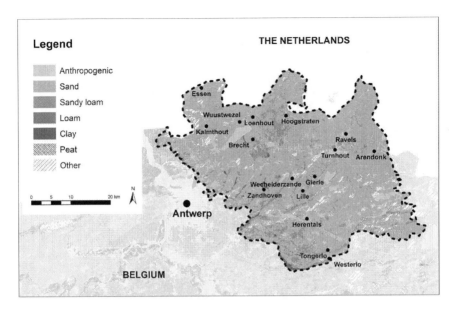

Figure 2.1 The Campine as Defined for This Research, Largely Corresponding to the Antwerp Campine Area

Image created by Iason Jongepier, GIStorical Antwerp (Uantwerpen/Hercules Foundation).

deposits were introduced which determined the Campine's surface geology.[5] Because of the sandy topsoil, together with an impenetrable clay layer beneath it, much of the region suffered from extremely poor drainage. In the parts where the clay layer was absent, the soil was characterised by arid conditions.[6] As a result, only a limited area was suitable for grain production and some grains, wheat for example, could barely be cultivated. In the wet regions, open spaces consisting of peat bogs, swamps with reeds and alders were dominant. Initially a mixed forest was able to develop on the dryer areas.[7] These forests were a mixture of oak and beech trees, scrubland and open heath. As soon as too much pressure was put on this ecosystem, the woodlands were transformed into a mixture of scrub interspersed with sturdy grasses and heathland (see Figure 2.2).[8]

The heathlands could either be sustained or transformed. If left without either cultivation or grazing, even for only a brief period, the forest would regenerate. On the other hand, continued exploitation might further degrade the ecosystem and turn heathland with a diversity of plant cover into ground with poor heather cover or ultimately a sand bowl.[9] The transformation from woodland into progressively open space started quite early, long before the arrival of the common pool institutions. Throughout the Neolithic period, the Roman occupation and from the eighth century onwards, heather gained ground at the expense of woodland because

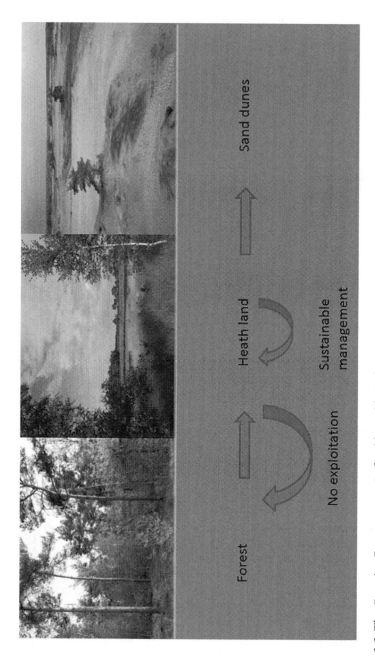

Figure 2.2 The Campine Ecosystem, as Defined by Hilde Verboven

of increasing human intervention.[10] Although the extent of the woodland cover of the early and high Middle Ages is difficult to assess, the Campine was predominantly a heathland area by the beginning of the period under investigation. As Guido Tack has argued, the later medieval era was one of the least densely forested periods in our history.[11] Open spaces which generated sand drifts seem to have already been a problem during the Roman and early medieval periods but one which did not fundamentally worsen during the later Middle Ages. The purple heather heathland, dominated by ericaceous vegetation and few grasses, which has become synonymous with the Campine in our collective memory, probably only developed from the end of the seventeenth century when more intensive plaggen fertilisation was needed and digging for sods became more intensive—and destructive of the vegetation cover.[12] (By 'plaggen' is meant the practice of digging turf from the common and using the sods mixed with manure as fertiliser on arable land.) Theo Spek has called the open spaces during the Middle Ages 'groene heide' or green heath fields. The landscape was by then dominated by grasses, herbs and heather vegetation with several shrubs and varieties of vegetation.[13]

Overcrowded or Extensive Occupation? Late Medieval Occupation History

The Campine has an extraordinary population history. The late medieval period (from the twelfth century) witnessed continuous growth. First of all, the population was constantly on the rise, with only a few setbacks towards the end of the fifteenth century and during the Eighty Years' War (1568–1648). The earliest extant rent registers, for example the one for Bergeijk of 1210, show that during this period only 20 per cent of the land cultivated during the ancient regime was then either cultivated or rented. The rent register of 1340, however, shows 90 per cent of the total cultivable land as then being privatised and rented. By the middle of the fourteenth century, therefore, virtually all the area privatised by the eighteenth century had already been brought into cultivation.[14] Jean Bastiaensen has analysed all the rent registers of Kalmthout and paints a similar picture (see Figure 2.3).

The late medieval period is the most fundamental in the pre-modern history of the Campine area. Because of rapid population expansion, internal growth, agricultural transformations, urban growth and commercial opportunities, Campine villages were transformed from small hamlets or dispersed farmsteads into concentrated settlements in the stream valleys with arable fields and meadows, surrounded by open waste. The fertility of the soil limited the possibilities of exploitation for arable production and pastures to approximately 25 per cent of the total surface area. The most important changes occurred in a first phase between 1210 and 1350 when large-scale land reclamations went hand-in-hand with a population rise of more than 100 per cent.[15] Both the influx of immigrants from the

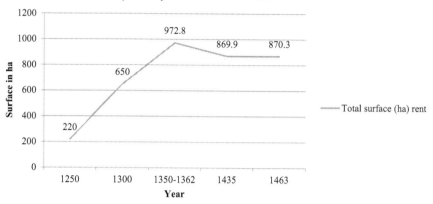

Evolution of land held in customary rent (in ha) in Kalmthout

Figure 2.3 Evolution of the Area of Land Held in Customary Rent in Kalmthout
Graph based on calculations of Jean Bastiaensen.

over-populated County of Flanders and other bordering regions, and the opportunists attracted by the new ruler, the Duke of Brabant, changed the Campine from a sparsely-populated region into a rapidly developing area (see Figure 2.4).[16]

The second phase, between 1350 and 1550, was characterised by interrupted growth.[18] The late medieval crisis had devastating effects throughout Europe, even within the Low Countries. Overall, population declined, urban and rural economies dwindled and disease and wars ravaged almost continuously.[19] Nevertheless, Campine society largely escaped this crisis. In Bergeijk, the total number of households tripled from around 100 to a little over 300.[20] As Figure 2.4 shows, the population did witness a dip from 1480 onwards, but had already recovered by 1526. In the other parts of the Low Countries, this decline started much earlier and took much longer to recover.[21]

As more than 90 per cent of the fertile land was already exploited, expansion became a challenge. Between 1350 and 1526, only 10 per cent more land was exploited while the amount of households grew. Inevitably this brought about an increase in number of rented plots of land without increasing the exploited surface area. The area of arable became fragmented and all the fertile land privatised and cultivated.[22]

The most radical response to these pressures was to reduce the amount of fallow to a bare minimum and turn towards intensive fertilising, which was achieved by keeping cattle inside and mixing their manure with sods from the common wastelands.[23] In order to feed the animals, fodder crops

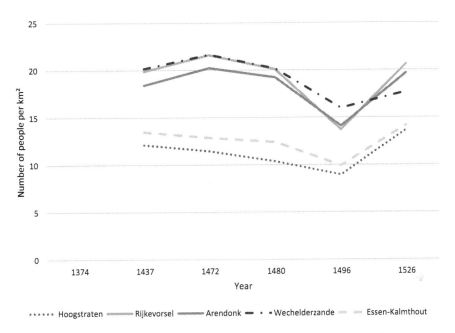

Figure 2.4 Population Density per Square Kilometre Between 1374 and 1565 in a Number of Representative Campine Villages

Source: Cuvelier, Les dénombrements. The surface area of the villages is based on the historical database of www.hisgis.be/nl/start_nl.htm.[17]

were introduced.[24] Second, the economy changed from one mostly based on arable farming, where were cattle the dominant animal, towards a mixed economy of arable production alongside commercial sheep breeding on the common wastelands for wool, meat and hides.[25]

Finally, the surrounding cities probably functioned as an outlet for surplus rural population. By the fifteenth and sixteenth century Antwerp was the main hub of rural immigration. As partible inheritance created increasingly inadequate plots of land, migration to the city offered an alternative to the inadequacy of rural livelihoods. Jan De Meester has shown that people from the Campine dominated the rural influx into Antwerp. Some Campine apprentice craftsmen made a step-by-step migration from the Campine villages via local towns to cities such as Antwerp.[26] After a short period of crisis at the end of the fifteenth century, with a temporary population decline and economic downturn, the sixteenth century ushered in a revival with population levels, together with economic activity, reaching their former levels.

The fourteenth and fifteenth centuries were therefore actually the highest point of population density for the Campine area. After the small-scale setback at the end of the fifteenth century, the population recovered quickly and remained high until the end of the research period, that is, 1580.[27] After the Eighty-Year's War, the population density and composition changed fundamentally. The crisis affected almost all aspects of society, which is one of the main reasons to exclude the seventeenth century from the analysis.

Population was on the rise, but compared to the surrounding regions, population densities remained low. Population density is a relative concept. According to Wim Blockmans, the Campine, with 19 inhabitants per square kilometre, was far less populated than core regions such as Flanders, Holland and the southern part of Brabant.[28] Nevertheless, figures like this can only be fully understood when both the ecosystem and the fact that only 25 per cent of the land was fertile and productive are taken into consideration. Therefore, given the ecological circumstances, together with the absence of sufficient arable land, these numbers can be considered quite high. This becomes clear if we compare the Campine with the Veluwe, which had a similar ecosystem and commons but only 10 inhabitants per square kilometre. Thus, the population pressure in the Campine was significant. During the second half of the fifteenth century, the general malaise brought about a decline, yet only in moderation, and the upward trend resumed after 1496. Although the Campine might not be the most densely populated region within the Low Countries, pressure on the environment was nonetheless high and village communities were expanding. Consequently, the region cannot be compared with Alpine communities or Swedish villages, where commons survived because of the enormous extent of the natural resources together with extremely low population densities.[29]

Rye and Sheep: Mixed Farming

Due to the challenging ecological circumstances, the agricultural strategies available to the inhabitants of the Campine were rather limited. It could never become a grain-producing region such as the Nord-Pas-de-Calais, or provide the meadows required to fatten oxen.[30] Even attempts to fertilise the region by introducing canals and irrigation during the eighteenth and nineteenth century failed.[31] The acidic sandy soils, together with poor water management, limited the surface area available for cultivation to approximately 25–35 per cent. These patches of soil were limited to the sandy elevations, furthest from the marshy meadows that were already fully exploited by 1350.[32] Here rye was the dominant grain. The fifteenth- and sixteenth-century tenant registers of the abbey of Tongerlo show that the largest part of its rent was paid in rye, followed by oats, barley and millet.[33] In some districts buckwheat also became popular, but this was mostly used as a fodder crop, rather than as grain for consumption.[34] Spurrey was another vital crop, mainly sown on the stubble after the harvest and serving as green manure. It was also used as fodder, mainly for cattle.[35]

In order to produce rye, the sandy arable fields required an abundance of fertiliser and common wastelands were therefore required. This was called an infield-outfield system, whereby the infields were intensively cultivated and the outfields functioned as extensive pastures or wastelands, where sheep could graze and sods could be harvested to be mixed with manure to be spread on the infield.[36] Cattle were kept indoors for most of the year so as to maximise the quantity of available manure. Sheep dung, however, was superior for fertilising acid sandy soils. Sheep were therefore kept in 'kooien' or folds on the heathlands at night in order to collect their dung.[37]

The Campine did not focus on arable production alone. From the twelfth century a transformation towards a mixed farming system with animal husbandry and arable production took place. According to Daniel Vangheluwe, this development was necessary because, by 1350, the maximum extent of productive land had been reached and more intensive agricultural practices had to be adopted.[38] Plaggen fertilisation was introduced, and more animals were kept to provide manure as well as dairy products, meat and wool, which could be sold so as to supplement the family income.[39] Therefore, the meadows (the strips of regularly-flooded grassland in the stream valleys), patches of pasture and even the sturdy wastelands were extremely important to the peasant communities. Their extent diverged significantly between different villages. Figures are difficult to obtain for common meadows, but the heathland could cover between 60 to 90 per cent of the village surface area.[40]

The most defining characteristic of the Campine was that heathlands were not privatised, but remained common for the largest part of the year. Commons were omnipresent in most pre-modern societies, apart from some exceptional regions that had abandoned communal property by the later Middle Ages. Nevertheless, the presence of commons could differ significantly. Within the Campine a remarkably large proportion of the total surface area remained common throughout the late medieval and pre-modern periods. During the sixteenth century between 75 and 90 per cent of the surface area was common land (Table 2.1).[41] This calculation does not include the common meadows that were open to village herds on a seasonal basis. The Campine commons consisted predominantly of common heath fields, providing grazing land, peat, wood and building materials. Arable plots had common rights attached to them, but there was no real open field system, such as was found in large parts of England, including the Breckland. Arable fields and pastures were privately owned and no communal rotation of crops existed. Opinion differs as to whether there were grazing rights for communal cattle after the harvest. Although stubble grazing is often assumed, no real evidence of this practice has been found.

An Egalitarian Society?

The Campine was a true peasant society, with remarkable levels of equality between the thirteenth and eighteenth century. This society had evolved from a feudal society into a peasant one with strong communal privileges after the twelfth century. This development was aided by the power shift

Table 2.1 Common vs. Private Land in a Selection of Villages During the Sixteenth Century

Village	Total surface area (to nearest ha)	Total surface area of private land (to nearest ha)	Surface area of common wasteland (to nearest ha)	Per cent common
Lichtaart	2518	325	2193	87.0
s-Gravenwezel	1499	312	1187	79.2
Gierle	1775	400	1375	77.5
Kalmthout	11,586	4293	7294	58.3
Wommelgem	1274	474	799	63.0
Tongerlo	2045	498	1546	75.6

Source: SAA, Ancien regime Archief van de stad Antwerpen, Andere overheden, Lokale over-heden en heerlijkheden, België, Hertogdom Brabant, Toestand der dorpen in het markgraafsc-hap in 1593. RAA, OGA Gierle, 344; RAA, OGA, Tongerlo 896; AAT, Section II, 373–400, rent register 1518, Kalmthout. The surface area of the villages is based on the historical data-base of www.hisgis.be/nl/start_nl.htm

that occurred in the larger region. By 1190 the Dukes of Brabant had ambi-tions to exploit their position on the periphery of the Holy Roman Empire. Initially they wanted to integrate the Campine as a military buffer between their core area and the Duchy of Holland and Geldre, but the Campine also possessed features beneficial for the expansion of their wealth.[42] For this reason they started a campaign to incorporate the area into their territory. They coerced local lords and ecclesiastical bodies to sell their allods to them, or forced them to accept the Dukes as their feudal lord.[43] As a result of this push by the Dukes, local feudal lords who had previously been relatively independent and had possessed their land without any control or overlord-ship were degraded to vassals of the Dukes.

Moreover, their position vis à vis their subjects was fundamentally weak-ened because of the Duke's policies towards the rural inhabitants within their realm. To consolidate their power and ensure the payment of their rents, the Dukes needed the support of the local population, which they rapidly secured by founding 'nova oppida' and granting liberties which abolished serfdom, introduced charters with civil rights, founded village governments with aldermen's benches and granted market rights to entire rural communities.[44] In addition to granting them the power to govern themselves, they granted the use of the common wastelands via communal rights.[45] In order not to lose their subjects, the feudal lords were forced to grant similar rights. Nevertheless, they did not adopt the practice of issuing charters, but conferred liberties by oral grant.[46] Although they were able to retain more control over the governance of their seigniories, serfdom appears to have disappeared and liberties regarding the right to use the com-mons, the foundation of aldermen's benches and the diminishing of feudal dues were conceded.[47] Certain seigneurial rights, such as obligatory feudal grain mills, remained.

The granting of these liberties was quite extraordinary by comparison with other regions. In Flanders barely any rural communities were given such formal rights and powers,[48] nor in the Breckland, where the power of the manorial lords increased after the Black Death.[49]

The rural communities of the Campine were the winners in this story. As the Dukes had a constant need for money, communities were able to secure their rights and even receive charters as proof of their newly-acquired liberties, by paying a one-off sum of money or annual rents and taxes.[50] These dues were, however, were less oppressive than the former feudal dues, as these monetary sums diminished in value quite quickly due to inflation. By granting them their freedom and right to self-government, the villages developed as cohesive village communities with a strong group identity. It cannot be claimed that the village communities were made up of uniform rural households, with equal status and values, as Blickle has stated,[51] but despite their internal differences, they were well aware of the advantages of forming collectives.[52] The willingness to set aside differences gave them a strong position within late medieval society. They were a group to reckon with, and often proved to be the decisive factor in the power struggle between the other political powers in the region.

There were few towns within the core region of the Campine. Despite the foundation of several 'vrijheden' or liberties with city and market rights, most 'nova oppida' within the core Campine remained essentially rural communities.[53] All these newly founded liberties retained their arable fields and common wastelands. A majority of their inhabitants were always engaged in agricultural activities. Some undoubted towns existed on the borders of our research area. To the south, old urban centres such as Lier, Mechelen and Leuven were important craft centres with international markets. To the west, Antwerp was out-growing its status as a military fort and by the beginning of the sixteenth century was on its way to becoming the most important metropolis and trade centre in western Europe.[54] To the north, the Dukes of Brabant had founded or granted liberties to cities such as 's Hertogenbosch, Oisterwijk, Hilvarenbeek and Tilburg, all of which became important centres for the production of cloth.[55]

Despite the strength and uniformity of the Campine villages vis à vis their political opponents, they were not absolutely egalitarian. Since sources (tax records, rentals and field books for instance) which give us insights into the internal composition of the village community are only available from the sixteenth century, the medieval situation has to be inferred from quite late sources. We find that at that time, the Campine was a true peasant society dominated by small peasant proprietors cultivating plots of land of between 1 and 5 hectares. Despite this apparent equality, Eline Van Onacker has argued that we must distinguish several different interest groups within this peasant majority.[56] We can discern four main social groups. First, the micro-smallholders with one hectare or less constituted one of the largest groups within late medieval peasant society. As most holdings were continuously divided due to partible inheritance, this group had grown significantly in numbers between 1350 and 1550. Depending on the village, they made up between 20 and 36 per cent of the population during the sixteenth century.[57] These micro-smallholders generally held a cottage and small garden or arable plot. In general they did not own cattle except for from one or two cows, which were vital for their survival.

Cottagers owning between one and three hectares formed the second group: they represented between 20 and 33 per cent of village communities during the sixteenth century. Like the micro-smallholders, they held cottages and garden plots. These cottagers invested in arable fields, pasture and meadows. Next to their arable land, they possessed at least a couple of cows and some of them even possessed a horse.

The group most characteristic of the Campine were the independent peasants. In large parts of Flanders and Breckland this middle group was disappearing from the later Middle Ages onwards, giving way to societies polarised between large farmers and small cottagers.[58] In the Campine, however, this socioeconomic group maintained its central position. Just like their cottager neighbours, they held their land in customary tenure with a mix of arable land, pasture and meadows. The distinctions between the micro-smallholders, cottagers and even independent peasants were not absolutely fixed. Households could quite easily rise or fall between categories: over the life-cycle of a household it was possible to belong to all three categories. While a young couple may only have had a tiny parcel of land at the time of their marriage, through the possibility of inheritance and the availability of land for lease, they might be able to raise their social and economic standing to that of independent peasant. Afterwards old age might change their status again.[59]

The Campine's independent peasants are distinguishable by their possession of cattle, draft horses and sheep flocks. While they owned barely more land than the cottagers and micro-smallholders, it was their possession of significant flocks of sheep, typically four or five cows and a draft horse which made them independent. They had the means of production, diverse income strategies and sufficient food and animal products to safely reach and even exceed the level of subsistence.[60]

Finally, there were the rural elites. All peasants farming over 5 hectares of land can be thought of as an elite within their communities (although most of them continued as peasants). The majority never obtained more than 10 ha of land. They were not more commercially orientated than any of the other social groups in the Campine.[61] Whilst the concept of rural elites is a relative one, these larger peasants were an exceptional group within Campine communities. In the village of Minderhout, not a single household with more than 10 ha was encountered by Van Onacker. It was in Gierle that the largest concentration of 'large landowners' was discovered, but here only 5.5 per cent of households owned more than 10 ha (Table 2.2).[62] In fact, this elite group can be divided into two distinct categories. First, there

Table 2.2 Property Distribution in Gierle, 1554

Total surface area of farm	Percentage of households in Gierle
< 1 ha	37.2
1–5 ha	38.2
5–10 ha	10.6
≥ 10 ha	5.5
Unknown	8.5

Source: data supplied by Eline Van Onacker.

were peasant households who rented significantly more land and owned large herds of cattle and sheep.[63] They have exactly the same socioeconomic profile as the average independent peasant and developed a similar attitude towards the commons. Second, some communities included a very different socioeconomic group: the tenant farmers. They are to be distinguished from peasants who held land in leasehold, most of whom only held the same amount of land as those that paid customary rent. Leaseholders of this sort should be considered to be independent peasants or cottagers.[64]

Tenant farmers were characterised by the fact that they rented land from external institutions, townspeople or lords: they held far more land than any other socioeconomic group. Ecclesiastical or manorial land had been directly exploited by the abbeys or lords themselves, employing monks, unfree labourers or laymen to farm the land, but by the fourteenth century, these demesne farms were leased out to tenants.[65] Their tenants were therefore the 'odd ones out' within Campine society. In fact most villages did not have a single tenant farmer. They are only found where ecclesiastical institutions, lords or burghers had invested in the development of leasehold farms. Although some of these tenants were recruited from outside of the village, they were members of the village community. They contributed to its taxes and had access to the village's commons. Once they had lived in the village for five years, they were able to participate in all aspects of village life. Their formal membership in the village, however, did not necessarily lead to informal acceptance by the village communities as we will discuss in Chapter 4.

The most striking feature of these tenant farms was their size.[66] The smallest farm in Kalmthout measured 8.6 ha, while the largest, called 'in Vorst' and belonging to the abbey of Tongerlo and located in the village of Tongerlo, extended to 82.5 ha. Due to the surviving accounts, land registers and farm descriptions, we can achieve a detailed description of the agricultural exploitation of the abbey's estates. Since their farms measured on average around 40 ha, these farmers were the true economic elite within the Campine. Other than their size, these tenant farmers were not that different from their peasant neighbours. They shared the same agricultural strategy as the independent peasants, but on a larger scale. They owned flocks of sheep, cattle, horses and engaged in grain production.

The Campine area was an ecologically-fragile region which posed important challenges for its rural communities. Just like the other regions in the coversand belt, such as Breckland, the land was easily overexploited and degraded, leading to soil erosion and sand drifts. In addition, the region was relatively densely populated and becoming more so until the sixteenth century. As opposed to the general European trend, pressure on the landscape was rising throughout the later Middle Ages. The rural communities were made up of true peasants and smallholders, managing their land in a communal way. The most distinctive character of the Campine communities was their level of inclusiveness in the long run.

Notes

1 Koster, 'Aeolian environments'.
2 Daniel Vangheluwe and Theo Spek, 'De laatmiddeleeuwse transitie van landbouw en landschap in noord-brabantse kempen', *Historisch geografisch tijdschrift* 26, no. 1 (2008).
3 Karel A. H. W. Leenders, *Van turnhoutervoorde tot strienemonde. Ontginnings—en nederzettingsgeschiedenis van het noordwesten van het maas-schelde-demergebied (400–1350)* (Zutphen: Walburg Pers, 1996); Willy Steurs, *Naissance d'une région: Aux origines de la mairie de bois-le-duc, recherches sur le brabant septentrional aux 12e et 13e siècles* (Académie royale de Belgique, Memoire de la classe des lettres, III, 1993).
4 The archives of the Dutch regions are located in Dutch archives. For this book we have limited ourselves to the numerous Belgian archives and therefore Belgian village communities. The boundary is a porous one, however, and references to Dutch cities are found in the Belgian ecclesiastical and ducal archives.
5 Eduard Koster, 'Origin and development of late holocene drift sands: Geomorphology and sediment attributes', in *Inland drift sand landscapes*, eds Josef Fanta and Henk Siepel (Zeist: KNNV Publishing, 2010).
6 Leenders, *Van turnhoutervoorde*; Karel A. H. W. Leenders, 'Van wolvenput naar de ellendige berk. Het landschap van de kempense wildernis, 1200–2000', *Post Factum. Jaarboek voor geschiedenis en Volkskunde* 1 (2009).
7 Nico Arts et al., 'De middeleeuwen en vroegmoderne tijd in zuid-nederland', *Nationale onderzoeksagenda Archeologie* 22 (2007); Jan Bastiaens et al., *Inheemse bomen en struiken in nederland en vlaanderen herkenning, verspreiding, geschiedenis en gebruik* (Amsterdam: Boom, 2007); Jan Bastiaens and Koen Deforce, 'Geschiedenis van de heide. Eerst natuur en dan cultuur of andersom?', *Natuur. focus* 4, no. 2 (2005).
8 Hilde Verboven, Kris Verheyen, and Martin Hermy, *Bos en hei in het land van turnhout (15de–19de eeuw): Een bijdrage tot de historische ecologie* (Leuven: Ministerie van de Vlaamse gemeenschap, Monumenten & Landschappen en het Vlaams, Instuut voor het Onroerend Erfgoed, 2004).
9 Ibid.
10 Bastiaens and Deforce, 'Geschiedenis van de heide'; Henk Hiddink, *Opgravingen op het rosveld bij nederweert, 1, Landschap en bewoning in de ijzertijd, romeinse tijd en middeleeuwen* (Zuidnederlandse archeologische rapporten, Amsterdam: Vrije Universiteit Amsterdam, 2005); Alde Verhaert et al., 'Een inheems-romeinse begraafplaats te klein-ravels', *Archeologie in Vlaanderen* 8 (2001–2); Arts et al., 'De middeleeuwen en vroegmoderne tijd in zuid-nederland'; Evert Van Ginkel and Liesbeth Theunissen, *Onder heide en akkers:*

De archeologie van noord-brabant tot 1200 (Utrecht: Matrijs, 2009); Leenders, *Van turnhoutervoorde.*

11 Guido Tack, Paul Van Den Brempt, and Hermy Martin, *Bossen van vlaanderen, een historische ecology* (Leuven: Davidsfonds, 1993); Guido Tack, Anton Ervynck, and Gunther Van Bost, *De monnik-manager, abt de loose in zijn abdij 't ename* (Leuven: Davidsfonds, 1999).
12 J. Bastiaens and C. Verbruggen, 'Fysische en socio-economische achtergronden van het plaggenlandbouwsysteem in de antwerpse kempen', *Tijdschrift voor ecologische geschiedenis* 1, no. 1 (1996); Erik Thoen and Eric Vanhaute, 'The "Flemish husbandry" at the edge: The farming system on small holdings in the middle of the 19th century', in *Land productivity and agro-systems in the north sea area (Middle Ages-20th century): Elements for comparison*, eds Bas Van Bavel and Erik Thoen (Turnhout: Brepols, 1999).
13 Theo Spek, *Het drentse esdorpenlandschap. Een historisch-geografische studie* (Utrecht: Stichting Matrijs, 2004).
14 Vangheluwe and Spek, 'De laatmiddeleeuwse transitie', 8.
15 Vangheluwe and Spek, 'De laatmiddeleeuwse transitie'.
16 Steurs, *Naissance d'une région.*
17 Since January 1, 2016, HISGIS is no longer online. The data files have been transferred to LOKSTAT, the Historical Database for Local Statistics in Belgium (nineteenth and twentieth centuries). More information is available on the website Census 1900 (www.lokstat.ugent.be/lokstat_start.php), where a selection of the data files and maps can be consulted.
18 Vangheluwe and Spek, 'De laatmiddeleeuwse transitie', J. Cuvelier, *Les dénombrements de foyers en brabant (xiv–xvi siècle)* (Brussel: Librairie Kiessling et C. P. Imbreghts, 1912).
19 Wim Blockmans, 'The social and economic effects of plague in the Low Countries, 1349–1500', *Belgisch tijdschrift voor filologie en geschiedenis* 58 (1980); Kristof Dombrecht, 'Plattelandsgemeenschappen, lokale elites en ongelijkheid in het brugse vrije (14de–16de eeuw)' (Unpublished thesis, University of Ghent, 2014); Erik Thoen, *Landbouwekonomie en bevolking in vlaanderen gedurende de late middeleeuwen en het begin van de moderne tijden* (Ghent: belgisch centrum voor landelijke geschiedenis, 90, 1988); Erik Thoen and Isabelle De Vos, 'Pest in de zuidelijke nederlanden tijdens de middeleeuwen en de moderne tijden: Een status quaestionis over de ziekte in haar sociaal-economische context', *Academia Regia Belgica Medicinae. Dissertationes. Series Historica* 7 (1999).
20 Vangheluwe and Spek, 'De laatmiddeleeuwse transitie'.
21 Dombrecht, 'Plattelandsgemeenschappen'; Dirk Peter Blok (ed.), *Algemene geschiedenis der nederlanden*, vols 2, 3, 4 (Haarlem: Fibula-Van Dishoeck, 1977–83).
22 Jean Bastiaensen, 'Landbouwstatistiek uit de 14de eeuw', *De Spycker* (1990).
23 Bastiaens and Verbruggen, 'Fysische en socio-economische achtergronden'; Spek, *Het drentse esdorpenlandschap*; H-P. Blume and P. Leinweber, 'Plaggen soils: Landscape history, properties and classification', *Plant Nutrition and Soil Science* 167 (2004); W. van de Westeringh, 'Man-made soils in the Netherlands, especially in sandy areas ("plaggen soils")', in *Man-made soils*, eds W. Goenman-van Waatering and M. Robinson (Oxford: British Archaeological Reports, Int. Ser., 410, 1988).
24 Cedric Heerman, 'Het abdijdomein van de abdij van tongerlo in de 15de-16de eeuw (met speciale aandacht voor de pachthoeves van de abdij)', *Taxandria, Jaarboek van de Koninklijke geschied- en oudheidkundige kring van de Antwerpse Kempen* 78 (2006), 121–224.
25 Vangheluwe and Spek, 'De laatmiddeleeuwse transitie'.

26 Jan De Meester, 'Gastvrij antwerpen? Arbeidsmigratie naar het 16de-eeuwse antwerpen' (Unpublished thesis, University of Antwerp, 2011).
27 Source: Cuvelier, *Les dénombrements*. The surface area of the villages is based on the historical database of www.hisgis.be/nl/start_nl.htm
28 Holland = 47.0 inhabitants/square kilometre in 1514; Flanders 44.9 inhabitants/ square kilometre in 1469; Brabant = 27.3 inhabitants/square kilometre in 1473. Figures from Wim P. Blockmans et al., 'Tussen crisis en welvaart: Sociale veranderingen 1300–1500', in *Algemene geschiedenis der nederlanden*, ed. Dirk Peter Blok (Bussum: Unieboek bv, 1980).
29 S. Brakensiek, 'The management of common land in north-western Germany', in *Management of common land*, eds De Moor, Shaw-Taylor, and Warde.
30 Hugues Neveux, *Les grains du Cambrésis (fin du xive, début du xvii siècles): vie et declin d'une structure economique* (Lille: Service de reproduction des thèses université de Lille, 1974); Erik Thoen and Tim Soens, 'Elévage, prés et paturage dans le comté de Flandre au moyen age et au début des temps modernes: Les liens avec l'économie rurale régionale' (paper presented at the Prés et pâtures en Europe occidentale: 28e journées internationales d'histoire de l'abbaye de Flaran, 2008).
31 Erik Vanhaute, 'De mutatie van de bezitsstructuur in kalmthout en meerle, 1834–1910', *Bijdragen tot de geschiedenis* 71, no. 1 (1988); id., *De invloed van de groei van het industrieel kapitalisme en van de centrale staat op een agrarisch grensgebied: De noorderkempen in de 19de eeuw (1750–1910)* (Brussels: Gemeentekrediet, 1990).
32 Vangheluwe and Spek, 'De laatmiddeleeuwse transitie'.
33 Cedric Heerman, 'Het abdijdomein van de abdij van tongerlo in de 15de–16de eeuw (met speciale aandacht voor de pachthoeves van de abdij)' (Unpublished thesis, University of Ghent, 2003).
34 Paul Lindemans, *Geschiedenis van de landbouw in belgië*, I, 2 vols (Antwerp: De Sikkel, 1952).
35 Eline Van Onacker, 'Leaders of the pack? Village elites and social structures in the fifteenth and sixteenth-century campine area' (Unpublished thesis, University of Antwerp, 2014).
36 Erik Thoen and Tim Soens, 'Land use and agricultural productivity in the north sea area: Introduction', in *Struggling with the environment: Land use and productivity*, eds Erik Thoen and Tim Soens (Turnhout: Brepols, 2015)
37 Lindemans, *Geschiedenis van de landbouw in belgië*; Blume and Leinweber, 'Plaggen soils'; Bastiaens and Verbruggen, 'Fysische en socio-economische achtergronden'; Van Der Westeringhe (ed.), *Man-made soils*.
38 Vangheluwe and Spek, 'De laatmiddeleeuwse transitie'.
39 Bastiaens and Verbruggen, 'Fysische en socio-economische achtergronden'; Vangheluwe and Spek, 'De laatmiddeleeuwse transitie'.
40 SAA, Ancien Regime archives of the city of Antwerp, other governments, Local governments and seigniories, Belgium, Duchy of Brabant, 5, Condition of the villages in the margraviate of Antwerp in 1593 (from now on referred to as SAA, 5, condition) and RAA, OGA Gierle, 344, 1554; RAA, OGA, Tongerlo 896, 1569; AAT, Section II, 373–400, Rent register, Kalmthout, 1518. The surface area of the villages is based on the historical database of www.hisgis.be/nl/ start_nl.htm
41 Ibid.
42 P. J. V. Dekkers, 'Brandend zand. Hoe de hertog van brabant zijn heerschappij op de kempense zandgronden verwierf ten koste van de lokale en regionale adel', *Noordbrabants historisch jaarboek* 12 (1995).
43 Astrid De Wachter, 'De opname van de kempen in het hertogdom brabant (elfde tot dertiende-veertiende eeuw): Een politiek-geografische probleemstelling', *Tijdschrift van de Belgische vereniging voor aarderijkskundige studies*, no. 1

(1999); Piet Avonds, 'De brabants-hollandse grens tijdens de late middeleeuwen', *Regionaal-historisch tijdschrift* 14, no. 3–4 (1982).

44 Willy Steurs, 'Les franchises du duché de brabant au moyen age: Catalogue alphabetique et chronologique provisoire', *Handelingen van de Koninklijke commissie voor geschiedenis* 25 (1971–2); De Wachter, 'De opname van de kempen': Peter Hoppenbrouwers, 'De middeleeuwse oorsprong van de dorpsgemeenschap in het noorden van het hertogdom brabant', *Noordbrabants historisch jaarboek* 17–18 (2000–1).

45 Steurs, *Naissance d'une région*; Verboven et al., *Bos en hei*; Diederik Theodorus Enklaar, *Gemeene gronden in noord-brabant in de middeleeuwen* (Utrecht: Kemink, 1941); Hoppenbrouwers, 'De middeleeuwse oorsprong'.

46 Enklaar, *Gemeene gronden*.

47 Steurs, *Naissance d'une région*.

48 Wim Blockmans, Jos Mertens, and A. Verhulst, 'Les communautés rurales d'ancien regime en Flandre: Caracteristiques et essai d'interpretation comparative', *Les Communautés rurales: Recueils de la Société Jean Bodin* 44 (1987).

49 Bailey, *Marginal economy*.

50 Enklaar, *Gemeene gronden*; Herman Van Der Haegen, 'Hoe de kempense gemeenschappen hun aard verkregen, gebruikten . . . En verloren. Een overzicht', *Post Factum: Jaarboek voor geschiedenis en Volkskunde*, no. 1 (2009).

51 Van Onacker, 'Leaders of the pack?'.

52 Dyer, *Everyday life*.

53 Harry De Kok, *Turnhout: Groei van een stad* (Turnhout: Culturele Raad Turnhout, 1983); J. R. Verellen, 'Lakennijverheid en lakenhandel van herentals in de 14e, 15e en 16e eeuw', *Taxandria* 27, no. 3–4 (1955); Raymond Van Uytven, 'Brabantse en antwerpse centrale plaatsen (14de–19de eeuw)' (paper presented at the Het stedelijk netwerk ik België in historisch perspectief, 1350–1850, 1990); Verboven et al., *Bos en hei*.

54 A. Bousse, 'De verhoudingen tussen antwerpen en het platteland', *Bijdragen tot de geschiedenis* 58, no. 1–2 (1975); Michael Limberger, *Sixteenth-century Antwerp and its rural surroundings: Social and economic changes in the hinterland of a commercial metropolis (ca. 1450–1570)*, Studies in European urban history 14 (Turnhout: Brepols, 2008); Thijs Alfons, 'Structural changes in the Antwerp industry from the fifteenth to the eighteenth century', in *The rise and decline of urban industries in Italy and in the Low Countries*, ed. Herman Van Der Wee (Leuven: Leuven University Press, 1988); Herman Van Der Wee, *The growth of the Antwerp market and the European economy (14th–16th centuries)* (The Hague: Martinus Nijhoff, 1963).

55 Leo Adriaensen, 'Een zestiende-eeuws vluchtelingenprobleem', *Brabants heem* 53, no. 4 (2001); Leo Adriaensen, 'De plaats van oisterwijk in het kempense lakenlandschap', *THB* 41 (2001).

56 Van Onacker, 'Leaders of the pack?'.

57 Ibid., 91–4.

58 Thoen, 'A "commercial survival economy"'; Reinoud Vermoesen and Annelies De Bie, 'Boeren en hun relaties op het vlaamse platteland (1750–1800)', *Tijdschrift voor geschiedenis* 121 (2008); Dombrecht, 'Plattelandsgemeenschappen, lokale elites en ongelijkheid in het brugse vrije (14de–16de eeuw)'.

59 Van Onacker, 'Leaders of the pack?'.

60 Maïka De Keyzer and Eline Van Onacker, 'Beyond the flock: Sheep farming, wool sales and social differentiation in a late medieval peasant society: The Campine in the low countries', *Agricultural History Review* 64 (2016).

61 Lies Vervaet, 'Het brugse sint-janshospitaal en zijn grote hoevepachters in de 15e en 16e eeuw: Wederkerigheid en continuïteit in functie van voedselzekerheid', *Revue Belge de Philologie et d'Histoire* 90, no. 4 (2012).

62 Van Onacker, 'Leaders of the pack?', 91–4.
63 De Keyzer and Van Onacker, 'Beyond the flock'.
64 Van Onacker, 'Leaders of the pack?'. She found that approximately 20 per cent of land in sixteenth-century villages was leased.
65 Heerman, 'Het abdijdomein van de abdij van tongerlo'.
66 For the following, AAT, Section II, 292–3, Tenant farm descriptions of the abbey of Tongerlo, 1510–1653, 1239–1600.

3 Inclusive Commons

Inclusive commons should not be regarded as simply offering open access to the entire population, the situation described by Hardin, but as CPIs which allowed regulated access to the common pool resources to all or most of the community's members. The development of these inclusive commons in the Campine has a long history, but the later medieval period was of especial importance. During this period, collective action changed from taking the form of informal practices into formal institutions. Inclusive rules were introduced, moulded and tested. Initially, historians thought that common property dated back to the Germanic past, when communal societies shared risks and supplemented cultivation with resources from the commons.[1] This perspective has, however, been discarded by medieval historians.[2] According to Van Looveren, commons have their roots in the feudal domain structure. A domain consisted of hundreds of hectares of land, containing arable, pasture, woods and uncultivated wastelands. The 'servi' or serfs could—in exchange for their services—use those wastelands. Formally speaking, those wastelands remained part of the 'communia' which belonged to the lord, yet use rights attached to them which belonged to the 'servi'.[3]

According to Tine De Moor, the start of formalised commons—her 'silent revolution'—is to be located in the twelfth or thirteenth century. During the later Middle Ages, several regions within northwestern Europe opted to manage, exploit and regulate natural resources in a collective way via common pool institutions. This revolution took place because of the growing pressure on rural communities throughout Europe. Cities started to develop and grow, commercial opportunities and market transactions increased and these influences secured a firm grip on the rural countryside. As the market institutions were still underdeveloped and prone to crises, rural communities sought to protect themselves from their influence by forming institutions and engaging in collective action.[4] Northwestern Europe was very particular in the sense that they not only acted collectively, but that collective action was formalised. Institutions such as 'marken', 'genossenschaften' and 'meenten' were recognised as legitimate institutions by the local and central governments, were granted charters and were allowed to self-regulate via councils and written regulations contained in by-laws.[5]

There is evidence of such an institutional shift in the Campine area. The earliest indication of formal common pool institutions in this region is found in the thirteenth century. Before informal collective action was common, the vast wastelands, at that time densely wooded, were used as a common resource.[6] In fact, many of the rules for the management of their ecological benefits must have resembled those that were later formalised by being written down. During the thirteenth century this informal system came under pressure. Willem Droesen has argued that it was the disappearance of serfdom which was the factor that forced the redefinition of the status of the commons.[7] In addition, the power balance within the region was fundamentally altered. With the intervention of the Dukes of Brabant into the Campine, the long-term symbiosis that had existed between the local lords and their subjects was profoundly shaken, while at the same time streams of immigrants forced local peasant communities to redefine the rules concerning common rights within their villages.[8]

While such changes of population pressure, commercialisation and urbanisation led inland Flanders, Holland and southern Brabant to abolish the commons and opt for systems of privatised and intensified agriculture, the Campine peasants not only maintained their common resources and action, but also formalised their institutions.[9] According to De Moor, peasants chose collective action to protect themselves from the negative effects of population growth, nascent markets and the negative effects of failing states. These external stimulants pushed rural, risk aversive communities to enlarge the scale of production, distribute risk, and reduce transaction costs by acting collectively.[10] Nevertheless, inland Flanders, even southern Brabant, took another path, although they were both located within the same market networks and were subject to political structures that were similarly equally receptive to bottom-up institutions.[11]

It was not only risk aversion that led to the establishment of collective institutions. Local peasant communities, who had already been granted privileges and held strong claims on their land, were powerful enough to negotiate with the Dukes of Brabant. They were able to exploit the dukes' need for money to purchase the grant of their communal rights. This could be obtained through the payment of a one-off sum, together with a perpetual rent. In Flanders and Brabant rural communities did not possess a similar power base and so were unable to secure grants of their commons. As such, the Campine peasant households received what they wanted: formalised use and access rights to the commons, while maintaining fluid and unwritten regulations. The formal recognition of rights by charter was deemed necessary by both the Dukes of Brabant and the Campine peasants, since sociopolitical turmoil posed a serious threat to the interests of all the parties.

The earliest grant was made by Duke Jan I who, in 1288, granted to Litoyen, near Oss and 's Hertogenbosch, a charter that sold the use rights to the common wastelands for the sum of 210 Leuven pounds and a perpetual and hereditary rent of four penningen of Cologne.[12] This precedent was

followed by his successors.[13] This was also the period when the Brabantine cities were able to obtain their most important privileges.[14] As a result,
communities in the core region belonging to the Dukes of Brabant, including the Land of Turnhout and the area surrounding Tilburg, Oirschot and
Oisterwijk, were able to secure grants of their commons underpinned by
authoritative legal documents.

These grants were always made to the village governments themselves
and represent the start of the 'gemeyntes' or 'meenten'. Peter Hoppenbrouwers defined 'meenten' as user corporations that were closely linked to one
specific local village. In contrast, several provinces within the Low Countries created 'marken'. These were similar user corporations, but set up and
operated separately from general local government.[15] Marken could range
in size and remit from just a tiny part of one village to a number of villages.
As institutions, they managed the interests of their members, who did not
necessarily have to be members of the same territorial entity.

These transfers of rights were made by charters called 'aardbrieven'.
A typical 'aardbrief' included several topics. There would be a statement
that the use rights to a certain delineated area were granted to the community concerned for a sum that needed to be paid. For example, the village of
Bergeik and Westerhoven received a charter in 1331 stating:

> We John, grant all the commons and wastelands situated between the
> limits and markers here described [. . .] with the exception of allodial or
> other private goods, to all men of our village of Eyck and Westerhoven
> for their benefit. [. . .] The use right [will be granted] for a payment of
> ten pound 'oude groten' and for an annual and hereditary rent of 5
> solidus grossorum.[16]

Not all communities were as fortunate, however. Some only received an
oral undertaking, instead of a formal written charter.[17] During the later
Middle Ages this had barely any practical significance. All villages used the
commons, formulated rules and patrolled the commons to prevent infractions and overexploitation. When challenged by internal interest groups,
such as the lord or external pressure groups, however, they struggled to
defend rights when they were only based on custom. Those communities
that could prove their possession by means of a charter were more secure,
as Miguel Laborda Peman and Tine De Moor have shown.[18] Nevertheless,
apart from some exceptions, the disadvantages of not having a charter only
fully manifested themselves in the eighteenth century when the commons
were abolished.

The commons went through a phase of rapid transformation between
the thirteenth and fifteenth centuries. While their day-to-day use remained
extremely stable, the formal recognition and development of common pool
institutions significantly strengthened the power base of the local peasant
communities and the place of the commons in the Campine. Thereafter, a

long era of stability began. Further charters were rarely granted, and the formal structures and institutions remained largely intact until Maria Theresa abolished the commons in 1772.[19] The characteristics that are described in the following pages therefore apply to the entire late medieval period.

What Was Common?

Communal property is mostly associated with marginal economies such as the Campine where the possibilities for intensive arable production were limited. Nevertheless, soil alone is not the determining factor, since in the English Midlands arable land was organised as open fields, while in the Low Countries grain-producing areas opted for absolutely privatised land. At the same time, regions dominated by commons did not necessarily organise their collective action in similar ways. Therefore, each common property type and its causal factors has to be analysed in its own terms.

As Table 3.1 shows, most of the land—60 to 90 per cent—of Campine villages was held in common. This is, however, the lowest estimate of communal property, since large parts of the hay meadows and pastures also had seasonal communal rights attached to them.[20] In general, three broad categories of common land—arable, pasture and common waste—can be distinguished, of which common waste was easily the most extensive and so is considered here first.[21]

The preponderance of common waste in the Campine was a general feature of the European coversand belt, since the majority of its surface area was incapable of intensive exploitation.[23] Wastelands refer to land used neither for the cultivation of crops, nor for hay, but principally for the grazing of animals or the gathering of fuel, turves, buildings materials etc.[24] As land books, tax registers and rent registers indicate, between 60 and 90 per cent

Table 3.1 Common vs. Private Land in a Selection of Villages During the Sixteenth Century

Village	Total surface area (to nearest ha)	Total surface area of private land (to nearest ha)	Surface area of common wasteland (to nearest ha)	per cent common
Lichtaart	2,518	325	2,193	87.0
s-Gravenwezel	1,499	312	1,187	79.2
Gierle	1,775	400	1,375	77.5
Kalmthout	11,586	4,293	7,294	58.3
Wommelgem	1,274	474	799	63.0
Tongerlo	2,045	498	1,546	75.6

Source: SAA, Ancien regime Archief van de stad Antwerpen, Andere overheden, Lokale overheden en heerlijkheden, België, Hertogdom Brabant, Toestand der dorpen in het markgraafschap in 1593. RAA, OGA Gierle, 344; RAA, OGA, Tongerlo 896; AAT, Section II, 373–400, rent register 1518, Kalmthout. The surface area of the villages is based on the historical database of www.hisgis.be/nl/start_nl.htm.[22]

of the total surface area of Campine villages remained waste even during the sixteenth century. This still remained the case when the earliest maps were made in the eighteenth century (Figure 3.1).[25]

All land that supposedly had no claims attached to it, such as wasteland, was part of the 'bona vacantia' which was a component of the royal domain.[26] As such, the Duke of Brabant—sovereign and lord of the area—possessed the most remote and unclaimed pieces of land. By charters or oral agreements, however, all local lords granted in one way or another the use rights on these common wastelands to their subjects.[27] Throughout the year, they were free to use the commons according to the local by-laws. The lord retained the bare ownership, but could no longer determine the type of land use, nor the management and control of the commons on his own.

These charters or agreements fundamentally curbed the power of the local lords to exploit the commons. By contrast, in the East Anglian Brecklands, manorial lords shifted from rent-seeking strategies towards rabbit rearing and sheep breeding via their lessees. Because they adopted these forms of explotation, large parts of the wastelands were transformed, with implications for the tenants. In the Campine, manorial explotation of the common wastelands was much more difficult to achieve. This might explain why rabbit warrens are never found as a commercial feature in the Campine.

Peasant communities, in their turn, could use the heathlands and promulgate regulations, but could not sell or rent the land without consent of the lord. Property and use rights were therefore detached from each other and came to be held by different parties. This type of fundamental division between ownership and use rights is what made the commons different from public land or more modern forms of collective property.

The second category of land is common pasture, grassland used for common grazing.[28] Within the Campine, half of the privatised land was categorised as pasture.[29] Only the hay meadows were treated as common pool resources after the hay harvest.[30] Depending on the number of streams and brooks, the proportion of the village area used as common hay meadows could vary significantly. By the fourteenth century, most hay meadows were owned by individual peasants and farmers. The village community could no longer determine how they were managed except for the part of the year when common use rights could still be exercised.[31] After the first harvest, the community of users possessed the right to put their livestock on the meadows. From the end of May until the following March, the private owners had to acknowledge the use rights that were possessed by the community. In Oostmalle the by-laws stated that 'the hay meadows and "de Aesten" will be freed and fenced from mid-March and the common "broek" from the second day of May until the holiday after the harvest'. 'Between that period nobody will drive his cattle in the common hay meadows, either his own or that of others'.[32] In the late medieval period, much private land still had some important use rights attached to it which could be exercised by different individuals or groups.[33]

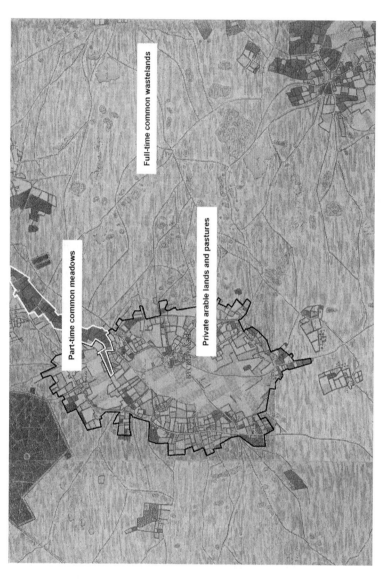

Part-time common meadows

Full-time common wastelands

Private arable lands and pastures

Figure 3.1 Ferraris's Map of Rijkevorsel (1771), Showing the Relationship Between Arable Meadow and Wasteland, Which Must Have Resembled the Late Medieval Situation

Source: Josef Johan Ferraris and Wouter Bracke, *De grote atlas van De Ferraris. De eerste atlas van België. Kabinetskaart van de oostenrijkse Nederlanden en het Prinsbisdom Luik* (Tielt: Lannoo, 2009).

Finally, there is the question of common arable land or open fields. Common arable refers to land that is primarily used as arable land within an individual or private ownership context, although collective sowing, harvesting and ploughing could be enforced and the whole might be made available to be grazed communally in fallow years.[34] In the Campine an open field system presumably developed from around the eleventh or twelfth century. Most scholars have agreed that these were organised as open fields once the dispersed arable plots were consolidated into larger units, but whether they really *functioned* as open fields, with communal sowing, ploughing, harvesting and the collective determination of the land use remains open to debate.[35]

The evidence for open fields in the Campine is not strong. First of all, scholars have relied on the literature regarding similar regions such as Drenthe,[36] or to the single reference to a village with open fields near Brussels in the magnum opus of Paul Lindemans.[37] The descriptions of tenant farms made by the abbey of Tongerlo in 1510 and 1539 reveal an altogether different picture.[38] As shown in Table 3.2, 78 per cent of all arable fields were enclosed by a hedge or ditch. In an open field, one would expect a large hedge surrounding the entire complex, which could be opened at crucial locations to allow cattle to enter. Individual enclosures were not compatible with open field agriculture. The surveys therefore indicate that by the beginning of the sixteenth century at the latest, a bocage landscape had emerged. It has to be stressed that these registers describe only monastic land, leased to tenant farmers. It is not absolutely certain that peasant land was enclosed at the same rate, but as the farm structure of tenant farms and the economic activities of ecclesiastical farmers did not diverge significantly from those other rural elites or even peasants, a fundamentally different approach to the enclosure of arable is unlikely.

Dating this enclosure movement is difficult. The estate registers of the abbey offer a date *ante quem* the hedges were created, yet not a single clue exists as to when they were introduced.[39] Looking at the fundamental

Table 3.2 Enclosure Rate of the Abbey of Tongerlo's Tenant Farms in Tongerlo During the Sixteenth Century

Land type	Total number of fields	Enclosed fields	Percentage of enclosed fields
Arable fields	81	63	78
Meadows	98	11	11
"Blok" or pasture	30	28	93
Woodlands	25	0	0
Heath fields	52	29	56
Pastures	67	27	40

Source: AAT, II, Registers, 292–293, Tenant farm descriptions of the abbey of Tongerlo, 1510–1653, 1239–1600.

transformations from the 1350s onwards,[40] and taking into account the fact that the first by-laws do not refer to such open field practices such as communal sowing, ploughing or the opening of the fences for the communal herds[41] prompts the suggestion that enclosure took place from the end of the fourteenth century onwards.

Privatised and enclosed land, however, was never completely free from use rights belonging to others. Since all arable plots were located in large complexes, without roads, most individuals needed to cross their neighbours' fields to reach their own land. Consequently they were granted right of access to drive their draft animals or carriages over the arable fields as long as those animals were harnessed and controlled, and crops were not damaged.[42] Although the right of passage was frequently disputed, the practice nonetheless survived.

Being predominantly common waste, the Campine commons were chiefly used for communal grazing but also provided important additional resources.[43] These rights offered fewer commercial opportunities than grazing, but helped secure the subsistence level of the poorest households who did not own any animals and were dependent on the exercise of other rights.[44] Because of the infertility of the soil, arable plots were fertilised through a combination of sods and manure. Those sods were made up of heather vegetation and perhaps a little bit of topsoil carried from the heathland (plaggen husbandry).[45] Although the question has been much debated, it is probable that thicker sods with humus attached, which were obviously more damaging to the heathland, were only harvested from the later seventeenth century onwards.[46]

Furthermore, the Campine area suffered from a serious shortage of wood.[47] By comparison with other parts of Flanders, the Campine might have been better supplied with wood than others: hedges and small copses or woodlands remained, or were maintained, on the commons. Nevertheless, firewood was scarce.

Organisation: Common Pool Institutions

Common pool resources were managed by what Elinor Ostrom has called Common Pool Institutions (CPIs). Douglas North defined institutions as the rules of the game in a society: They structure the incentives in human exchanges through formal rules and informal constraints.[48] Elinor Ostrom gave a very similar definition which is fitting for common pool institutions.[49] The most important aspect of the common pool institutions are the people involved in their governance. Where research has been undertaken on the actual guardians, monitors or governors, it has often been found that they were drawn from amongst the lowest level of the participants. This confirms one of the main design principles described by Elinor Ostrom. Labelling it as 'collective-choice arrangements', Ostrom stressed that in order to have an efficient and sustainable management of the commons, the individuals affected by the operational rules had to be given the opportunity to modify them.[50]

How they should be involved has remained rather vague and has prompted some debate amongst scholars concerned with both contemporary and historical communal institutions. Arun Agrawal, on the one hand, introduced the concept of 'environmentality', derived from Foucault's conceptualisation of 'governmentality'.[51] According to Agrawal, village communities would internalise rules and values that were introduced from the top down, as long as they could participate in local councils. That communities accepted and policed rules did not mean that they were involved in their formulation. Nevertheless, this concept of internalisation has been criticised. It has been suggested that communities only adopted these norms and values publicly, as a means to achieve their own goals, without ever really embracing them.

On the other hand, Tobias Haller has put the concept of 'constitutionality' on the agenda. According to Haller and others, all members of the community of users have to be required to be engaged in the institution-building process in order to acquire a sense of ownership of the institution and rules, without which they could not bind them. Haller calls this ownership of the institution-building process 'constitutionality', an instantiation of a bottom-up process of institution building. Passively witnessing the formulation of regulations in a council would not suffice. Rules have to be proposed and agreed at the grassroots level if they are to be accepted and obeyed by the whole community.[52] The same conclusion applies to historical communities. By-laws frequently refer to members of communities gathering in public meetings to discuss and agree rules in public meetings, the collective visiting of the boundaries and communal policing. Moreover, Tine De Moor has argued that having a broad base of community members participating in the commons as users, monitors or officials, was necessary for the survival of the system.[53]

The historical record reveals a combination of top-down and bottom-up processes. However small a village or hamlet was, it was controlled by a town council with village representatives and/or a local lord and his officials. In the opening section of several by-laws, there is mention of the 'gemeyne ingezetenen' or community members being present when the by-laws were formulated, thus strengthening the bottom-up image of the common pool institutions. But is this presence sufficient to prove a true agency of all, and most certainly the least influential, interest groups within the premodern communities? The lords in the Brecklands of Norfolk, for example, held a strong grip on the management of, and decision-making about, the commons, despite the existence of common pool institutions. Despite bottom-up protests, this system was reinforced and survived for more than two centuries.[54]

We find when looking at the formal leadership of the common pool institutions, namely the 'gemeynten' of Campine villages, that the bottom-up perspective is predominantly a case of discourse rather than reality. For example, the by-law of Hoogstraten, a town under the jurisdiction of the Van Lalaing family, stated that

> The by-law, statutes and ordinances that were drawn up by the renowned Lord Antoon van Lalaing of Hoogstraten in 1534 by the consent of the aldermen, sworn members and common inhabitants.[55]

Although the introductory clause of almost all by-laws includes a reference to the village community being present during their formulation, the power to create rules was largely out of reach of the ordinary peasant. First of all, the lord or at least his steward or bailiff, was often the one who created by-laws, or at least approved them. Even in the case of the village of Gierle, which had purchased the right to manage the commons, the introduction to its by-laws states that 'The old by-law, ordinances and statutes are known for time immemorial within the village as the ordinance handed over by His Majesty [the Duke of Brabant]'.[56] Where the lord did not directly interfere with the normative base of his seigniories, which must have been the case for those lords such as the Merodes who were absentee landlords residing on other estates, the responsibility was delegated to his bailiff or sheriff in combination with the local aldermen.[57] Negotiation between the lord's representative and the local village government was the most common way of creating village by-laws. In only one village are the inhabitants portrayed as being able to construct the rules themselves. In Terloo, a mere hamlet, a by-law was promulgated which omitted all criminal and economic rules and was concerned only with the management of the commons.

Despite the scarceness of evidence as to the social background of these lordly representatives and aldermen, it is quite probable that they were drawn from the upper classes of society. In the case of Brecht, we have the names of the aldermen who wrote down the by-laws. When cross-referenced with the tax registers, all of them can be placed in the highest quartile of the village's social ladder. With the exception of Willem Der Muyden, who could be found in the third quartile, all of the aldermen owned estates that placed them in the highest two quartiles of sixteenth-century Brecht.[58]

The villagers were often invited to confirm the rules, since their consent was required for the maintenance of peace and order in the village.[59] The main power the local villagers had in steering the management of the commons was the power to initiate new rules. One rule in the by-law of Retie shows this clearly:

> Whenever seven individuals of the same hamlet come to the lord in order to create a rule that would benefit the hamlet, the lord and four aldermen will be allowed to legislate this all year through. In case these men vow that it is in the interest of the hamlet, the rule will be found worthy and has to be abided by, just like the other rules that the jurors had made.[60]

The by-law of Vorselaar confirms this practice. Almost half the village by-laws refer to rules being introduced by the village community, either independently or with the co-operation of the aldermen and bailiff. Nevertheless, the bailiff and the aldermen possessed exactly the same prerogatives.[61] Moreover the power to legislate through by-laws was used far more often by the aldermen than by the villagers themselves. This is especially true when we consider the fact that almost half of the rules which are said to have been introduced by inhabitants come from one single village, Vorselaar.[62]

The lords and village governments tended to opt—as was the case in urban governments, guilds, and other forms of collective organisations—for a participatory model.[63] By being present at the village meetings and granting their explicit or implicit consent, it was presumed the inhabitants would comply with those rules and eventually internalise them. By-laws therefore demonstrate, especially when they are combined with social sources and tax registers, which interest groups were calling the shots within the formal common pool institutions. References to obligations to be present during the publication of by-laws, the annual village meeting and the communal duties are therefore illuminating but do not indicate the exercise of political power.

The same exercise of hierarchal power is found when we examine controlling and sanctioning activities. According to Elinor Ostrom, the introduction of strict and enforcable rules was vital when establishing a sustainable management system.[64] As shown by Haller, the involvement of the community in both setting the rules and sanctions and in their implementation is indispensable for the success of the institution. In modern-day Zambia, a tragedy of the commons was inevitable once the rules and fines had been introduced by the state, without any consideration for local communities.[65] Appointing members of the community as guardians and law enforcers ensures greater compliance with the rules. According to Tine De Moor, however, the best way to safeguard an efficient common pool regime, is not to sanction, but to prevent trespassing by implementing a system of social control within the community of users.[66] The ability to implement a purely democratic form of justice, policed by the community and judged by that community, was not possible during the early modern period. The punishment of important infractions, which attracted high fines, was always the prerogative of the lord.[67]

Most cases, however, had to be handled by the lord's bailiff and local aldermen. Whenever the bailiff detected an infringement of the rules, he had to summon the trespasser to the court, after which the aldermen had to hear and sentence the case. In Geel the function of the bailiff was set out as follows: 'The bailiff of the liberty of Geel and the aldermen are owing and responsible for securing justice for the inhabitants. The bailiff is the public prosecutor and the aldermen [the] judges'.[68] Afterwards the bailiff was responsible for determining and collecting the fine.[69] Although the majority of rules written down in the by-laws mentioned an exact fine, the bailiff usually set a fine which took into account the gravity of the offence, the social background of the trespasser and whether it was a first transgression (or not).[70] Although the aldermen were the direct representatives of the village community, selected from amongst their ranks, the most important figure in the justice system was the bailiff as the direct representative of the lord. Being judged by peers was ensured through the role of the aldermen, but as mentioned before, they were predominantly the elite of the village which reasoned according to a form of 'managerial logic' instead of following the peasants' interests.[71]

Imposing rules is one thing, but actually enforcing them is another altogether. Therefore, officials, called jurors and 'vorsters', whose duties included prosecuting trespassers, locking up stray cattle and collecting fines imposed by the bailiff or steward, were appointed. In Ravels and Eel the vorster was appointed by the bailiff and aldermen. They were charged with 'collecting [the lord's] fines from catching cattle and charging trespassers, as long as they concern the land and soil and will not intervene in the lord's matters'.[72] In addition, villagers were renowned for their expertise with cattle diseases and in containing pestilence. 'Good men' from the villages were therefore appointed to make frequent visits to the village's stables to check for sick animals. When precautionary measures had to be taken, their advice would be final. As in Ravels and Eel, these local officials were appointed and supervised by the bailiff and/or aldermen. On some rare occasions, however, the village community could determine who would patrol the commons and set fines. In Terloo, the one village that prescribed its own by-laws, the vorster was chosen by the community of users themselves.

> It is ordained by general election of the inhabitants of the hamlet [of] Loo that two commons' masters will be elected to serve two years like the church masters. When their term is over, they will have the opportunity of choosing other members of the community according to their understanding and judgement.[73]

Finally, the complete village community was charged with reporting any offences to the local officials or authorities. Although the vorsters were required to 'go around the common wastelands and boundaries every 14 days together and with each other', controlling every communal activity or straying shepherd was simply impossible.[74] In return for their collaboration, villagers could receive a portion of the fine.[75]

The Inclusive Access Regime: Everybody on Board

The combination of seigneurial involvement and elite management, however, did not lead to exclusive CPIs. From the later Middle Ages onwards, use rights were granted to all community members, or as the Duke of Brabant put it in the case of Oosterwijk:

The Duke concedes to the men of his freedom of Oisterwijk [the commons between the limits mentioned within the charter]. He concedes to his men [*homines*] that in case outsiders [*alienis*] use [the commons], his associates can prohibit the use by anyone, except those of Oisterwijk.[76]

Normative sources such as this charter are tricky to interpret. Oisterwijk was one of the quarters of the bailiwick of 's Hertogenbosch, a town and a collective of several inter-dependent hamlets or villages. Who exactly are the 'homines'? Are these all the inhabitants or households residing in one geographic area, or are these the '*Gemeine Männer*' who Blickle considers to be the families who owned a farm or piece of land and contributed to the village's taxes?[77] Although it is often held that such terminology was clear and obvious for the parties involved, the number of conflicts which appeared later, because of conflicting interpretations of these charters, suggests otherwise. Although '*alienis*' could be interpreted either in a very strict or broad manner, even in the most strict sense of the word it does not explicitly imply the exclusion of a specific subgroup within the village. In addition, it does not state that any preconditions must be met before access to the commons could be granted. One had to belong to the community, which could include both the centre and depending hamlets, or just the town or village mentioned by name.

By-laws do not paint a clearer picture, since the question of how the community of users was defined was never addressed by them. Some by-laws referred to the necessity of contributing to the general village taxes, 'schot and lot'.[78] In addition, individual by-laws often dealt with very specific questions, such as access to a defined area of the commons or a particular type of common pool resource. By-laws mostly elaborated on the 'alieni', that is, outsiders such as members of neighbouring communities or vagabonds. Consequently, it was made absolutely clear that non-residents of the village or peripatetic individuals did not possess access rights.[79] It is therefore difficult to decide whether there were subgroups within the village boundaries that were excluded. Overall, the evidence suggests that this was not the case. Cottagers are often explicitly mentioned when it comes to using the commons. For example, Rijkevorsel stated that

> Everyone, whoever he or she may be, either plough owners or 'cossaten' [cottagers without a plough], are permitted to dig peat for one day every year, without contradiction, and this after the announcement and consent given via the public declaration after Sunday's mass.[80]

Ultimately, by-laws remain enigmatic about the communal rights of landless or poor households.

Normative or institutional sources are therefore incapable of painting the full picture. Consequently, our attention will turn to administrative and economic sources, such as the 'heideboek' of Zandhoven, to supplement the information derived from normative sources. As Tine De Moor has shown for eighteenth-century Gemene Loweiden, the identity of the theoretical beneficiaries of commons and those permitted to use them could diverge fundamentally.[81] The same conclusion can be drawn from the example of the medieval Breckland in Norfolk. While access to the commons was granted to all peasants, farmers or manorial tenants that purchased the right of fold course, tenants and cottagers were denied the possibility of buying such rights from the late medieval crisis onwards. Without changing a single letter of the formal charters or by-laws, actual access rights were completely transformed and became restricted to the lords and their tenants.[82] Administrative documents such as membership lists or accounts, and indirect evidence drawn from legal or economic sources, offer the only viable option of getting a glimpse of the day-to-day practice behind the normative framework. For medieval northwestern European commons, however, evidence is thin on the ground. While some common pool institutions kept detailed membership lists, others did not, or any registers they kept have been lost. It was mostly CPIs which operated alongside village governments or introduced restrictive regimes, who were forced to record the basis of access rights and register the names of those entitled to use the common.[83] Most Campine 'gemeyntes', on the other hand, did not keep such records. Luckily one account has survived in the local archives, that of the village of Zandhoven.

Zandhoven: A Glimpse of the Actual Entitled Users

Zandhoven provides evidence of the exceptional inclusiveness of the Campine CPI's in the sixteenth century. While stopping short of allowing open access, all members of the community were able to benefit from the commons, even the landless and poorest members of society. Zandhoven was a village located at the heart of the Campine, next to the Land of Turnhout. Consisting of 81 households, it was rather small compared to the average sixteenth-century Campine village with 122 households, but it had a larger regional importance.[84] Enjoying the privilege of having the main 'hoofdbank' or appellate court next to Antwerp, a large part of the surrounding area relied on the statutes of Zandhoven. Lower village courts came to Zandhoven for legal advice and guidance.[85] The laws applied in Zandhoven were shared with 16 villages, while its legal influence covered over 60 villages within the Campine.[86] Whether Zandhoven determined the attitude of the other villages to inclusion and exclusion is unclear, but the likelihood of Zandhoven being completely anomalous is small.

Between 1559 and 1581, the village government of Zandhoven maintained an account book in which all payments to use the common wastelands were recorded together with payments for the purchase of hay and wood.[87] First they listed the names of the inhabitants who paid an annual rent to use the commons. The 'gemeyntenaren' or common inhabitants were required to contribute to the village taxes and burdens, if they wanted to use the commons. This practice is described in by-laws for other villages and mentioned in court records. The by-law of Westerlo, for example, stated in 1569 that:

> Everyone who comes to live in the quarter of Westerlo or in the jurisdiction of the external law court, will have to contribute to the 'schot en lot' [general village taxes] and 'horseman tax'. Those who refuse will be held as foreigners and de facto be excluded from using the commons.[88]

No reference to the payment of 'schot and lot' has been found in Zandhoven, but the 'heidecijns' was a general village tax paid at very low rates. A household was either exempt from paying it, or contributed a half or one 'braspenning'.[89] In 1559, at the start of the heideboek and the only year in which the 'heidecijns' was recorded, one 'viertel' (79.6 litre) of rye cost 71 'groten'.[90] Knowing that one 'braspenning' corresponds to 2.5 'groten', it becomes clear how minimal this amount was.[91] Surprisingly, only 23 names are recorded as paying the 'heidecijns', 13 of whom owned a 'stede' or house, and nine a 'hoeve' or farmstead. (One was undefined.) Three households which possessed either farmsteads or houses as well were listed, but did not contribute to the tax. Given that in 1526 81 households were counted in the village, at first sight this suggests that only a limited part of the community of Zandhoven could enter the commons.[92]

The account book continues by listing the names of all those who either collected heather, turves or peat, or paid to put cattle on the common wastelands. Using this, we can reconstruct how many users actively drew on the commons and in what ways. Every household that paid to collect heather and peat, or to graze cattle on the common wastelands, can be labelled as an 'active' and entitled member of the community. As Figure 3.2 indicates, the number of users fluctuated from year to year, but on average numbered around 79.5 names (see Figure 3.2). Considering that the household is the basic entity, and no more than one member per family would pay for the commons, we can infer that this refers to 79 or 80 households. Since the tax registers for Zandhoven are lost, we cannot link the names in the 'heideboek' to any other source that could identify the active users. It is possible that outsiders paid a sum in order to gain access to the common. Tine De Moor found for the 'Gemene Loweiden' that 'until the middle of the eighteenth century, non-commoners could request the management of the common to let some of their livestock graze for a certain period of time'.[93] To avoid unstable levels of exploitation, the managers of the 'Gemene Loweiden' allowed outsiders to use the common. This was, however, the practice at a time when the commons had an entirely different function for the majority of the community and a substantial sum had to be paid for their use. As a result, only a small percentage of the village community exercised their right to use the commons.[94]

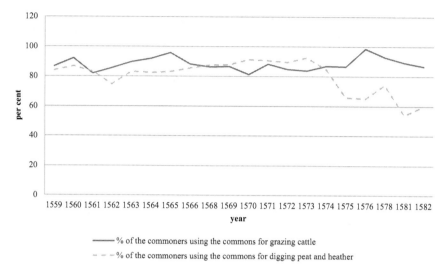

Figure 3.2 Number of Individuals Paying for Access to the Common Wastelands of Zandhoven, 1559–82

Source: RAA, OGA Zandhoven, 148, 'Heideboek', 1559–81.

This was not the practice in the sixteenth-century Campine. The Zandhoven by-laws suggest that outsiders were not welcomed. According to the by-laws, fines for trespassing animals on the common wastelands were twice as high for foreigners as for inhabitants.[95] Several Campine villages introduced rules to prevent the inhabitants of neighbouring villages from entering the commons. In Retie, for example, the by-law states:

> Nobody from Retie or other non-privileged individuals will take, bring, drove or feed any cattle or sheep onto, or on, the commons of Retie belonging to anyone outside the village or an unprivileged person, on the penalty of 3 karolus gulden.[96]

At Zandhoven the register never mentions the origin of the people paying for access to the common, nor does anybody have to pay at a different rate. It is therefore not impossible that outsiders paid to use the commons, but it is unlikely since the number of users corresponds perfectly with the total number of households in the village. Therefore, the 'heideboek' of Zandhoven shows that all the households of the village community of Zandhoven had access to and actively used the commons during the middle of the sixteenth century. This is remarkably inclusive when compared to other European commons, where a large part of the village community was often excluded on the basis of inheritance rights, property limitations, poverty or other restrictions.[97]

As the entire village community had access to the commons, this uncovers an apparent paradox about their inclusiveness. While the normative sources tend to stress the necessity of contributing to village taxes and burdens in order to secure access, on average 98 per cent of Zandhoven households belonged to the community of users and actively enjoyed their privileged position.[98] This is all the more remarkable since the ecological benefits were not free. Despite an absolute silence about entrance fees or contribution taxes in the local by-laws, the 'heideboek' listed the payments made by individual users for their use of the commons. On average a family had to pay 0.6 stuiver or 1.2 groten for every cattle unit they placed on the commons.[99] In addition, 1.75 stuiver or 3.5 groten was the fee required for a day spent collecting heather or digging peat. As 71 'groten' equals a 'viertel' of rye,[100] the price for using the commons was not that great. Nevertheless, monetary fees might have had the effect of excluding the poorest section of society from access. After all, a large proportion of any rural community in the Campine could be labelled 'poor' during the sixteenth century. According to Limberger, between 20–25 per cent of typical rural, Brabant community was exempt from taxes because of their financial status.[101] Nonetheless, as the registration rate in Zandhoven approached 100 per cent, it is certain that the poorest section of society was not excluded from using the commons.

Consequently, either the poor were exempted from paying the access fee, or the village dues were taken care of by the local Holy Ghost table. (Poor tables, called 'Heilige Geest tafels' in Dutch, were the institutions that collected the poor rates and distributed money or goods to the poor.) The findings of Hadewijch Masure and Eline Van Onacker support the latter scenario. In contrast with coastal and inland Flanders, the Holy Ghost tables in this district (in Rijkevorsel for example), were able to distribute 62 litres of rye per household. If we take only the poor households into account, each family could count on 190 litres or more. Most donations were distributed in kind, but assistance in money was also given. It is therefore possible that families who were unable to pay the village dues received help from the local poor relief system. Excluding families from the commons would, after all, increase the likelihood that those families would become dependent on poor relief.[102] Birtles described this strategy as follows: 'Property owners with an interest in common land preferred to allow certain use rights over their commons and wastelands rather than face the alternatives, which required far more trouble and expense to them personally'.[103]

Exclusive Tendencies: Groups on the Margin

Normative and even administrative sources tend to hide conflicts and discord. For Norfolk, Nicola Whyte showed that a restrictive reality was hidden behind the fold course system. Despite the theoretical opportunity for peasants to buy access to the commons, the lords reserved the licences for their own tenant farmers. None of the normative sources, however, gives any hint of this sixteenth-century practice. Only when the manorial lords were impeached for it before the manorial courts does the system become apparent to the historian. The court records reveal that not only were the tenants informally excluded, but complaints of their exclusion did not receive any support, either from the courts, or from complaints to the king seeking the overturning of these restrictions.[104]

To all appearances Campine communities were harmonious and inclusive. Exclusive tendencies were, however, not completely absent, but never developed very far, although the access rights of the larger tenant farmers and dependent hamlets were sometimes the subject of dispute. Both charters and court sentences were analysed to uncover any underlying forms of discord or conflict.[105]

The protection or re-evaluation of common rights, communal property and custom were recurrent conflicts in the late medieval Campine. In the Duchy of Brabant between the fourteenth and sixteenth centuries, several venues or juridical institutions were at the disposal of communities. The range of formal courts widened during this period, as new sovereign institutions and judicial officials were introduced with the arrival of the Burgundian Dukes.[106]

Within the late medieval Campine, conflicts about communal rights, access to the commons and the survival of common pool institutions fell within the jurisdiction of the highest formal court, the Council of Brabant. Since the ducal court was considered to be sympathetic in its attitude to communal rights, the Campine peasants took their grievances to this court with a remarkable frequency. Its records give us insights into the management of the commons.[107] Did all interest groups within the Campine possess and maintain their access rights to the commons in the way the normative and administrative documents suggest, or was inclusion a more contested issue during the later Middle Ages? Thanks to the judicial sources, it becomes clear that the access of tenant farmers and dependent hamlets was not invariably conceded.

Tenant farmers of large ecclesiastical institutions, or urban burghers leasing substantial farmsteads and land, were the subject of hostility from the 'common inhabitants and neighbours' ('gemeyne ingezetenen en geburen') of certain Campine villages. These tenant farmers were far from being small peasants leasing a plot of land or farmstead. They leased full farmsteads with their land, not from their neighbours or fellow peasants, but from ecclesiastical institutions such as the abbey of Postel and Sint Jan's in 's Hertogenbosch, or from 'poorters' or burghers from cities such as 's Hertogenbosch.[108] Tenants were, on many levels, the 'odd man out' within Campine communities.

In at least ten villages, the right of these tenant farmers to use the commons was disputed by the village community. The disputes between them turned on the questions that concern us. What conferred membership of the community of users? Who was an outsider? These questions were answered in fundamentally different ways by the tenant farmers and the village communities. For the communities, paying taxes or contributing to the village finances was the sine qua non of access to the commons. But most crucially, one had to be descended from the original peasants and farmers who had received a charter or privilege. For example, the community of Vroenhoeven pleaded that

> In the year of 1307 on Saint Servaes day, Lord Willem of Cramendonck and Lady Elizabeth his wife had legally sold to the inhabitants and their heirs of the hamlet called Bundel by name and surname in a letter their common hay meadows or marsh located in Bundel with all the wood that grew there.[109]

The inhabitants believed that the commons were not a 'meent' or CPI connected to the village government, but a 'marke'. This type of CPI operated independently from the village government and included only the original owners and their descendants. In addition, every member had to carry out common tasks, such as maintaining the commons, boundaries and fences, planting trees and hedges or clearing out the brooks.[110] Finally, one had to live within the village boundaries.

The contested tenant farmers did not meet all the preconditions prescribed for access. One village in particular made a very extensive case against the tenant farmers. The conflict arose in 1535 between the 'gemeyne ingesetenen' of Stiphout and the tenants of the 'fabrieksmeesters' of Saint John's in 's Hertogenbosch. The tenants had won a court case against the common inhabitants of Stiphout in 1526, which confirmed their entitlement to common rights on the wastelands of Stiphout. The common inhabitants, however, lodged an appeal before the Council of Brabant. According to Stiphout, the tenants belonged to the neighbouring hamlet of Hoochstrijpe which was under the jurisdiction of Aerle rather than Stiphout.[111] Another community, Vroenhoven, made an argument as follows: 'The use [of the commons] by the plaintiffs [the tenants] followed only from a plea and the consent of the defendants [the community of Vroenhoven] for a short time span or because of clandestine use'. Possessing property in the hamlet 'does not imply a lawful possession, privilege or use right for the owners and tenants nor their ancestors in the common hay meadow'.[112]

Clearly the community was not as inclusive as the administrative and normative sources seem to imply. In an almost xenophobic discourse, the tenants were portrayed as outsiders, living at the margins of society in both a literal and figurative sense. In the opinion of the village's inhabitants, owning or leasing property in the village did not make a person a member of the community of users of the commons. The tenants belonged either to a neighbouring community or, worse, were linked to urban or regional institutions rather than the local village community. Village communities regarded the rights of tenants to be a concession, a favour to them, and not an entitlement arising from the charters granted to the village communities.

Similar conflicts occurred between Campine village communities and another form of 'outsider': urban burghers owning property in the villages. For example, the Lord of Gaasbeke stipulated that 'nobody being burgher of the city of Brussels will be allowed to use the commons in any way'.[113] The plaintiffs, however, stated that the land of Leende and Heeze had been granted as a fief by the Duke of Brabant. Consequently, the inhabitants and neighbours of that land were citizens of Brabant, which placed them under the protection of the ordinances of the 'blijder incomst'.[114] The Lord of Gaasbeke, however, replied that he held a full fief and could therefore determine the requirements and terms as he wished, which included the exclusion of burghers. Every 16 years the terms of leasing the commons were discussed and re-evaluated by the lord and community. In addition, he stated that only the burghers themselves, who constituted the majority of the plaintiffs, opposed exclusion. The 'gemeyne ingesetenen', on the contrary, accepted the terms of leasing the commons. After all, he claimed that it was 'an ill-founded argument to presume that long-term usage would provide them an official privilege'.[115] Finally, the ducal court pronounced in its sentence that the Lord of Gaasbeke, as vassal of the Duke, held all rights to determine the terms for receiving the use rights, but declined the condition of excluding individuals, based on them being a burgher of Brussels or having the Saint Peter's 'manscap', as unseemly.[116] For the ducal institutions, an exclusion based on the membership of a Brabant city was unacceptable. As long as they leased or possessed estates in the seigniory, they were granted access to the commons.

Almost all tenant farmers and urban burghers secured a right of access through court actions.[117] According to the ducal court, contributing to the village's finances, whether through annual taxes or a separate payment by tenants to purchase access, was sufficient to make them a member of the community of users.

Similar conflicts occurred between dependent hamlets or jurisdictions and the main village communities. Practically every village consisted of a main nucleus, and several smaller hamlets. During the thirteenth and fourteenth centuries, however, hamlets and agglomerations were not as developed as they would become by the sixteenth century. Because of population growth, the hamlets grew and, as they did, they developed their own jurisdictions and institutions such as aldermen's benches, becoming practically independent villages, with their own governments and by-laws, as was the case for Terloo.[118] From that time onwards the issue of their access to the commons of the main village arose, and attempts to exclude hamlets were made in the sixteenth century. According to the dependent hamlets, the main villages would suddenly and wrongfully exclude them from entering and using the commons, although they had used them for centuries. As a result, the main villages were forced to defend their position and explain who was, and who was not, entitled to exercise common rights.

Here a less straightforward solution was found. In several cases the hamlets were proven to be independent from the main village and were from then onwards excluded from the main commons. Nevertheless, some of them already owned a piece of common land designated for the inhabitants of the hamlet. In the remaining cases the hamlets remained part of the larger village and maintained access to those commons.[119]

So despite rising population densities and growing commercialisation and urbanisation on the borders of the region, communal property was not only retained, but was institutionalised. The fruits of the commons continued to be enjoyed by all interest groups. Even when the population grew, the benefits continued to be divided among all the households of the village. Children born and settled in Campine villages were immediately accepted as members of the community of users. Immigrants, however, had to become formal members of the village community before being allowed access. Attempts to exclude parts of society or even interest groups from within the village are to be found in the records of the Council of Brabant. Large tenant farmers and urban burghers as well as dependent hamlets were often the target of the core village communities, comprising independent peasants, sometimes accompanied by the village government. As marginal groups on the edge of village society, they were often portrayed as literal or figurative outsiders who were not admitted into the community of users. Nevertheless, since the Campine area had a balanced distribution of power, smallholders, farmers and lords alike were able to influence the decision-making within the village, and the common pool institutions remained inclusive. As such they contrasted with societies such as Breckland in East Anglia, and the Geest region in Schleswig-Holstein, where one particular stakeholder was able to usurp the government and management of the village or common pool institution, disturbing the equilibrium to such an extent so as to fundamentally alter accessibility, resulting in an exclusive system.[120]

Notes

1 Martina De Moor, Leigh Shaw-Taylor, and Paul Warde, 'Comparing the historical commons of north west Europe: An introduction', in *Management*, eds De Moor, Shaw-Taylor, and Warde, 20.
2 Ibid.; Verboven et al., *Bos en hei*, 32.
3 E. Van Looveren, 'De privatisering van de gemeentegronden in de provincie antwerpen: Vier case-studies', *Bijdragen tot de geschiedenis* 66, no. 1 (1983).
4 De Moor, ' "Silent Revolution" '.
5 Ibid.; Laborda Peman and De Moor, 'Tale of two commons'.
6 Van Looveren, 'De privatisering van de gemeentegronden'.
7 W. J. Droesen, *De gemeentegronden in noord-brabant en limburg en hunne ontginning: Eene geschied- en landhuishoudkundige studie* (Roermond, 1927).
8 See Chapter 1.
9 For more information about the surrounding agrosystems: Bas Van Bavel and Erik Thoen (eds), *Land productivity and agro-systems in the North Sea area, middle ages-20th century* (Turnhout, 1999); Thoen, 'Social agrosystems'; Hoppenbrouwers, 'Use and management'.
10 De Moor, ' "Silent Revolution" '.
11 Similar critiques are formulated by Curtis, 'Tine de Moor's "Silent Revolution" '.

12 Enklaar, *Gemeene gronden*, 129.

13 Paul De Ridder, *Hertog jan i van brabant (1267–94)* (Antwerp: Vlaamse toeristenbond, 1978).

14 Piet Avonds, *Brabant tijdens de regering van hertog jan iii (1312–1356): De grote politieke crisissen* (Verhandlingen van de Koninklijke Vlaamse Aademie voor Wetenschappen. Letteren en Schone Kunsten van België 46, Brussels: Paleis der Academiën, 1984).

15 Hoppenbrouwers, 'Use and management', 92–3.

16 Original text: 'Nos Johannes [] quod nos omnes communitates et wastinas nostras, sitas infra limites seu palos infrascriptos [] bonis allodialibus necnon juribus et juridictionibus aliorum dominorum infra dictos palos [] exceptis universis et singulis hominibus nostris villarum nostrarum de Eyck et de Westerhoven ad opus eorum et omnium commorcancium infra dictos limites [] ad communes earum usus pro certe prelevio decem librarum grossorum turonensium antiquorum et pro annuo et hereditario censu quinque solidorum grossorum'. In addition, members of the community were often granted the right to sell certain plots of common land that would yield customary rent for the lord: 'propter nostram et eorum utilitatem vendidimus ab ipsis seu eorum heridibus ad dictam communitatem spectantibus jure heriditario obtinendas et habendas'. Free translation: 'For our and their benefit, they and their ancestors will sell the aforementioned commons keeping in mind the hereditary right' (ibid.).

17 Maïka De Keyzer, 'The common denominator. The survival of the commons in the late medieval Campine area' (Unpublished thesis, University of Antwerp, 2014).

18 Laborda Peman and De Moor, 'Tale of two commons'.

19 G. Dejongh, 'De ontginningspolitiek van de overheid in de zuidelijke nederlanden, 1750–1830. Een maat voor niets?', *Tijdschrift van het Gemeentekrediet* 210 (1999), 31–44.

20 Rosa Congost and Rui Santos, 'Working out the frame: From formal institutions to the social contexts of property', in *Contexts of property: The social embeddedness of property rights to land in Europe in historical perspective*, eds Rosa Congost and Rui Santos (Turnhout: Brepols, 2010).

21 De Moor, Shaw-Taylor, and Warde, 'Comparing the historical commons', 18–19.

22 Since January 1, 2016, HISGIS is no longer online. The data files have been transferred to LOKSTAT, the Historical Database for Local Statistics in Belgium (nineteenth and twentieth centuries)
      More information is available on the website Census 1900 (www.lokstat. ugent.be/lokstat_start.php), where a selection of the data files and maps can be consulted.

23 Poulsen, 'Landesausbau und umwelt in schleswig 1450–1550j'; Bailey, *Marginal economy*.

24 'Glossary', in *Management of common lands*, eds De Moor, Shaw-Taylor, and Warde, 261.

25 SAA, Ancien Regime archives of the city of Antwerp, other governments, Local governments and seigniories, Belgium, Duchy of Brabant, 5 Condition of the villages in the margraviate of Antwerp in 1593. From now on referred to as SAA, 5 condition and RAA, OGA Gierle, 344, 1554; RAA, OGA, Tongerlo 896, 1569; AAT, Section II, 373–400, Rent register, Kalmthout, 1518. The surface area of the villages is based on the historical database of www.hisgis.be/nl/start_nl.htm.

26 De Wachter, 'De opname van de kempen', Dekkers, 'Braband zand'.

27 Verboven et al., *Bos en hei*; Nico Paepen, 'De aard van de zes dorpen 1332–1822: Casusonderzoek naar de kempense gemene heide (deel 1)', *Taxandria, Jaarboek van de Koninklijke geschied- en oudheidkundige kring van de Antwerpse Kempen* LXXVI (2004); Van Der Haegen, 'Hoe de kempense gemeenschappen hun aard verkregen'.

28 De Moor, Shaw-Taylor, and Warde, 'Comparing the historical commons', 1.

29 RAA, OGA Gierle, 344, 1554; RAA, OGA, Tongerlo 896, 1569.

30 'It has been decided and by the village proclaimed with the consent of the bailiff and aldermen, that the hay meadow will be fenced and liberated like all other "vrede beemden". Before the harvest everyone can collect his hay and nobody will graze his animals as long as more than three individuals have to collect their hay. When everyone has done his harvest the hay meadow will be common. 17 January 1544'. E. H. A. Van Olmen, 'De keuren van vorselaar', *Taxandria* 7 (1910).

31 For example: AAT, Section II, Rent registers, 341–2, Tongerlo and its surroundings, 1566–1621; AAT, Section II, Rent registers, 335, General rent registers, 1435–53.

32 'Er is geordonneerd dat men in de beempden in het broek en de Aesten zal bevrijden en omheinen te half maart en het gemeen broek de tweede dag van mei. Daarna zal niemand meer mogen stouwen in het gemeen broek, op zijn eigen of op dat van iemand anders'. Source: Th. De Molder, 'Keuren van oostmalle', *Oudheid en Kunst* 26, no. 1 (1935).

33 Congost and Santos, 'Working out the frame'.

34 De Moor, Shaw-Taylor, and Warde, 'Comparing the historical commons', 18, 261.

35 Lindemans, *Geschiedenis van de landbouw in belgië*; Spek, *Het drentse esdorpenlandschap*; Vangheluwe and Spek, 'De laatmiddeleeuwse transitie'; Hans Renes, 'Grainlands. The landscape of open fields in a European perspective', *Landscape History* 31, no. 2 (2010).

36 Theo Spek, *Het drentse esdorpenlandschap: Een historisch-geografische studie* (Utrecht: Stichting Matrijs, 2004).

37 Lindemans, *Geschiedenis van de landbouw in belgië.*

38 AAT, II, Registers, 292–3, Tenant farm descriptions of the abbey of Tongerlo, 1510–1653, 1239–1600. The farmsteads were located in Tongerlo, Eindhout, Oevel, Zoerle, Wiekevorst, Oosterlo, Veerle, Meerhout, Hapert, Eersel, Wippenhout, Westerhoven, Bergeijk, Oostelbeers, Middelbeers, Tilburg, Alphen, Teteringen, Broechem, Mol, Massenhoven, Oelegem, Nijlen, Brecht, Kalmthout, Beers, Bladel, Loon, Mierlo, Chaam, Nieuwmoer, Duffel, Ravels, Oelegem, Viersel, Venloon, Udenhout, Goerle.

39 AAT, II, Registers, 292–3.

40 Vangheluwe and Spek, 'De laatmiddeleeuwse transitie'.

41 See database: by-laws.

42 See database: by-laws.

43 Vivier, *Proprieté collective.*

44 For more information on the possession of animals, see Chapter 4.

45 Spek, *Het drentse esdorpenlandschap.*

46 J. Bastiaens and J. M. van Mourik, 'Bodemsporen van beddenbouw in het zuidelijk deel van het plaggenlandbouwareaal: Getuigen van 17de-eeuwse landbouw intensivering in de blegische provincies antwerpen en limburg en de nederlandse provincie noord-brabant', *Historisch geografisch tijdschrift* 3 (1994).

47 Verboven et al., *Bos en hei*; Tack et al., *Bossen van vlaanderen.*

48 Douglas North, *Institutions, institutional change and economic performance* (Cambridge: Cambridge University Press, 1990), 2–3.

49 Ostrom, *Governing the commons*, 51.

50 Ibid., 93.

51 Arun Agrawal, *Environmentality: Technologies of government and the making of subjects* (Durham: Duke University Press, 2005).

52 Haller, Acciaioli, and Rist, 'Constitutionality'.

53 Tine De Moor, 'Participating is more important than winning: The impact of socioeconomic change on commoners' participation in eighteenth-and nineteenth-century Flanders', *Continuity and Change* 25, no. 3 (2010).

54   Whyte, 'Contested pasts'.

55   Original text: 'Het keurboek, statuten en ordonnanties die door de welgeboren heer Antoon van Lalaing van Hoogstraten in 1534 bij goeddunken van de schepenen, gezworenen en gemene ingezetenen van zijn vrijheid van Hoogstraten gesloten zijn geweest'. Source: Guillaume De Longé, *Coutumes d'herenthals, de casterlé, de moll, balen et deschel, de gheel, de hoogstraten, de befferen et de putte, et feodales du pays de malines, Recueil des anciennes coutumes de la belgique* (Recueil des anciennes coutumes de la belgique, Brussels: Fr. Gobbaerts, 1878).

56   Harry De Kok, 'De aard van zes dorpen: Beerse, vosselaar, lille, wechelderzande, gierle en vlimmeren. Een casusonderzoek van een kempense gemene heide', *Post Factum. Jaarboek voor geschiedenis en Volkskunde*, no. 1 (2009).

57   'Keuren gemaakt geordonneerd en gestatueert door de schout en schepenen van de heerlijkheid en jurisdictie van Oostmalle en geapprobeerd door de edele en welgeboren heer Fredericus de Renesse, heer van het dorp Oostmalle'. De Molder, 'Keuren van Oostmalle'.

58   J. Michielsen, 'Keuren van brecht', *Oudheid en Kunst* (1907); RAA, OGA Brecht, 2431–82, Accounts of the ducal (later royal) aides, 1523–76.

59   This is also noticed by Arun Agrawal and Clark C. Gibson, 'Enchantment and disenchantment: The role of community in natural resource conservation', *World Development* 27, no. 4 (1999).

60   'Wanneer zeven personen van een heertgang komen naar de heer om enige zaken die profijtelijk zouden zijn voor de heertgang in een keure gezet te worden, zal men het hele jaar door mogen ordineren en zetten bij de heer en vier schepenen. Indien de mannen affirmeren bij eed dat dezelfde keur naar hun vijf zinnen profijtelijk is dan zal de keure waardig zijn om te onderhouden zoals de andere keuren die bij de gezworenen gezamenlijk gemaakt zijn en onverbrekelijk onderhouden moeten worden'. I. Helsen, 'Het dorpskeurboek van retie', *Bijdragen tot de geschiedenis* 1, no. 1 (1949).

61   Van Olmen, 'De keuren van vorselaar'.

62   Ibid.

63   Maarten Prak, *Gezeten burgers. De elite in een hollandse stad leiden 1700–1780* ('s Gravenhage: De Bataafse Leeuw, 1985).

64   Ostrom, *Governing the commons*.

65   Tobias Haller (ed.), *Disputing the floodplains. Institutional change and the politics of resource management in African wetlands* (Leiden: Brill, 2010).

66   René van Weeren and Tine De Moor, 'Controlling the commoners: Methods to prevent, detect, and punish free-riding on Dutch commons in the early modern period', *Agricultural History Review* 62, no. 2 (2014), 256–77.

67   See for example Ravels: 'Niemand zal ontvreemden of wegdragen andermans heymsel, horden oft tuinen of vekens op pene van gecorrigeerd te worden door de heer' ('Nobody will steal or carry away another's hedge, fence, bushes or locks, on pain of correction by the lord'). Milo Koyen, 'Keuren van ravels', *Oudheid en Kunst* 41, no. 2 (1958).

68   'De drossaard van de vrijheid van Geel en de schepenen zijn schuldig en behoren de onderzaten recht en justitie te doen. De drossaard is maander in alle zaken en de schepenen rechters en wijzen'. J. Ernalsteen, 'Keuren van gheel', *Oudheid en Kunst* 26 (1935), 19–66.

69   D. A. Berents, 'Taak van schout en schepen', *Maandblad Oud Utrecht* 45, no. 8 (1972); B. C. M. Jacobs, *Justitie en politie in 's-hertogenbosch voor 1629: De bestuursorganisatie van een brabantse stad* (Assen: Van Gorcum, 1986); Walter Van Den Branden, 'De schout of officier van de landsheer te lille, wechelderzande en vlimmeren: Aspecten van het dorpsbestuur in het land van turnhout in

het ancien régime, vooral in de zeventiende en achttiende eeuw', *Heemkundige kring Norbert de Vrijter Lille* 79 (1989), 57–99; J. Van Rompaey, 'Het compositierecht in vlaanderen van de veertiende tot de achttiende eeuw', *Tijdschrift voor rechtsgeschiedenis* 44 (1961).

70 José-Antonio Espín-Sánchez, 'Let the punishment fit the crime: Self-governed communities in south-eastern Spain' (unpublished conference paper, Utrecht, 2012).

71 Maïka De Keyzer, Iason Jongepier, and Tim Soens, 'Consuming maps and producing space. Explaining regional variations in the reception and agency of cartography in the Low Countries during the medieval and early modern periods', *Continuity and Change* 29, no. 2 (2014).

72 'zal zijn boeten van het schutten en aanklagen, innen zo ver deze de grond en bodem aangaan en zal zich niet onderwinden in enige zaken de overheer aangaande'. Koyen, 'Keuren van ravels'.

73 'Is geordonneerd dat bij gemene stemmen van de ingezetenen het gehucht van loo dat er altijd 2 aardmeesters gekozen zullen worden om 2 jaar te dienen zoals kerkmeesters. Als hun termijn beëindigd is zullen zij de keuze hebben om uit de gemeente van Loo twee andere uit te kiezen naar hun verstand en goeddunken'. J. Van Gorp, 'De aartbrief van terloo', *Bijdragen tot de geschiedenis* 18 (1927).

74 'alle 14 dagen tezamen en met elkaar in de heide en rond de palen van Ekeren te gaan'. A. Gielens, 'Keuren van ekeren', *Oudheid en Kunst* 30, no. 1 (1939).

75 In Arendonk the by-laws stipulated 'that everybody is allowed to report [a trespasser] and will receive half of the fine' ('iedereen mag klagen en de breuk voor de helft hebben'). Floris Prims, 'Keuren der vreyheyt van arendonk', in *Feestbundel H. J. Van de wijer, den jubilaris aangeboden ter gelegenheid van zijn vijfentwintigjarig hoogleeraarschap aan de R. K. Universiteit te leuven 1919–1943*, ed. H. Draye (Leuven: Instituut voor Vlaamse topynomie, 1944).

76 Original text: 'hominibus nostris nostre ville d'oisterwijk'. [. . .] 'Concede hominibus nostris predictis quod hominibus alienis usum possint dicte co[mm]itatem prohibere qua nulli licitum sit perfrui nisi solum hominibus nostril de oisterwijk'. Alphonse Verkooren, *Inventaire des chartes et cartulaires des duchés de brabant et de limbourg et des pays d'outre-meuse*, I (Brussels: Archives générales du royaume, 1961), no. 202.

77 Peter Blickle, *Kommunalismus: Skizzen einer gesellschaftlichen organisationsform* (München: Oldenbourg, 2000).

78 In the village of Westerlo, a by-law of 1569 states: 'everyone who comes to live in the quarter of Westerlo or in the jurisdiction of the "buitenbank" (external law court), will have to contribute to the "schot en lot" [general village taxes] and "horseman tax". Those who refuse will be held [to be] foreigners and de facto be excluded from using the commons' ('Iedereen die komt wonen in enig kwartier van de heerlijkheid van Westerlo of onder de buiten banken die de gemeyn aarden van Westerlo gebruiken, zullen contribueren in alle schot, lot, ruitergelden etc. indien men weerspannig is zal men hen houden voor buitenlieden de facto gepriveerd van aarden, vroenten en bij overtreding steeds verbeuren 16 stuivers'). J. Lauwerys, 'Keuren van westerloo', *Oudheid en Kunst* 28, no. 4 (1937).

79 See database: by-laws.

80 Rijkevorsel: 'Iedereen wie hij ook zij, een gespan heeft of een cossaat is, zal elk jaar 1 dag turf mogen slaan, zonder meer, na het uitgeven en consenteren bij openbaar kerkgebod'. Herenthout had a more general rule that 'every household of Herenthout will be permitted according to the by-laws to dig peat on the waste lands or commons for two days per person, without one day more' ('Elk huisgezin van herenthout zal alle jaren volgens de oude costuimen mogen turf

steken op de heide en vroente, twee dagen vor 1 persoon zonder meer'). Geel displays a different perspective, granting access and rights to everybody, however, in terms of the collection of fodder on the wastelands, they did grant a larger share to plough owners than cottagers: 'Each plough can collect one voeder per week and cottagers every 14 days. Those who plough go every Thursday, while cottagers go on Monday' ('Elke ploeg een voerder per week en de keuters per 14 dagen een voerder. De ploegers op donderdag en de keuters op maandag'). RAA, OGA, Herenthout, 3, by-law; RAA, OGA rijkevorsel, 8, by-law; De Longé, *Coutumes*; Ernalsteen, 'Keuren van gheel'.

81 Tine De Moor, 'Avoiding tragedies: A Flemish common and its commoners under the pressure of social and economic change during the eighteenth century', *Economic History Review* 62 (2009).

82 Allison, 'Sheep-corn husbandry'; Whyte, 'Contested pasts'.

83 Casari, 'Gender-biased inheritance systems'; Kos, *Van meenten tot marken*.

84 This average is calculated from the survey of hearth sizes in 1526 collected by Cuvelier including all Campine villages from the districts of Geel, Herentals, Land of Arkel, Land of Bergen op Zoom, Land van Rijen, 'Vrijheid' of Hoogstraten, 'Vrijheid' of Turnhout and Zandhoven; Cuvelier, *Les Dénombrements*.

85 E. Sabbe, 'De hoofdbank van zandhoven', *Tijdschrift voor geschiedenis en folklore* 7, no. 1–2 (1954); Guido Van Dijck, 'Het landbouwleven in de antwerpse kempen volgens de dorpskeuren (speciaal de hoofdbank van zandhoven)' (Unpublished thesis, Catholic University of Leuven, 1965).

86 The by-laws of Zandhoven were directly adopted by: Zandhoven, Viersel, Massenhoven, Halle, Broechem, Oelegem, Ranst, Rillegem, Borsbeek, Westmalle, Zoersel, Oostmalle, Pulle, Pulderbos, Grobbendonk, Bouwen en Olmen. In addition, the by-laws were closely linked with those of Baarle-Hertog, Sprundel, Groot en Klein Zundert, Warehout, Nispen, Rozendaal, Meerle, Meir, Minderhout, Buitenbank of Hoogstraten, Weelde, Wuustwezel, Rijkevorsel, Vosselaar, Beerse, Rode-bij-Turnhout, Kasterlee, Gierle, Halle, Lille, Poederlee, Zandhoven, Massenhoven, Lichtaart, Grobbendonk, Viersel, Vorselaar, Oostmalle, Wechelderzande, Zoersel, Vlimmeren, Brecht, Deurne, Borsbeek, Broechem, Hemiksem, Merksem, Oelegem, Schilde, Schoten, Wommelgem, Emblem, Millegem, Ranst, 's-Gravenwezel, Wijnegem, Herselt, Herenthout, Kesseland Olmen. Sabbe, 'De hoofdbank'; M. W. Van Boven, 'De verhouding tussen de raad van brabant en de hoofdbanken inzake de appelrechtspraak in civiele zaken', in *Hoven en banken in noord en zuid*, eds B. C. M. Jacobs and P. L. Nève (Assen: Van Gorcum & Comp., 1994); R. Van Uytven, 'Landen en 's hertogenbosch: De hoofdvaart', in *Brabandts recht is . . . Opstellen aangeboden aan prof. Mr. J. Pa. Coopmans ter gelegenheid van zijn afscheid als hoogleraar nederlandse rechtsgeschiedenis aan de katholieke universiteit brabant*, eds Th. E. A. Bosman et al. (Assen: Van Gorcum, 1990).

87 RAA, OGA Zandhoven, 148, 'Heideboek', 1559–81.

88 'Iedereen die komt wonen in enig kwartier van de heerlijkheid van Westerlo of onder de buiten banken die de gemeyn aarden van Westerlo gebruiken, zullen contribueren in alle schot, lot, ruitergelden etc. indien men weerspannig is zal men hen houden voor buitenlieden de facto gepriveerd van aarden, vroenten'. Lauwerys, 'Keuren Van Westerloo'.

89 RAA, OGA Zandhoven, 148, 'Heideboek', 1559–81.

90 Data Prices and wages, Robert Allen: www.iisg.nl/hpw/data.php

91 K. Lemmens, 'Rekenmunt en courant geld', *Jaarboek van het Europees genootschap voor munt- en penningkunde* 59 (1998).

92 Source: Cuvelier, *Les dénombrements*.

93 De Moor, 'Avoiding Tragedies', 13.

94 Ibid.
95 G. De Longé, 'Coutumes de Santhoven, de Turnhout et de Rumpet', in *Coutumes du pays et duché de brabant: Quartier d'anvers*, ed. G. De Longé (Recueil des anciennes coutumes de la belgique, Brussels: Gobbaerts, 1870–8); F. Verbist, *Costuymen van de hoofdrechtbank van zandhoven, uitgave 1664: Keuren en breuken, uitgave 1665* (Zandhoven: Gemeentebestuur Zandhoven, 2007).
96 'Niemand van binnen Retie of andere ongeprivilegieerde zullen geen hoornbeesten of schapen van iemand buiten of andere ongeprivilegieerde aan nemen, brengen, stouwen, drijven, voederen of weiden op enige gemeynte van Retie of zulks laten doen, op boete van 3 karolus gulden'. Helsen, 'Het dorpskeurboek van retie'.
97 Leigh Shaw-Taylor, 'The management of common land in the lowlands of southern England circa 1500 to circa 1850', in *Management of common land*, eds De Moor, Shaw-Taylor, and Warde; Leigh Shaw-Taylor, 'Labourers, cows, common rights and parliamentary enclosure: The evidence of contemporary comment, *c.*1760–1810', *Past and Present* 171 (2001); Maïka De Keyzer, 'The impact of different distributions of power on access rights to the common waste lands: The Campine, Brecklands and Geest compared', *Journal of Institutional Economics* 9, no. 4 (2013).
98 Cuvelier, *Les dénombrements*; RAA, OGA Zandhoven, 148, 'Heideboek', 1559–81.
99 No information about the composition of these cattle units is given in the account itself. It was deduced, however, via information regarding herd compositions and numbers of Wuustwezel and Wortel, that one horse or cow, or four sheep formed one head or unit. SAA, 5, condition.
100 1 viertel rye corresponds to 79.6 litres. Data Prices and wages, Robert Allen: www.iisg.nl/hpw/data.php
101 Limberger, *Sixteenth-century Antwerp.*
102 Van Onacker, 'Leaders of the pack?'.
103 Sara Birtles, 'Common land, poor relief and enclosure: The use of manorial resources in fulfilling parish obligations, 1601–1834', *Past and Present* 165 (1999), 78.
104 Allison, 'Sheep-corn husbandry'; Whyte, 'Contested pasts'.
105 In order to limit the number of charters considered in this study, only those ducal charters analysed by Verkooren in the series *Chartes et cartulaires des duches de Brabant et de Limbourg et des Pays d'Outre-Meuse* and the clerical charters of the abbey of Tongerlo until the end of the fifteenth century have been considered. Verkooren, *Inventaire des chartes*; A. Erens, *De oorkonden der abdij tongerloo*, 4 vols (Tongerlo: St.-Norbertusdrukkerij, 1948); AAT, Section I; Court cases: RAB, Conseil de Brabant, Archives of the registry, General sentence registers, 1498–1517, 1529–55, 1574–80.
106 Robert Stein, *De hertog en zijn staten. De eenwording van de bourgondische nederlanden ca. 1380–ca. 1480* (Hilversum: Verloren, 2014).
107 For an elaborate overview of the jurisdiction of courts and peasant access to courts in late medieval Brabant, see Maïka De Keyzer, 'Access versus influence: Peasants in court in the late medieval Low Countries', in *Handbook of rural life*, ed. Miriam Müller (London: Routledge, 2018).
108 For more information about tenant farmers, see Chapter 4. Meesters godshuis van Postel (zommeren) RAB, VB, 553, 10 (end of 15th century), Zommeren; hoevenaar en leenman in Deurne RAB, VB, 558, 40 (1508) Deurne; Pachter (Vroenhoven) RAB, VB, 561, 16 (1510) Vroenhoven; pachters eppegem RAB, VB, 565, 81 (1516) Eppegem; kerkmeesters van 's Hertogenbosch (stiphout) RAB, VB, 581, 48 (1526) Stiphout; Poorter 's Hertogenbosch (Schijndel) RAB,

VB, 586, 94 (1533) Schijndel; Fabrieksmeesters Sint Jan's RAB, VB, 581, 48 (1526) Stiphout, Rentmeester Postel (Kerkkasteel) RAB, VB, 583, 274 (1535) Kerkkasteel.

109 'Inden jaere 1307 op sint Servaes dach heer Willeme heere van Cramendonck ende vrouwe Elizabeth sijne huysvrouwe hadden wettelijck verkocht den ingesetenen van Bundel bij naeme ende toename inden brieve daer af sijnde ende huere erfgenamen huere gemeyne beemde oft broeck gelegen tot Bundel met allen den houte dat inden voorschreven weyde oft broecke wassen was'. RAB, VB, 561, 16 (1512) Vroenhoven.

110 RAB, VB, 585, 198 (1535) Stiphout.

111 'Dat het waerachtich waere notoir ende oepenbaer dat die ingesetenen van hoochstrijpe ende die gronde van erven aldaer gelegen ende particuliere persoenen toebehoiren nyet en waeren gelegen noch resorterenden onder die prochie, justicie oft dingbanck van stiphout maar onder die prochie van Aerle'. RAB, VB, 585, 198 (1535) Stiphout.

112 'Sulcken gebruyck als doe voorschreven impetrant mochte hem seggen te hebben alleene waeren geweest vuyt beden tot zijn versuecken ende bij consente vanden voorschreven gedaeghden voere een cleyne oft cortten tijt oft anderssins heymelic'. 'Niet bevonden en souden wordden dat die voorschreven impetranten oft hueren pachteren huys of hoff hadden onder buedel dat oick hij oft zijn pachteren noch sijn voorsaten oft huere pachteren eenige wettelijke possessie oft gebruycke gehadt hadden'. RAB, VB, 561, 16 (1512) Vroenhoven.

113 'Heeren ende zijne officieren van zijnen wegen gewilt dat niemandt poirtere wesende onser stat van brussele die voorschreven gemeynte en zouden moegen gebruycken in eeniger manieren'. RAB, VB, 576, 3 (1522) Leende. The citizens of Brussels were probably 'buitenpoorters', rural subjects that had purchased the 'poorterschap' or urban rights of the city of Brussels. For more information on 'buitenpoorters', see Erik Thoen (ed.), *Rechten En Plichten Van Plattelanders Als Instrumenten Van Machtspolitieke Strijd Tussen Adel, Stedelijke Burgerij En Grafelijk Gezag in Het Laat-Middeleeuwse Vlaanderen. Buitenpoorterij En Mortemain-Rechten Ten Persoonlijken Titel in De Kasselrijen Van Aalst En Oudenaarde Vooral Toegepast Op De Periode Rond 1400* (Handelingen Van Het 13de Internationaal Colloquium Spa, 1991).

114 'Tlandt ende dorp van heeze ende van leende werdde te Leene gehouden van ons als Hertoge van Brabant soe dat die ondersaten nabueren ende ingesetenen vanden selven lande waeren ingesetenen des selfs land van brabant ende onsen ondersaten soe dat sij stonden onder onse protectie ende waeren gecomprehendeert inde ordinantiën van onser blijder incompst'. RAB, VB, 576, 3 (1522) Leende.

115 'Het soude nochtans ongefundeerd zijn dat zij onder tdexele van desen langen gebruyck zouden willen naemals recht pretenderen te hebben'. RAB, VB, 576, 3 (1522) Leende.

116 'Afslaende die eene vanden voorschreven conditiën als onbehoirlijk bijden gedaeghde doende die pachtinge vander heyden contentieux [] niet rechts plagen met poerteren van brussele oft sinte peeters manscap van Loeven ende aldaer'. RAB, VB, 576, 3 (1522) Leende.

117 RAB, VB, 586, 94 (1533) Schijndel.

118 Leenders, *Van turnhoutervoorde*; Vangheluweand Spek, 'De laatmiddeleeuwse transitie'; Van Gorp, 'De aartbrief van terloo'.

119 De Keyzer, 'Access versus influence'.

120 K. J. Allison, 'Flock management in the sixteenth and seventeenth centuries', *Economic History Review* 11 (1958); Poulsen, 'Landesausbau und umwelt in schleswig 1450–1550j'; Carsten Porskrog Rasmussen, 'An English or

a continental way? The great agrarian reforms in Denmark and Schleswig-Holstein in the late eighteenth century', in *Contexts of property in Europe*, eds Congost and Santos; Martin Rheinheimer, 'Umweltzerstörung und dörfliche rechtssetzung im herzogtum schleswig (1500–1800)', in *Dünger und dynamit: Beitrage zur umweltgeschichte schleswig-holsteins und dänemarks*, eds Manfred Jakubowski-Tiessen and Klaus-J. Lorenzen-Schmidt (Neumünster: Wachholtz Verlag Neumünster, 1999); Martin Rheinheimer, *Die dorfordnungen im herzogtum schleswig: Dorf und obrigkeit in der frühen neuzeit* (Stuttgart: Lucius & Lucius, 1999); De Keyzer, 'Impact of different distributions of power'.

4 Successful Commons
What's in a Name?

Inclusive commons existed in the Campine until at least the end of the six-teenth century and probably much longer: No evidence suggests that access to the commons became more restrictive during the seventeenth and eigh-teenth centuries. But was the distribution of benefits among all members of the community, even a growing community, a success? Indeed, what makes common pool institutions successful? This question has seldom been posed in commons studies. Success is often implicitly assumed. Elinor Ostrom her-self used a rather vague definition. Institutions are successful when they 'enable individuals to achieve productive outcomes in situations where temptations to free-ride and shirk are ever present'.[1] Others have looked more at the length of time the commons survived. If collective action took institutional form and the institution endured for a long time span, then the CPI is deemed to have been successful. Only when institutions for collective action falter or are abolished is the question of success (or the lack of it) considered.

Nevertheless, we can identify two elements in the historiography which are read as indicating success.[2] First, a CPI has been regarded as successful if it was able to prevent free riding or overexploitation and maintain the ben-efits of the asset being governed for future generations. In this way a CPI is deemed to be successful if it avoided a 'tragedy of the commons'. Second, it has been regarded as being successful if the institution itself was long endur-ing. Van Weeren and De Moor hold that 'although longevity is just one way to measure institutional success, a lifespan of over two centuries at least indicates that the commoners were able to bridge several generations, whilst dealing with changing circumstances, both internally and externally'.[3]

These definitions or preconditions are broad to the point that they include CPIs whose claim to success is questionable. First, the definition of longev-ity poses some problems. What is the minimum length of time an institution must exist before it can be termed successful? Can short lived institutions never be successful? More importantly, is longevity actually a measure of success? This has been contested. Sheilagh Ogilvie was concerned by the tendency to explain institutions as an efficient and beneficial response to the needs of the economy (or for that matter ecology), the view that 'whatever is, is right'. Inefficient or unsuccessful institutions could—and did—last. Ogilvie refers to feudalism as an example of an institution that had no economic rationale, but survived for a very long time. While all institutions arise out of rational decisions, they do not necessarily have to be the most efficient or successful entities to endure. In the conflict approach to institutional economics, institutions affect not just the efficiency of an economy but also how its resources are distributed; that is, institutions affect both the size of the total economic pie and who gets how big a slice.[4] So long as the dominant groups within society receive the share of resources to which they see themselves as being entitled, institutions will last, regardless of the detrimental effects these institutions might have on other parts of society or the general efficiency of the institution itself.[5]

This understanding of institutions in general can be applied to historical commons. While CPIs' main functions are to protect common resources, develop the means for their sustainable management and distribute the benefits among the members of the community, many long-lasting historical commons failed to do so. In pre-modern Breckland, lords and their lessees were able to monopolise the benefits of the common heathlands and open fields, while undermining the rights of the small tenants by overgrazing and degrading the landscape.[6] Nevertheless the CPIs survived into the eighteenth century without significant formal alterations. In addition, in the Netherlands, marken were CPIs established to manage forest resources, but they were unable to prevent progressive deforestation. Having failed in their original purpose, these CPIs were not abolished but evolved into institutions for the management of pastures and wastelands.[7]

Second, sustainable management is seldom defined. The idea of maintaining similar levels of ecological benefit is rather elusive. Landscapes changed significantly over time. At what point can we say that an ecosystem was so degraded that its management had failed? When Clark argued that open fields were common sense and the most efficient way of organising and managing the landscape, no evaluation of the ecological state of open fields through time was offered.[8] The same applies to practically every study of commons. While levels of deforestation, erosion and degradation are often described as increasing from the later Middle Ages onwards, even in regions with strong and long-lasting commons, the success of CPIs in resisting damaging change is almost invariably assumed. Since interdisciplinary research, in the form of pollen analysis and environmental archaeology, is needed to paint a picture of historic landscapes, the issue is rarely addressed.

Defining Success

A clear definition or at least demarcation of 'success' is needed for the concept to have any academic value. The conceptual mist that has obscured past discussions needs to be cleared by having well-defined criteria by which standard CPIs and historical commons can be tested and evaluated. Instead of a temporal evaluation, we propose three main criteria should be met before a CPI is judged to have been successful (Figure 4.1).

First, CPIs should be able to achieve ecological resilience, or in other words maintain the ecological value of their common pool resources. In order to move beyond a vague definition of maintenance or sustainability, a more rigid evaluation should be implemented. 'Ecological resilience is measured by the capacity of a system to absorb disturbance and re-organise while undergoing change so as to still retain essentially the same structure, function, identity and feedbacks'.[9] This definition implies that a landscape should not be fossilised, rather that an ecosystem must not be pushed out of its stability domain. As Figure 4.2 shows, a stability system is the stable state in which a system exists, with only modest or no disturbance.[10]

The example of a common meadow can illustrate this. The proportion and relationship between grasses and vegetation types may change, but only to such an extent that the same structure and function, namely providing grazing for the same type of animals in similar quantities, remains. A shift towards heather vegetation or a forest landscape is a shift of stability domain and cannot be considered to be a sign of ecological resilience. Deliberate decisions to alter the landscape, by, for instance drainage projects or woodland clearance, do not constitute faltering management.

Second, the benefits of the commons should be divided fairly among the community of users. Obtaining access to the commons is one thing, acquiring a fair share or useful share of the commons is another. Fair can be defined in two ways. In the first case the same benefits are distributed to every household, regardless of their socioeconomic status or interests. In the second, each household is allowed to use the commons up to a certain limit, regardless of the fact that different amounts or types of resource are then used per community member. An egalitarian division of resources among all the members is therefore no precondition of success, as long as the

Figure 4.1 Model for Successful Commons

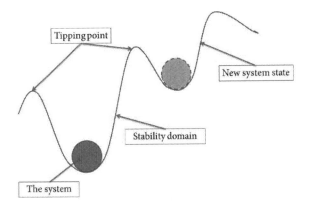

Figure 4.2 Ecological Resilience as Defined by Walker et al. (2004) and Gunderson (2000)

commons provide benefits that fit the needs of every interest group within the community of users. Such a fair distribution of benefits was not obvious in historic commons. As Lana Berasain has demonstrated, a very unbalanced distribution of power in the kingdom of Navarra led to an unequal distribution of the benefits derived from the commons. This unjust system, however, did not lead to the disappearence of the commons, or to unsustainable management, but an equilibrium was achieved on both a social as well as an ecological level.[11] In several cases, for instance the mountain pastures in the Spanish Pyrenees, communal resources such as the best grazing spots and long distance trails were reserved for a handful of wealthy farmers, while peasants were limited to smaller and less desirable pastures in the village and valleys.[12] In the Breckland, tenants were completely excluded from the communal flocks grazing the open fields by the sixteenth century, therefore making peasant sheep ownership impossible.[13] In other cases, common rights were available, but of no use to the community members. In the Gemene Loweiden in Flanders, grazing rights were often not used by members of the community because of their changed economic profile, forcing the CPI to attract outsiders to the commons in order to prevent grazing levels from dropping too low.[14]

Finally, communal property and management should prove to be resilient towards other forms of appropriation or management. The communal management of ecological resources has always co-existed with forms of private property and commercialised societies. Attempts to change communal structures into private property have been manifold. Waves of enclosure have occurred in practically every century since the thirteenth. Successful commons, were however able to fend off moves to enclose them and maintain their communal resources and management. As with ecological resilience, moderate disturbances and changes, such as piecemeal enclosure, could be absorbed without fundamentally changing the function and identity of the system. We cannot claim, however, that communities that privatised or enclosed the larger part of their commons, but still maintained a CPI to manage a small residue of common land, were successful guardians of their commons.

The Proof of the Pudding: Evaluating the Campine Case

In the light of this new tripartite definition of success, was the late medieval Campine an area with successful CPIs? After all, they refused to limit the community of users in a context of scarce and fragile common pool resources. Their approach is contrary to what most scholars have considered to be vital to maintain sustainable management and so achieve success as a CPI.[15] Nevertheless, the Campine scores remarkably well on all three criteria.

First of all, Campine CPIs were able to reach and maintain high levels of ecological resilience. This is remarkable since a consensus has emerged that the Campine failed to protect its ecosystem from the fourteenth century onwards. One of the most basic characteristics of the area remains the prevalence of easily exposed sandy soils. When the vegetation was destroyed or degraded, the topsoil could easily start to drift. Once a sand dune had formed, it could regenerate itself quite easily, so that it was difficult to stop sand drifting. Sand drifts not only eroded the soil and destroyed productive land, but in the process covered other fields and pastures and even whole villages with loose sand. These layers of arid and infertile sand prevented arable production and threatened the survival of even the sturdiest heather vegetation. Sand drifts were a continuous process in the entire cover belt area, creating what Bankoff called a landscape of risk.[16] According to Koster, local re-sedimentation of terrestrial deposits by wind occurred on a large scale from the beginning of the Neolithic period up to the present mainly in the western part of the sand belt.[17] One of the main tasks of the Campine CPIs was therefore to design a system that would prevent the exposure of the soil, maintain sturdy vegetation on the wastelands and limit the open spaces that encouraged gusts of wind. The degree of sand mobility and the extent to which sand dunes were created is therefore a good indication of the ecological resilience of the region.

The dominant view is that CPIs throughout the coversand belt failed to achieve ecological resilience. It has been established that the topsoil was sufficiently degraded for major drifts to form from the late medieval period onwards.[18] Due to the expansion and intensification of agriculture through the use of large grazing herds and plaggen fertilisation, the heather and grass vegetation of the common wastelands was degraded to such a degree that sand drifts began to threaten the region.[19] In addition, the growing number of roads and increased levels of transport have been considered to be damaging to the ecology.[20] According to Hein Vera, a number of rent registers which list the fields lost to sand show that sand-drifting became an acute problem from the fourteenth century onwards. Charters issued during the fourteenth and fifteenth centuries by the Dukes of Brabant stipulate penalties against communities that failed to stop the drifting of sand.[21] Jan Luiten Van Zanden has reported similar findings for the provinces of Overijssel, Groningen and Drenthe. He found that the disappearance of woodland cover in these regions resulted in a serious deterioration of the environment, particularly during the sixteenth century. The main causes, according to Van Zanden, were a rising population which could not be halted by the Marks, as well as the failure to manage or apply rules effectively. Consequently, sand drifts were a later medieval and early modern phenomenon that were only halted in the eighteenth century.[22]

Nevertheless, new research, and especially new methods of dating sand deposits (and in particular optically stimulated luminescence (OSL) dating), has altered our perspective on pre-modern sand drifts. Before the emergence of this technique, establishing the exact date at which sand started to drift had been extremely difficult but sand layers without archaeological elements or organic matter suitable for carbon dating can now be dated quite accurately.[23] Two important findings have been made because of the new technique. First, the periods prior to 1300, when village communities and CPIs had not yet developed, were not as stable as presumed. In fact they suffered the worst disasters before the eighteenth century. By contrast, the late medieval Campine CPIs were able to reduce the risk of sand drifting and achieve a high level of ecological resilience.

Jan Sevink and his colleagues have studied the Groot Wasmeer near Hilversum in the region of het Gooi which is, ecologically speaking, extremely similar to the Campine. They have discovered that the prehistoric period was not characterised by stabilised soils. A major drift sand phase took place about 3000 BC, coinciding with the first intensive period of land exploitation.[24] Later periods witnessed very similar processes. According to Verhaert, Roman settlements also suffered from drifting sand, as indicated in the village of Ravels, within the Campine.[25] During the excavation of a burial place in Ravels-Weelde, it was discovered that the entire site (as well as a nearby fen), had been covered by a sand layer which was big enough to protect the graves at the site from later disturbance.[26] The most disastrous sand flood occurred during the high Middle Ages. In a recent excavation in the Campine, Cilia Derese and her colleagues discovered an abandoned habitation site near present-day Pulle. The site was inhabited from the fifth until the end of the ninth century but was subsequently covered by a 2.5 m thick layer of drift sand. After OSL dating, it was discovered that the entire layer had approximately the same age (1.2 ± 0.1 ka, or around AD 800), indicating that Pulle witnessed a short period of sand drifts, covering part of the settlement, which would have forced the inhabitants to abandon the site. This led Derese to the conclusion that the early Middle Ages can no longer be considered to be a stable period, with only minor sand drifts.[27]

The first colonisers and early medieval communities reclaimed vast and unenclosed arable fields and introduced herds of livestock which induced sand drifts large enough to threaten entire villages. These drifts, however, predated the introduction of CPIs and effective collective action. While communal property was present, villages had not formed nucleated settlements, with strong collaborative ties. In addition, colonising communities and new forms of exploitation always faced high levels of risk, since understanding of the inherent challenges of the landscape was still lacking.[28]

Nonetheless, it is still widely accepted that major sand drifts occurred during the late medieval period, from the thirteenth century onwards, during the period when CPIs were fully developed.[29] After all, the Campine witnessed a sustained growth after the thirteenth century, which lasted until the second half of the fifteenth century. The culmination of the ecological pressure was reached in the fourteenth and continued during the fifteenth century. A combination of population growth, arable production, cattle grazing and sod cutting ensured a high level of ecological pressure. According to Van Zanden, unstoppable immigration and population growth were the most devastating phenomena for the commons.[30] Consequently, these were the perfect conditions in which an ecological crisis could develop.

Historical evidence of landscape degradation, however, is thin on the ground. Vera relies on evidence from a limited number of rent registers and charters.[31] These are, however, sources that only appear from the fourteenth century and therefore give only a periodisation *ante quem*. Rent registers list all plots once granted by the duke or lord, even those that were lost because of sand drifts. However, the date at which the land was lost to the sand might be any time after the lord secured possession of these lands. Van Zanden has linked historical evidence of population pressure, intensive agricultural practices and the presumed malfunctioning of the common pool institutions to the references to sand dunes in the charters. These dunes are shown on historic maps and exist in the present landscape, but Van Zanden is unable to offer a date for their creation. He is therefore unable to connect the dunes to the pressures on the landscape which he envisages led to their creation.[32]

Geological evidence for a degradation of the landscape and the occurrence of disastrous sand floods from the later Middle Ages onwards is missing. Sand drifts were certainly a significant risk during the late medieval period, as they must have been in the early medieval period. Nevertheless, it is mistaken to claim that they worsened from the thirteenth century onwards. The early medieval sites that have been discovered had arable fields and farmsteads, huts and wells, all of which were subsequently covered by thick layers of sand. We do not have evidence for abandoned or destroyed villages after AD 1000. Documents would certainly report such major events. Beatrijs Augustyn has discovered sources which showed the loss of coastal dune villages and cities during the fifteenth and sixteenth centuries, but there are no parallels to this in the Campine.[33] The sand dunes investigated in the Campine villages of Mol, Lille and Vosselaar are all located either in the wastelands surrounding the hamlet and its arable plots or next to the wooden fences or hedges which protected the arable fields from drifting sand.[34]

While comments over the location of the dunes might come across as splitting hairs, it is vital to distinguish between a disaster that is beyond human control and threatens the presence and occupation of the local population and sand that was halted and stabilised by windbreaks, hedges and other technological interventions, introduced by the CPIs to manage the landscape and prevent large-scale drifts. These measures certainly helped to halt the sand and stabilise the landscape. The thin sand layers discovered in the plaggen soils of the arable plots of late medieval communities such as Mol and Lille were evenly dispersed within the plaggen layers, suggesting that the sand was continuously ploughed into the existing soil. Cultivation was therefore permanent and not fundamentally disturbed by surges of sand. In addition, large-scale sand drifts, showing as thick layers of sand, have not been discovered.[35] As the layer sequence of Mol demonstrated, constant re-sedimentation of thin layers of sand took place.[36] Given that sand dunes were lasting entities that could barely be halted and continued to drift on a small scale,[37] the landscape must have become more enclosed and the soil better protected by vegetation or windbreaks by the thirteenth century.

The Campine communities were therefore able to turn the tide and change a highly disturbed and mobile landscape into a stabilised system. The institutions for collective action that had developed to organise the commoners and manage the environmental challenges were successful in turning the region's inherent danger of drifting sand into a manageable hazard. In contrast to previous studies, we would advance the argument that late medieval sand drifts were continuous drifts, but not necessarily disasters. No new dune sites on productive land and habitation sites were created, nor did new regions become eroded or degraded. Existing dune sites were resedimented and caught the traces of drifting sand that was common in the coversand belt. Campine communities understood the risks and problems connected with living in a cover-sand belt.[38] According to Franz Mauelshagen, strategies for coping with risk environments are based on the expectation of repetition drawn from the experience of repeated disasters.[39] It has been recognised that natural hazards and catastrophes have a history: 'They are anticipated long in advance and they are remembered, often for a long time after the actual event takes place'.[40] Having learned from the first swift and irreversible drifts in the early Middle Ages, late medieval Campine communities adapted their agricultural practices and infrastructure. Given the disappearance of disastrous sand floods and the stabilisation of the landscape, it is fair to conclude that the CPIs were successful in their struggle with the landscape and achieved their goal of a sustainable management.

A Fair Share of the Pie: The Common Denominator

The second criterion we proposed for a successful common is a fair division of the benefits to be drawn from the common amongst its community of users. For most CPIs this distribution was very important, as is shown by the abundance of rules regulating it. According to Rodgers et al., a fair distribution of benefits was vital to secure 'good neighbourhood', which was one of the most vital issues for CPIs.[41] In general scholars have considered the distribution of fixed and maximum shares of common pool resources as the main principle to distribute benefits fairly, while maintaining a sustainable management.[42] Limitations on use rights predominantly took the form of limits on herd sizes, but could equally be applied to other types of use rights, such as timber, peat and hay harvests. Winchester has distinguished two principles that could be employed to control and limited the number of livestock on any common pasture. First, there is the rule of 'levancy and couchancy' which allowed a commoner to place on the commons as many animals as he was able to sustain over the winter from the produce of his holding. A second option was the introduction of stints. CPIs that applied stints allowed each household to put a fixed number of animals on the commons, regardless of their socioeconomic status or landownership where levancy and couchancy was more focussed on equitable access. Not all households held the same privileges, but their grazing rights were in relationship with their economic needs. Stinting actively responded to the carrying capacity of the common field. Rich community members had reduced privileges, but the benefits were distributed in a purely egalitarian way.

A third distribution strategy was possible in which no prohibitions were introduced and no strict numerical limitations were applied, but without creating an open access situation. In this third strategy the benefits to be obtained from the commons were clearly defined and measures to prevent overexploitation were employed, but community members were not granted a fixed share of the benefits. This meant that different types of resources and diverging quantities could be used per household or member. In all three options communities introduced rules to limit overexploitation. In addition, according to McCarthy, engaging in collective action immediately restricts individual peasants from overstocking and has a negative effect on herd sizes.[43]

The use of fixed stints and even restrictive stints per household is often considered to have become dominant way of allocating resources from the fifteenth and sixteenth centuries onwards. Only upland regions, or areas with vast commons such as Sweden, refrained from introducing such restrictions and then because of the extent of their wastelands.[44] Nevertheless, the third option was more common than assumed. For example as much as 46 per cent of England and Wales remained stint-free.[45] The Campine was also stint-free, despite the fact that it was exactly the sort of area where one could have expected stinting to have been introduced.

If we take a look at the local by-laws, which are the only sources available for this analysis, only 14 rules out of 1143 deal with the question of a maximum number of animals allowed.[46] Not a single village, however, imposed a rule of a fixed number of a specific type of animal throughout their entire seigniory. Where they existed, such rules were mostly concerned with particular places within the village, where one type of animal could be restricted. The hay meadows in particular were protected against overgrazing. For example, Westerlo limited the number of sheep in the reeds next to the brook to six, and in the common hay meadows a maximum of 10 'hamelen' or male sheep were allowed.[47] Apart from those rare rules, community members could put as many animals on the commons, and most certainly the common wastelands, as they possessed. The renting or buying of cattle or sheep for a short period to fatten them on the common wastelands or meadows was, however, prohibited. The by-law of Arendonk of 1627 stated 'Nobody will, under the pretence of a purchase, bring foreign animals of strange folk unto the common meadow or the common wastelands on the penalty of 20 stuiver, unless they can attest on their honour that they have purchased the animals without guile'.[48]

Nor do the by-laws refer to levancy or couchancy. By-laws did not formally limit the number of animals in any way. In practice, however, the extent of private land and fodder production did place a limit on the number of sheep each household could sustain. Sheep remained out doors for the larger part of the year, but shelter and additional fodder were always required and therefore restricted the size of flocks. In addition, informal regulations regarding the number of animals could have been employed which would escape our attention. As McCarthy had indicated, 'the capacity of co-operation is critical. Co-operation has a direct negative impact on stock densities and land allocated to private pastures'.[49]

In the Campine the benefits were distributed unevenly but tailored to the needs of all interest groups. The common pool resources were inventoried and the manner of exploiting them was strictly regulated. Especially for depletable resources, maximum shares were introduced. The absence of fixed stints did not prevent a fair distribution of the benefits of the Campine commons. Equitable rather than equal access was preferred. Farmers, with larger flocks or bigger arable plots, were able to put more cattle units on the commons and collect more turves than micro-smallholders without any animals. Nevertheless, rich farmers and rural elites were not able to dominate or monopolise the commons, whether by overstocking or prohibiting the access of other interest groups. During the late medieval period, every subgroup had very specific interests and basic needs, which were met thanks to the inclusive as well as unrestricted access to the commons.

As we showed earlier, the Campine had four main groups who were interested in the commons: micro-smallholders, cottagers, independent peasants and the rural elites. The micro-smallholders and cottagers had similar interests. As small landholders, they were predominantly in search of resources to enable them to survive as independent households. They required peat as fuel and wood for fires, building and making tools, and heather clippings and sods for fertilising their infields from the common wastelands. These requirements were met, since all community members were able to collect as much as they needed for their own use.[50] In most villages, apart from in Geel and Rijkevorsel, the same maximum amount was introduced for all community members. This was often called 'weekheide'. In Geel 'weekheide' was described as follows:

> Nobody of the six hamlets will try to mow more than his 'weekheide' between the Mass of St John and the Bamisse. The farmers owning a plough will receive one 'voeder' every week and the cottagers not owning a plough a carriage load each week. The farmers will go on Thursday, and the cottagers on Monday. Nobody will collect, dig, mow or harvest heather or sods under the pretence of taking a friend's share.[51]

What is remarkable here is the distinction between farmers and cottagers regarding the quantity of heather and sods that could be collected. This is, however, the exception. The by-law of Tongerlo even expressed the equal rights of every household by stating that nobody could collect more than could be dug in one day by one man, which was the equal share of each household.[52] At Arendonk every inhabitant could harvest seven voeder.[53] In general, every household possessed equal rights, regardless of the amount of land they cultivated. As such, these micro-smallholders and cottagers who owned no arable land had an advantage over the independent peasants or rural elites whom owned arable fields. Despite the equal shares, in reality not all households took the same quantity of turves.

In addition, cottagers needed fodder or access to common pastures. Possessing at least a single milch cow was a necessity for micro-smallholders and cottagers: It could make the difference between being able to survive as peasant or becoming a labourer or having to move to a town. Cottagers invested in cattle to supplement their supply of grain and to produce manure. As Neeson argued, the ownership of and potential gains to be made from of a single animal during the eighteenth century were worth almost half as much as the wage of a fully employed male agricultural labourer.[54]

All the extant animal counts, such as that from Rijkevorsel made in 1608 (Figure 4.3), indicate that an average Campine household possessed a significant number of cattle. Even micro-smallholders could own up to four cows. We calculate that cottagers could own herds of up to six units of cattle.[55] To keep cattle well-nourished, peasants needed sufficient quality fodder. While sheep could roam the barren wastelands and graze heather and sturdy grasses, cattle needed more nutritious grass and hay.[56] Consequently, we find examples of micro-smallholders who possessed a parcel of meadow which they could cut for hay. While in Alphen only 2 per cent of the micro-smallholders owned a parcel of meadow, 10 per cent of their

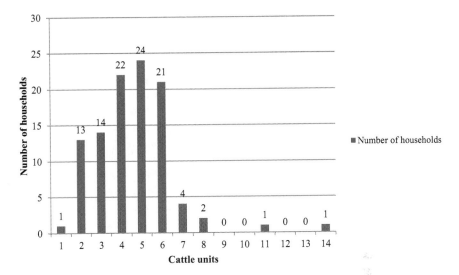

Figure 4.3 Cattle Herd Sizes in Rijkevorsel in 1608
Source: RAA, OGA Rijkevorsel, 3141–9, animal counts, 1608.

counterparts in Gierle possessed one.[57] These hay meadows were by far the most productive and valuable pieces of land in the Campine.

It seems unlikely that the average peasant household was unable to provide from its own resources all required fodder it needed. According to Moriceau, pre-modern farm animals were fed far less than modern animals. He suggested that they received approximately a third of the fodder we feed our animals today, which was just enough to keep them alive.[58] Only cattle kept for commercial purposes, such as oxen fattened for urban consumption, would have received better fodder and in larger quantities.[59] As such, he calculated that the average cow would need to receive 625 kg of dry mass of fodder during the winter months. If the cows were kept inside for most of the year—as happened in the Campine—the amount required would be much greater.[60] Estimating the yield of grass and hay is, however, much more challenging. Anna Dahlström provided some calculations based on south-central Sweden.[61] Drawing on her estimates, we have attempted to calculate what the average Campine meadow, pasture and heathland could provide.

Given the soil quality, which was a little worse than that of south-central Sweden, I estimate that the average hectare of meadow provided 1200 kg of dry mass, a pasture 520 kg and, finally, a heather patch 100 kg. Given the fact that micro-smallholders owned less than one hectare of land, of which probably no more than a half was pasture or meadow, they were unable to feed a cow all the year round. Eline Van Onacker has posited that 43 per cent of land belonging to meadow-owning micro-smallholders was meadow and they were therefore able to sustain 0.8 cattle units. Cottagers possessed more meadow and in fact, of all the interest groups, had the greatest proportion of meadow in their holdings but only between 23 and 40 per cent of a cottager's total acreage. This was able to sustain between 1.3 and 2.2 cattle units.[62] As Campine herds transcended the actual carrying capacity of the private hay meadows, they required additional grazing. That this was possible was because of the right to graze private meadows after the first hay harvest in May. Both the micro-smallholders and cottagers were able to graze any number of their cattle on the entire 'broeken' or hay meadows, and it was this which secured their required yields of fodder. For the micro-smallholders and cottagers especially, this common right was indispensable.

The independent peasants had other interests in the commons. They were more concerned with the common wastelands than the common hay meadows. Although we see the number of cattle units steadily rising the further we go up the social ladder, as demonstrated in the 'heideboek', independent peasants did not invest in ever-larger herds of cattle, instead diversifying and enlarging their livestock with horses and sheep. Therefore, the average independent peasant must have possessed between five and eight units of cattle.[63] Possessing significant amounts of private meadows as they did, they could probably provide sufficient fodder for their cattle if they were able to generate a second harvest of hay on enclosed private meadows. As such, the independent peasants were almost certainly not supporters of the communal access rights on private meadows.

Independent peasants were distinguished from the micro-smallholders and cottagers by their sheep flocks. Sheep possession was not directly linked to immovable wealth. Nevertheless, not all interest groups within the Campine communities possessed sheep. They were exclusively the possession of the better-off peasants, namely the independent peasants and rural elites.

Families who owned sheep had a flock rather than individual animals as was the case with cattle. In Wortel, a family with sheep owned 48.7 on average. This was similar to Rijkevorsel in 1608, where the average flock numbered 45.2 animals (see Figure 4.4).[64] The reason for large numbers of sheep has been the subject of some discussion. Sheep could be kept simply for their manure which was indispensable for fertilising sandy soils in pre-modern farming regimes. In the sheep-corn region in Norfolk, countless sheep were grazed on the open fields and brecks, which were temporarily cultivated and extensively used as pastures or arable fields out into the wastelands. As acid, sandy soils benefit from sheep dung rather than from cattle manure, sheep played a vital part in making it possible to cultivate these ecosystems. Regardless of the importance of their manure, however, sheep were first and foremost kept for their wool, hides and meat.[65] The same was true for the Campine peasants. Although sheep were kept in 'schaapskooien' or folds which enabled the peasants to collect their manure and spread it on their fields, they were predominantly kept for their commercial value.[66]

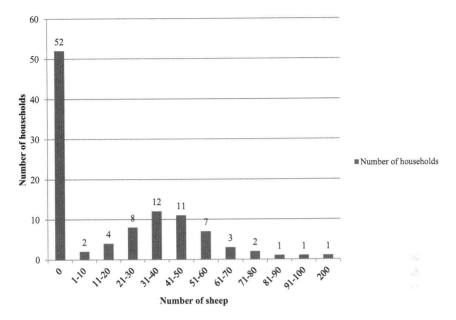

Figure 4.4 Size of Sheep Flocks in Rijkevorsel in 1608
Source: RAA, OGA Rijkevorsel, 3141–9, animal counts, 1608.

Although sheep were far less demanding than cattle in terms of the type and quantities of fodder needed to sustain them, maintaining sheep flocks of 40 animals or more was a challenge for Campine peasants. They became reliant on the commons and more specifically the vast common heathlands. Each sheep required at least 500 kg of dry mass per year according to Moriceau's estimates.[67] If they possessed 45 sheep, every independent peasant had to find a staggering 22,464 kg of dry mass.

Despite the fact that we do not know the exact composition of an independent peasant's estate, it is clear that it was impossible to generate this amount of forage from less than 5 ha of private property, especially when only half was pasture or heathland. In fact the difference was so great, that purchasing enough private pasture to support their animals was simply impossible for these independent peasants. The grazing capacity of the heathlands was, after all, extremely low, and vast, extensive fields were necessary to maintain a substantial herd of sheep permanently. The yields from sheep keeping were simply insufficient to make the transformation from extensive grazing on practically free common wastelands to intensively managed private pastures possible. The necessity of using common wastelands is therefore obvious. By maintaining vast, open and diverse heathland and grasslands as common wastelands, the village herds could easily be moved from area to area to allow each area to recover. The Campine case seems to confirm Clark's argument that purchasing the land in order to enclose and improve it enough to transform it into good pasture was in itself such a large investment that pre-modern peasants could not really profit from such a manoeuvre.[68] Consequently, it was the independent peasants who had most to gain from the survival of vast common wastelands, uninterrupted by temporary incursions of arable or pasture.

When it comes to the commons, tenant farmers resembled the independent peasants. In general, they have been considered as the opponents of common property regimes. The fact that numerous cases of enclosure, depopulation, and large-scale land transformation were instigated by feudal lords throughout the medieval and early modern period has encouraged this image. The feudal lords' tenant farmers are considered to be their partners in crime: Whilst the lords enclosed the land, it was their tenant farmers who leased and managed the newly-established or enlarged farms. In contrast to the traditional peasants, the tenant farmers had the advantage of scale and the ability to invest capital allowing them to run commercial, specialised or even capitalistic enterprises.[69] Scholars such as Bas Van Bavel, Tim Soens and Erik Thoen have also demonstrated that in large parts of the late medieval Low Countries, tenant farmers became increasingly specialised. They commercialised and intensified their agricultural production because of the rise of competitive land and commodity markets.[70]

In the Campine, however, tenant farmers were dependent on the common wastelands for their commercial sheep breeding enterprises and therefore did not press for enclosure. The profits of their sheep farming were not sufficient to encourage them to enclose heathland. The tenant farmers were not the owners of their livestock but had a specific contract with the abbey, called '*Kempisch stalrecht*'. This was a form of share-cropping, since half of the flock was owned by the tenant farmer and the other half by the lessor, or landlord. The costs and profits of these flocks were shared between the parties. As a result, each year a steward of the abbey's had to be attend to witness the shearing of the flock, after which some of the animals would be sent to the abbey, and a new herd established.[71] Through this system, the abbey of Tongerlo and its tenants owned between 1000 and 1600 sheep and more than 250 head of cattle per seignory. The average flocks were big, but not proportionally when compared to those of the independent peasants' herds. Whilst owning incredibly large farms, with 5 to 16 times as much land as the typical peasant, they 'only' possessed herds double or triple the size of their peasant neighbours.

As with the composition of their farms, the tenant farmers' animal husbandry strategies resembled those of the Campine peasants' rather than capitalistic tenant farmers. The key word here is 'diversification'. Some farms do show a slight over-representation of one kind of cattle, but to label those farms as being 'specialised' would be a step too far.[72] The tenants possessed equal numbers of dairy cows and oxen, together with herds of cattle, consisting of heifers, calves and beef cattle. This differs from the general tendency to invest either in dairy cattle or the fattening of oxen, so as to export either high quality dairy or beef products.[73]

These tenant farmers were therefore a peculiar group. Looking at the composition of their estates, they resembled the independent peasants. However, the scale on which they could operate was fundamentally different. They were truly large-scale farmers, with extensive herds that were, on the one hand, used to provide the basic necessities for the abbey of Tongerlo whilst on the other, they could engage in the regional markets and trade with a wide range of merchants and artisans. Yet they were subject to the same shortages of meadow. Although the ratio of land to cattle units was far better for the tenant farmers than the independent peasants, they were still incapable of generating sufficient fodder to maintain these flocks. In Figure 4.5 the required and obtained fodder yields of the ecclesiastical tenant farms have been estimated by combining information for the production of dry mass on different types of farm land and assessments of dietary needs of animals in the pre-modern period. This shows the farmers' heavy reliance on the commons. Looking at the pastures, yields and cattle units it becomes clear that on average only 43 per cent of the required fodder was actually produced. Certain farms possessed nearly enough private property to cope, while others could not provide even 10 per cent of the required hay. There was no easy way out of this dilemma. Their commercial activities were insufficient to cover all the costs that would accompany a transformation from an estate relying on the commons to a self-sufficient farm. Purchasing enough pastures, turning infertile and sturdy heathlands into productive, hay-producing fields, enclosing land and paying higher rents would squander their entire potential earnings.

The benefits from the commons were distributed according to the principle of a common denominator (Figure 4.6). This was an equilibrium that satisfied the most important interests of each subgroup while not fundamentally disadvantaging any group. The micro-smallholders and cottagers were able to regulate the commons through inclusive common pool institutions, secure the survival of common hay meadows for the entire community, and maintain a diverse range of appropriation rights on the common wastelands. They, nevertheless, were not able to steer the common pool institutions towards a stinted system, where the upper stratum of society would be restricted in their commercial strategies. The independent peasants and rural elites consequently accepted inclusive CPIs and common hay meadows, but enforced the acceptance of unstinted common wastelands so as to graze their extensive flocks of sheep in order to engage in commercial activities. This is a less egalitarian system than a stinted system, but as all interest groups received the benefits they needed, the distribution mechanisms can be judged to have been fair.

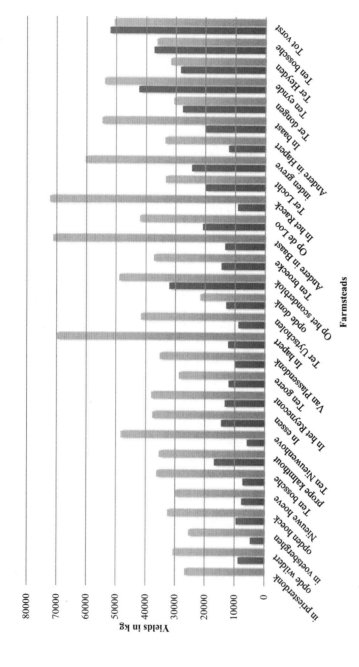

Figure 4.5 Required Versus Achieved Hay Yields of the Tenant Farmers of Tongerlo in 1510

Source: AAT, Section II, Registers, 292, Tenant farm descriptions of the abbey of Tongerlo, 1510–1653; AAT, Section II, Registers, 293, Tenant farm descriptions of the abbey of Tongerlo, 1239–1600.

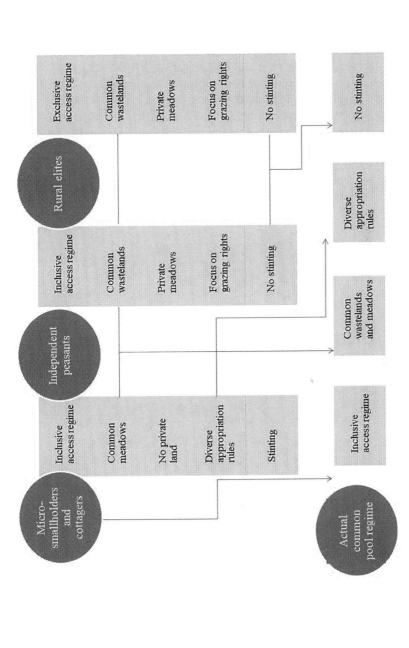

Figure 4.6 Diagram Depicting the Interest Groups' Interests and the Actual Common Property Regime, Suggesting Which Group Was Able to Influence Which Aspect of the CPI

To Enclose or Not to Enclose?

The third criteria by which we measure the success of a CPI was its ability to defend itself from alternative modes of appropriation. In the case of pre-modern commons, that usually meant either privatisation or enclosure. Although privatisation and enclosure often went hand-in-hand, it is important to define them clearly. Privatisation refers to the buying, leasing or the renting of land which was formerly part of the 'bona vacantia'[74] or communal land owned or managed by a community or common pool institution. Enclosure is the action of closing off property, either common or private land, from the surrounding environment with a hedge, ditch, fence or other delineation. Our view of enclosure is formed by the hedges and walls which emerged within the former open fields of central England.[75] We assume its unpopularity and envisage angry crowds of peasants filing complaints or attempting to impede the planting of hedges.[76] In the Campine nothing like this took place: There was no enclosure movement or any attempt to privatise the commons between the formation of the common pool institutions and their demise in the later eighteenth century. Enclosure came only after Maria Theresa abolished common wastelands in 1772 in response to the physiocratic philosophy that extensive heathlands should be turned into productive arable land.[77] The basic disposition of land, where at least between 60 and 90 per cent of the total surface area of the Campine was common throughout the year, with seasonal common rights attached to other types of land, such as hay meadows, did not fundamentally change during the later Middle Ages or early modern period. The exceptions will be discussed here, in order to understand the challenges faced by village communities and their response to alternative allocation strategies.

The longevity of the common pool regime does not preclude the existence of actors within society who believed that they, whether as individuals or representatives of sectional interests or the community as a whole, would benefit from privatising and enclosing commons. When looking for those actors, landlords are often the main suspects. Mostly living off their rents, their income could be increased by enclosing arable fields or meadows. Nevertheless, Nicola Whyte has stressed that lords could be the champions of open field systems. Being involved in capitalistic sheep breeding via the customary practice of fold course, the manorial lords in Breckland fiercely opposed peasant efforts to enclose their arable fields in order to be able to continue grazing their manorial sheep flocks on the open fields, brecks and wastelands.[78]

The literature shows, therefore, that identifying a single interest group as the main driving force behind privatisation or enclosure is impossible. While in one region during a certain timeframe, lords granted charters, privileges and by-laws providing access and control over the commons to their communities, their successors could turn out to be the greatest opponents of communal rights. Equally, peasants were most often supporters of communal systems, yet could just as well argue for the division and enclosure of commons. Therefore, we cannot simply refer to enclosure as a fixed process always driven by the same interest groups. Instead we need to focus on the different types of enclosure and the actors behind those diverging movements.

In the Campine there were three periods when attempts were made to change the structure and use of common property. Only a few attempts succeeded, and in all cases the area whose status was changed constituted only a small fraction of the total common surface area. The first attempt to enclose happened during the sixteenth century. It was started by the wealthiest independent peasants and rural elites with the goal of abolishing communal grazing over their hay meadows. These were private plots of land that remained common for most of the year. Only during spring were the meadows enclosed to allow the hay to grow. For example, the village of Westerlo wrote in its by-law of 1554:

> That everybody will hang and maintain a praiseworthy 'veken' or sign on the moat of the hay meadow called schaapswas in the south near Zoerle, like the way those of Herselt ordained. It will start from the time that the meadows will be closed till they are reopened again, on the penalty of 16 stuiver.[79]

According to the by-law of Oostmalle, this period of closure ranged from the middle of March until the second day of May.[80]

By the sixteenth century this practice was under pressure. Hay meadows were the most expensive and sought after plots of land in the Campine area.[81] Such fields, if not grazed by communal herds, were able to provide more crops of hay than just the first cut in May. For this reason the owners of hay meadows pressed the common pool institutions to limit the common rights and end collective grazing. However, their arguments were only successful in a few cases or villages. The village of Wuustwezel, for example, added a new rule in 1563 to their by-law, stipulating that 'The hay meadows will remain free for the entire year'.[82] Here the word 'free' refers to the liberating of the land from communal grazers. The village of Oostmalle agreed in 1665 that 'In the case where anybody would want to liberate and improve its meadows, he can do so without any consideration for others'.[83] Complete enclosure of the meadows did not necessarily occur, but individual community members were allowed to enclose their particular field if they considered it in their interest.[84]

This attempt to overthrow communal rights did not pass without being contested.[85] Enclosing one meadow does not, of course, fundamentally change the common use rights in other meadows, but in some cases they could disturb the privileges of certain community members. In the case of Peter Pynaerts in Turnhout, the enclosure of a meadow prevented him from using his 'erfweg', a road crossing the field of a neighbour to reach another field or a road. Although the plot was completely private and communal use was forbidden all year round, Pynaerts needed to use the road to access his own land. 'He and his ancestors had possessed the privilege to cross the meadow for as long as nobody could remember the opposite and any restrictions were completely new'.[86] The right to cross a neighbour's field was based on customary law. Although these customs were under pressure by the eighteenth century, such claims were powerful in practice.[87] As such, all cases regarding the communal rights of way, whereby the private nature of a meadow was not contested, were decided in favour of the individuals claiming passage.[88]

The discussion of the communal use of meadows took a more complex turn. In Koersel, in 1512, a group of meadow owners apparently enclosed their meadows although the common pool institution of the village had not decided to turn the meadows into private property. The village community decided that the enclosure of these meadows was illegal, destroyed the fences and drove their cattle into the meadows. Consequently the meadow owners took their complaint to the Council of Brabant and petitioned it to restore their private rights and punish the trespassers. They testified that they were in possession of the land and therefore had always used these meadows privately. The village community of Koersel replied that all private meadows were still common after the hay harvest and they therefore had the right to graze their cattle. In this case the court favoured the owners and granted them the right to enjoy the meadows privately even after the first harvest.[89] In 1514, a very similar case occurred in Westerlo but with the opposite outcome. Practically the same arguments were made, but here the ducal administration decided that the inhabitants of Holken were correct and could use the meadow once the harvest was removed.[90]

Some hay meadows were gradually being transformed from being unfenced private property (apart from the communal fence around the entire complex), to something akin to enclosed arable fields. It was, however, not a uniform process that happened in all Campine villages. The larger part of hay meadows continued to be used in common after the first harvest. This is shown by by-laws of other villages. For example the village of Vorselaar, introduced a new rule in 1544, explicitly stating that the meadows should remain common after the harvest.[91] Most villages retained communal rights in the hay meadows after the harvest, despite the grumbling of the rural elites and the wealthiest independent peasants.

Whilst this attempt to change the common property regime and reduce communal use rights arose from within the village, threats to the commons also came from outside. From the late fourteenth, and especially during the fifteenth and sixteenth centuries, the attitude of the Campine lords to commons changed. It is, nevertheless, important to state that there was not one uniform strategy towards commons shared by all the different types of lords present in the Campine. Nor did all lords have an unwavering policy. In general, lords were not involved with agricultural practice: Most of them did not even have farms that were managed by tenants. Consequently, most of them were not seeking to enclose land, but they welcomed new income arising from peasant initiatives.

In the Campine, enclosure was largely the initiative of the abbey of Tongerlo, a powerful and wealthy institution, which had a very proactive agricultural policy. In 1544 the abbot Arnoldus Van Diest and the monks granted to Hubrecht De But the right to turn 1149 gemeten or 482.6 ha of heath- and wasteland, belonging to the common wastelands of Kalmthout-Essen, into privatised land.[92] Hubrecht was a rich Antwerp lawyer and investor in property. On several occasions he made investments in real estate in partnership with Gilbert Van Schoonbeke.[93] Nevertheless, the community members of Kalmthout and Essen were convinced that the wastelands surrounding the villages had always been and remained unenclosed and common to all the community members. Seven witnesses, all over 60 years old, contributed to a written statement saying that as long as they had lived the wastelands had always been seen and used as common and unenclosed land.[94] Whilst the outcome of this case is uncertain, the abbey maintained that it had previously made grants of land to individuals (as indeed, we shall show they did in 1518).

In 1624 conflict occurred again when the abbey issued a charter prohibiting the community of Kalmthout and Essen from using parts of their commons.[95] Unsurprisingly, a lawsuit was initiated which was decided in favour of the abbey. The abbey acknowledged that the peasant community were allowed to use non-privatised parcels of wastelands, although it stated that digging for peat was not allowed and, by doing so, community members had acted contrary to the by-law. For evidence, the abbey meticulously referred to the by-laws and all its charters and privileges, proving that the abbey was the landlord and therefore could decide on all matters concerning the regulation and management of the seigniory. It accepted that at times a blind eye might have been turned towards illegal use, but nonetheless it maintained that the communities did not possess the right to take peat. In this particular case the Council of Brabant supported the abbey and prohibited further digging of peat by the communities of Kalmthout and Essen.[96] Consequently, a new charter was published by the bailiff on the door of the church that it was forbidden to dig peat and heather turves, as defined by the by-laws. The community of Kalmthout-Essen, however, did not leave it at that. In 1627, they filed a complaint before the Council of Brabant requesting that they retain their right of using the commons, 'as was custom for as long as nobody could remember the opposite'. Ultimately they received the court's ruling which granted them that right.[97] The abbey, as landlord, established that it had the right to privatise and enclose parts of the commons, but restricting the peasants' access to the remaining common wastelands was a step too far.

This attempt to abolish communal rights was part of the abbey's policy of privatising and enclosing land in the region around Kalmthout-Essen. This was, after all, an unusual region because large parts of the soil consisted of peat. This was a valuable fuel since, by the later Middle Ages, the majority of woodland in the Low Countries had been cleared.[98] The exploitation of peat started in Flanders, but once the peat there had been exhausted, attention turned to Brabant.[99] Starting from the northern part of the peat layers (around Rosendaal), Flemish and Brabantine investors began exploiting the moors and peat fens commercially. By the fourteenth century, the abbey was actively engaged in the process, with a peak of activity occurring during the fifteenth and sixteenth centuries.[100] This commercial process fundamentally affected the extent and outlook of the Kalmthout commons. In 1518 alone, 70 hectares of moor and heathland was privatised and registered in the rent registers of Kalmthout-Essen (Figure 4.7).[101] A concession to exploit 90 hectares of peat mostly around Hotmeer was granted about the same time.[102] The total area exploited between 1300 and 1600 has never been calculated, but, as indicated by a map prepared by Leenders shows, the area affected was huge.[103] Whereas some, and probably most, parts of the former peat bogs were given back to the communities as common wastelands after the peat had been removed, areas such as Nieuwmoer were transformed into private, enclosed fields and pastures.[104] As such, large parts of the commons were progressively privatised by the abbey. Kalmthout and Essen, cannot really be seen as a representative case, for it was the value of the peat that triggered enclosure. In the other parts of the Campine, no comparable exploitation and privatisation took hold.

The third and ultimately unsuccessful attack on the commons was launched by the governess of the Low Countries, Mary of Hungary. The Dukes of Brabant and later the Burgundian and Habsburg rulers had an inconsistent and unpredictable attitude towards the commons, shifting between institutionalising and protecting communal rights, forcing privatisation and enclosure and encouraging commercial exploitation. Under the rule of Charles V, the Habsburg Netherlands was governed by his sister Mary of Hungary from 1530 to 1555. In addition, she was the Lady of Turnhout and so direct landlord to the core area of the Campine.[105]

Under her government, a more active involvement in the management of the ducal domains and earnings was clearly intended. This was manifested through encouraging, one could say practically demanding, the privatisation of parcels of land from the 'gemeynte' of Turnhout.[106] Two strategies were employed. First, whilst between 1436 and 1475 several plots were registered as being privatised, in 1540 the administration complained that 250 bunders or 325 ha still needed to be privatised. Unsurprisingly, around 1549 several plots of heathland peat lands were registered.[107] The second was the most far-reaching and invasive. Like the manorial lords in Breckland, the Governess decided that an active commercial enterprise should be pursued in her domain. One Willem Wils was made responsible for the management of a farm measuring 10 ha for which detailed accounts are extant.

Wils invested large sums on the establishment of the farm in 1550. He started with as many as 900 sheep and, as a result, he was able to generate

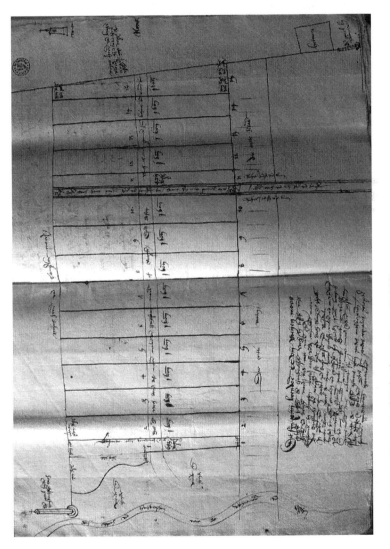

Figure 4.7 Folio From the 'Nova Census' of Kalmthout-Essen (1518)

Note: The map depicts the Tongerlo peat concessions divided by a pathway each measuring 1 bunder. They are located in the seignury of Kalmthout-Essen between the boundary marker of Huybergen in the south-east (upper left corner) and the hamlet of Hotmeer in the north-west (lower right corner).

Source: AAT, Section II, 377 Nova census Kalmthout-Essen, 1518. © Abdij Archief Tongerlo.

70,000 denier of income that year (which corresponded to 100,000 litre of rye). Costs, however, were just as substantial as earnings. The farm only measured 10 ha and was apparently not well equipped. From the very beginning, Wils needed to invest large sums to keep the estate running. He needed additional labour to sow the fields, mow the meadows and tend the animals. In addition, the pastures were inadequate to support the livestock. Although the animals could graze on the common wastelands, Wils rented some additional pasture, a barn and a sheep cote. He also had to purchase manure, animal equipment, ploughs, carts and large quantities of animal fodder. In 1554 these expenses amounted to no less than 30,764 deniers.[108] Mary of Hungary had to take steps to reduce costs. In 1552 she forced the aldermen of Turnhout and Arendonk to grant her a part of the wastelands that her forefathers had given to those communities. The aldermen wrote a charter stating 'that it was Her Majesty of Hungary and Bohemia's wish, as Lady of Turnhout, that a certain quantity of commons would be exploited as farm land'. Therefore, they granted her 260 ha of wasteland.[109] This could no longer be used by the members of the community for grazing their animals. Trespassers would be subject to the standard fine. Her tenants, however, were to contribute to the village taxes and would therefore be able to use the remaining commons. Although the charter was issued by the aldermen of the 'vrijheden' of Turnhout and Arendonk, the initiative for this privatisation almost certainly did not stem from them. Although villages and cities had privatised plots of common land to raise money to allow them to settle debts, this transaction brought no advantage to Turnhout and Arendonk. The area of wasteland was probably enclosed, since trespassing was fined. No court records or sources survive to reveal any tensions caused by this grant but it hard to believe that it was not resented.

Despite this enlargement of his farm, Wils was still unable to make a profit from it. The number of animals declined. Enthusiastically starting with 900 sheep, the number had dropped to around 600 in 1554, to 370 in 1557 and they disappeared entirely a year later. In 1556 the community of Turnhout and Arendonk granted an additional parcel of 12 ha of wasteland. Nothing could save the enterprise, and later that year Mary of Hungary was forced to acknowledge the fact, returning the land to the aldermen of Turnhout and Arendonk and stating: 'We restitute the 144 bunder that we received from the "vrijheden" Turnhout and Arendonk in the state that it was before it was granted by those "vrijheden", so as to use them in common as before, to graze animals and mow, without any further claim from us or our descendents'.[110]

Mary of Hungary and Willem Wils had learned by experience that a capitalistic enterprise, focussed on animal husbandry on privatised wasteland, was not a profitable strategy in the type of ecosystem present in the Campine region. As Clark argued for the English Midlands, transformation required large-scale investments in the form of labour as well as capital which was not returned via higher yields.[111] As a result, the manorial lords in Breckland maintained the communal fold course system, whereby the manorial tenant farmers monopolised the concessions of folds. They could therefore profit from the vastness of the area they were able to graze and did not need to invest in enclosures or tolerate the communities on the commons. These farmers, together with the manorial lords, got away with it because they were much more powerful than their equivalent in the Campine. They had the backing of the monarchy and royal courts. Protesting peasants had no help from the courts that nearly always favoured the manorial lords and therefore strengthened their position.[112] However, in the case of Turnhout and Arendonk, whilst the power of resistance and underlying tensions cannot be underestimated, what defeated the project was its failure to turn a profit. Once the vision of a successful enterprise had vanished and Mary of Hungary returned to Spain, the experiment was abandoned, and the 260 ha of land was reinstated as common.[113]

Therefore, the Campine peasants were not able to fend off all privatisation and enclosure attempts. The abbey of Tongerlo and a couple of rural elites were able to privatise or enclose communal plots of land. Nevertheless, this affected only a tiny proportion of the Campine area, such as the village of Kalmthout. In other villages the communal response enclosures was strong enough to resist similar challenges, such as for instance the village of Koersel shows. The Campine CPIs were therefore successful in fending off alternative modes of appropriation, although only narrowly.

Conclusion: Three Forms of Success

A clear definition of what constituted a successful common is needed to assess the functioning of commons in the past and present. Only when a fixed and comparable set of indicators is used, can commons be compared and success can be evaluated in a scientific way. After all, despite the positive evaluation of most common pool institutions, successful commons should not be taken for granted or taken at face value. The case of the late medieval Campine is used here as an example to test the level of success. In light of the three-fold definition of success we have proposed, the Campine can be held as an example of a locality where common pool institutions were successful, although some enclosure did take place. The Campine communities were able to combine high levels of ecological resilience, inclusive access rights with a fair distribution of the benefits, while at the same time being able to defeat alternative modes of appropriation.

First of all, the heathlands were not disturbed fundamentally. The ecosystem of heathlands was maintained and a shift from this stability domain into either a forest or sand dune situation was prevented. The Campine communities invested significantly in preventing environmental degradation. Second, the benefits from the commons were distributed fairly. In the Campine, benefits were not distributed in an egalitarian way, but equitably. Every household was allowed to obtain depletable resources to fulfil subsistence needs and to graze their animals on the common wastelands and meadows. As such, not everybody collected the same amounts or types of resources, but all interest groups were able to obtain the required resources. Third, privatisation attempts and enclosure movements were fended off. Some communities lost access to certain commons or saw their common land reduced from the sixteenth century. For example Kalmthout-Essen was fundamentally affected by privatisation projects from the abbey of Tongerlo, and some villages enclosed their common hay meadows. But in the end, the majority of the common wastelands and meadows were defended by the local communities. As a result, the Campine communities maintained a successful system from the fourteenth until the eighteenth century.

Acknowledgements

Parts of this chapter were originally published as Maïka De Keyzer, "All we are is dust in the wind: 'The social causes of a "subculture of coping' in the late medieval coversand belt", *Journal for the History of Environment and Society*, vol. 1 (2016), pp. 1–35.

Notes

1 Ostrom, *Governing the commons*, 15.
2 Shaw-Taylor, 'Management of common land'; Van Zanden, 'Paradox of the marks'; Marco Casari and Charles R. Plott, 'Decentralized management of common property resources: Experiments with a centuries-old institution', *Journal of Economic Behavior & Organization* 51, no. 2 (2003); Angus Winchester, 'Common land in upland Britain: Tragic unsustainability or utopian community resource?', in *Umwelt und geschichte in deutchland und grossbritannien—environment and history in Britain and Germany*, eds Franz Bosbach, Jens Ivo Engels, and Fiona Watson (Munich: Prinz-Albert-Studien Band 24, 2006); Winchester and Straughton, 'Stints and sustainability'.
3 Van Weeren and De Moor, 'Controlling the commoners', 260.
4 For a discussion of this topic see Ensminger, *Making a market*.
5 Ogilvie, ' "Whatever is, is right?" '
6 Bailey, *Marginal economy*; Postgate, 'Historical geography'; Whyte, 'Contested pasts'; Nicola Whyte, *Inhabiting the landscape: Place, custom and memory, 1500–1800* (Oxford: Oxbow Books, 2009).
7 Hein Vera, '. . . Dat men het goed van den ongeboornen niet mag verkoopen. Gemene gronden in de meierij van den bosch tussen hertog en hertgang 1000–2000' (Unpublished thesis, Radboud University, 2011); Kos, *Van meenten tot marken*.
8 Gregory Clark, 'Commons sense: Common property rights, efficiency, and institutional change', *Journal of Economic History* 58, no. 1 (1998).
9 Carl Folke, 'Resilience: The emergence of a perspective for social-ecological systems analyses', *Global Environmental Change* 16, no. 3 (2006), 259.
10 Lance H. Gunderson, 'Ecological resilience in theory and application', *Annual Review of Ecology and Systematics* 31 (2000).
11 Lana Berasain, 'From equilibrium to equity'.
12 Esther Pascua, 'Communautés de propriétaires et ressources naturelles à Saragosse lors du passage du moyen âge à l'époque moderne', and Xavier Soldevila I

Temporal, 'L'élevage ovin et la transhumance en catalogne nord-occidentale (xiiie–xive siècles)', both in *Transhumance et estivage en occident: Des origines au enjeux actuels*, ed. P-Y. Laffont (Toulouse: Presses universitaires du Mirail, 2006).

13 Allison, 'Sheep-corn husbandry'.

14 De Moor, 'Avoiding tragedies'.

15 Mckean, *People and forests*.

16 Greg Bankoff, 'The "English lowlands" and the North Sea basin system: A history of shared risk', *Environment and History* 19 (2013).

17 Koster, 'Aeolian environments', 145.

18 Derese et al., 'Medieval settlement', 340.

19 K. Beerten, K. Deforce, and D. Mallants, 'Landscape evolution and changes in soil hydraulic properties at the decadal, centennial and millenial scale: A case study from the Campine area, northern Belgium', *Catena* 95 (2012); Vera, '. . . Dat men het goed'; Josef Fanta and Henk Siepel (eds), *Inland drift sand landscapes* (Zeist: Publishing, 2010).

20 Beatrijs Augustyn, *Zeespiegelrijzing, transgressiefasen en stormvloeden in maritiem vlaanderen tot het einde van de xvide eeuw* (Brussels: Algemeen Rijksarchief, 1992), 260–1.

21 Vera, '. . . Dat men het goed'.

22 Van Zanden, 'Paradox of the marks'.

23 For more information see Ann Wintle, 'Luminescence dating of quaternary sediments—introduction', *Boreas* 4 (2008).

24 Jan Sevink et al., 'Drift sands, lakes, and soils: The multiphase holocene history of the laarder wasmeren area near Hilversum, the Netherlands', *Netherlands Journal of Geosciences* 92, no. 4 (2013), 260.

25 Verhaert et al., 'Een inheems-romeinse begraafplaats'.

26 Ibid.

27 Derese et al., 'Medieval settlement', 337.

28 Harm Jan Pierik et al., 'Controls on late holocene inland aeolian drift-sand dynamics in the Netherlands', *The Holocene* (in press).

29 Ibid.; Anna Broers, 'Drift sand activity phases in northwest Europe' (unpublished Ph.D thesis, Wageningen University, 2014).

30 Van Zanden, 'Paradox of the marks'.

31 Vera, '. . . Dat men het goed'.

32 Van Zanden, 'Paradox of the marks'.

32 Augustyn, *Zeespiegelrijzing*, 325.

34 Beerten, Deforce, and Mallants, 'Landscape evolution', Dixit Jan Bastiaens.

35 Ibid.

36 Ibid.

37 Koster, 'Aeolian environments'.

38 Regarding such collective knowledge and subcultures of disaster: Bankoff, 'Cultures of disaster'; Bankoff, 'The "English lowlands"'.

39 Franz Mauelshagen, 'Flood disasters and political culture at the German north sea coast: A long-term historical perspective', *Historical Social Research* 32, no. 3 (2007), 134.

40 Uwe Lübken and Christof Mauch, 'Uncertain environments: Natural hazards, risk and insurance in historical perspective', *Environment and History* 17 (2011), 1.

41 Christopher P. Rodgers et al., *Contested Common Land: Environmental Governance Past and Present* (London: Earthscan, 2011).

42 De Moor, Shaw-Taylor, and Warde (eds), *Management*; Winchester and Straughton, 'Stints and sustainability'.

43 McCarthy, Kamara, and Kirk, 'Co-operation', 236.

44 Ibid.; Winchester and Straughton, 'Stints and sustainability'.

45 Ibid.

46 See databases: by-laws.
47 Lauwerys, 'Keuren van westerloo'. Similar rules are found for the villages of Veerle and Vorselaar.
48 Original text: 'niemand zal onder het deksel van een pretense koop mogen vreemde beesten of vreemde lieden toebehorende brengen of hoeden in het gemeen broek of op de vroente op de boete van 20 s. [tenzij zij] doen hun behoorlijke eed deze beesten gekocht te hebben zonder arglist'. Source: Prims, 'Keuren'.
49 McCarthy, Kamara, and Kirk, 'Co-operation', 236.
50 See database: by-laws.
51 Original text: 'Niemand van de zes heerdgangen zal voorderen te maaien meer dan zijn weekheide, van sint jansmisse tot bamisse: de ploegers elke week een voeder en de keuters die geen ploeg hebben elke week een kar. De ploegers donderdag en de keuters maandag. En zij zullen gehouden zijn de heide te halen en maaien overdag. [. . .] Niemand zal enige russen, schadden, heide steken, maaien, halen of laten halen onder de pretext van zijn vrienden die geen heide of russen nodig hebben, op de pene van 20 stuivers'. Source: Ernalsteen, 'Keuren van gheel'.
52 '2 januari 1800 niemand zal in de toekomst mogen rus of schadden hakken of laten hakken op de sterschotsheide, tenzij zijn gelijke portie voor ieder huishouden, zoals een man op 1 dag kan afhakken, maar niet anders dan werd geordineerd door de heer en de schepenen. Zij die geen inboorling zijn van tongerlo zullen ook niet mogen hakken tenzij hij daar eigenaar of leenman is van de heer van tongerlo en zal hetzelfde geconfisceerd blijven telkens men ter contrarie bevonden wordt, bovenop de boete van 10 stuiver'. Source: AAT, Bundel Tongerlo I: Rules for the village of Tongerlo, Copy.
53 Prims, 'Keuren'.
54 J. M. Neeson, *Commoners: Common right, enclosure and social change in England, 1700–1820* (Cambridge: Cambridge University Press, 1993); J. L. Hammond and Barbara Hammond, *The village labourer, 1760–1832* (Stroud, 1995); Jane Humphries, 'Enclosures, common rights, and women: The proletarization of families in the late eighteenth and early nineteenth centuries', *Journal of Economic History* 50, no. 1 (1990).
55 Based on the animal counts of Rijkevorsel, we have estimated that the bottom socioeconomic stratum of the community did not possess any sheep or horses. As such, the cattle units referred only to cattle. Again, considering the animal counts of Wortel and Rijkevorsel, our conclusion is that the cattle units could not consist of bovine cattle only, but also included horses and sheep. I have therefore determined the composition of the cattle units by calculating that the upper stratum must have had three units or six head of cattle which were deducted from the total number of cattle units. Most Campine households, even the elites, did not possess more than two horses, as indicated by Loenhout. Therefore, it is possible that possessing only one unit could refer to draft animals. Finally, the remaining units were divided by 5 in order to calculate the number of sheep owned by each household. RAA, OGA Rijkevorsel, 3141–9, animal counts, 1608.
56 Lindemans, *Geschiedenis van de landbouw in belgië*.
57 Van Onacker, 'Leaders of the pack?'.
58 Jean-Marc Moriceau, *Histoire et géographie de l'élevage français: Du moyen âge à la révolution* (Paris: Fayard, 2005), 209.
59 Wilhelmina Maria Gijsbers, *Kapitale ossen: De internationale handel in slachtvee in noordwest-europa (1300–1750)* (Hilversum: Verloren, 1999); Carsten Porskrog Rasmussen, 'Innovative feudalism: The development of dairy farming and *koppelwirtschaft* on manors in Schleswig-Holstein in the seventeenth and eighteenth centuries', *Agricultural History Review* 58, no. 2 (2010).
60 Moriceau, *Histoire et géographie de l'élevage*, 209 (75 per cent of one kg of hay corresponded to dry mass).

61 Anna Dahlström, 'Pastures, livestock number and grazing pressure 1620–1850: Ecological aspects of grazing history in south-central Sweden' (Unpublished thesis, Swedish University of Agricultural Sciences, 2006).

62 Van Onacker, 'Leaders of the pack?', 99.

63 RAA, OGA Zandhoven, 148, 'Heideboek', 1559–81.

64 SAA, 5, condition, 1593; RAA, OGA Rijkevorsel, 3141–9, Animal counts, 1608, analysed by Eline Van Onacker.

65 Allison, 'Sheep-corn husbandry'; Bruce M. S. Campbell, 'The regional uniqueness of English field systems? Some evidence from eastern Norfolk', *Agricultural History Review* 29 (1981); Mark Overton and Bruce M. S. Campbell, 'Norfolk livestock farming, 1250–1740: A comparative study of manorial accounts and probate inventories', *Journal of Historical Geography* 18, no. 4 (1992); Edward I. Newman, 'Medieval sheep-corn farming: How much grain yield could each sheep support', *Agricultural History Review* 50, no. 2 (2002).

66 Lindemans, *Geschiedenis van de landbouw in belgië*; De Keyzer and Van Onacker, 'Beyond the flock'.

67 Moriceau, *Histoire et géographie de l'élevage*, 209.

68 Clark, 'Commons sense'.

69 Robert C. Allen, *Enclosure and the yeoman: Agricultural development of the south Midlands, 1450–1850* (Oxford: Clarendon Press, 1992).

70 Van Bavel, *Transitie en continuïteit*; Van Bavel, *Manors and markets*; Soens and Thoen, 'Origins of leasehold'.

71 Heerman, *Het abdijdomein*, 68–75.

72 AAT, II, 206, Lease accounts of the abbey of Tongerlo, 1504–1513.

73 Jan De Vries, *The Dutch rural economy in the golden age, 1500–1700* (New Haven: Yale University Press, 1974); Rasmussen, 'Innovative feudalism'; Gijsbers, *Kapitale ossen*.

74 A component of the royal domain.

75 Allen, *Enclosure and the yeoman*; Humphries, 'Enclosures'; R. I. Hodgson, 'The progress of enclosure in county Durham, 1550–1870', in *Change in the countryside: Essays on rural England, 1500–1900*, eds H. S. A. Fox and R. A. Butlin (London: Institute of British Geographers, 1979); Leigh Shaw-Taylor, 'Parliamentary enclosure and the emergence of an English agricultural proletariat', *Journal of Economic History* 61, no. 3 (2001).

76 Heather Falvey, 'Voices and faces in the rioting crowd: Identifying seventeenth-century enclosure rioters', *Local Historian* 39, no. 2 (2009); Stephen Hipkin, ' "Sitting on his penny rent": Conflict and right of common in Faversham Blean, 1595–1610', *Rural History* 11, no. 1 (2000).

77 Van Looveren, 'De privatisering van de gemeentegronden'.

78 Whyte, 'Contested pasts'.

79 Original text: 'Men zal wel en loffelijk onderhouden en hangen een veken op de oude vest van het broek of daar geheeten het schaapwas in het zuiden naar zoerle, zoals die van Hersel geordineerd houden. Beginnende van de tijd dat het broek gesloten wordt tot de tijd dat het met de gemeynte weer open gaat, op de boete van 16 stuivers. Dit veken zal onderhouden worden door de zeven heerdgangen die de straat en Liese gebruiken van alle oude tijden tot nu'. Lauwerys, 'Keuren Van Westerloo'.

80 Th. De Molder, 'Keuren Van Oostmalle', *Oudheid en Kunst* 26, no. 1 (1935), 3–15.

81 In Loenhout in 1602 a hay meadow cost, on average, 525 stuiver per bunder. By comparison arable was 245 stuiver/bunder, pasture 216 stuiver/bunder and poor grazing land 208 stuiver/bunder. RAA, OGA Loenhout, 3823, Land book, 1602. Eline Van Onacker found similar high values for Wuustwezel in 1581, while Gierle and Tongerlo show average values. Van Onacker, 'Leaders of the pack?', 96–7.

82 Original text: '16 mei 1563 de heer philips vander meeren heeft geordineerd dat alle beempden het gehele jaar door vrij zullen staan'. K. C. Peeters,

De wuustwezelsche dorpskeuren (xve–xviie eeuw) (Verslagen en mededelingen van de koninklijke Vlaamsche academie voor taal en letterkunde, 1932); K. C. Peeters, 'De wuustwezelsche dorpskeuren (xve–xviie eeuw)', *Wesalia, Tijdschrift voor plaatselijke Geschiedenis en Folklore* 8, no. 1–2 (1933).

83 Original text: 'Indien iemand zijn beempden wil bevrijden en verbeteren, dit zal mogen doen zonder aanzien van iemand'. De Molder, 'Keuren van oostmalle'.

84 In the sample of by-laws, only one village refers to a permanent enclosure of the common hay meadows. Nevertheless, the juridical sentences that follow in the following paragraphs give some additional evidence of enclosure. See database: by-laws.

85 RAB, VB, 565, 9 (1509) Turnhout.

86 Ibid.

87 R. W. Hoyle (ed.), *Custom, improvement and the landscape in ealy modern Britain* (Farnham, 2011); Peter King, 'Legal change, customary right and social conflict in late eighteenth-century England: The origins of the great gleaning case of 1788', *Law and History Review* 10 (1992); Graham Rogers, 'Custom and common right: Waste land enclosure and social change in west Lancashire', *Agricultural History Review* 41, no. 2 (1993); E. P. Thompson, *Customs in common* (London: The Merlin Press, 1991); Whyte, *Inhabiting the landscape*; Angus Winchester, 'Statute and local custom: Village byelaws and the governance of common land in medieval and early-modern England', in *Rural societies and environments at risk: Ecology, property rights and social organisation in fragile areas (middle ages-twentieth century)*, eds Bas Van Bavel and Erik Thoen (Turnhout: Brepols, 2008); Whyte, 'Contested pasts'.

88 RAB, VB, 557, 63 (1507) Mechelen; RAB, VB, 565, 9 (1510) Turnhout; RAB, VB, 581, 11 (1534) Meldert; RAB, VB, 581, 19 (1534) Retie; RAB, VB, 594, 98 (1541) Veerle; RAB, VB, 595, 103 (1545) Unknown; RAB, VB, 595, 121 (1545) Putte; RAB, VB, 595, 67 (1546) Aarschot; RAB, VB, 595, 58 (1548) Berlecom; RAB, VB, 602, 225 (1549) Wijnegem.; RAB, VB, 597, 8 (1549) Zeelst.

89 RAB, VB, 563, 76 (1512) Koersel.

90 RAB, VB, 564, 53 (1513) Oplinter.

91 'Er is gesloten en door de gemeente overgedragen bij consent van de meier en schepenen dat men het broek zal omheinen en bevrijden zoals de andere vrede beemden en dat men in hetzelfde broek zal mogen voor de oogst hooien en dat niemand zijn beesten daar in zal stouwen zolang er 3 lieden hooi in het broek hebben. Als de lieden hun hooi daaruit hebben zal het wederom gemeen zijn. Dit zou drie jaar duren om dit mede te proeven. 17 januari 1544'. Van Olmen, 'De keuren van Vorselaar'.

92 AAT, IV, Fund of Kalmthout-Essen-Huibergen, 324, Privatisation of a piece of the commons by Hubrecht de But, 1544.

93 He was born in Brussels in 1518 out of the marriage between the lawyer Cornelis and Marie van Oolen. In 1541 he married Mechtelt de Vogeleer, daughter of Adriaen and Adriana Boots. They both received large estates in the regions surrounding Antwerp and Breda as dowry. H. Soly, *Urbanisme en kapitalisme te antwerpen in de 16de eeuw: De stedebouwkundige en industriële ondernemingen van gilbert van schoonbeke* (Brussels: Gemeentekrediet van België, 1977), 152. In Antwerp he also purchased goods from the Abbey of Baudeloo in Antwerp, Caroline Luypaers, ' "Le goût pour les spectacles est tellement devenu à la mode . . .". Spektakelcultuur in het achttiende-eeuwse antwerpen' (Unpublished thesis, Catholic University of Leuven, 2001).

94 The document is undated, but is probably of 1544. AAT, IV, Fund of Kalmthout-Essen-Huibergen, 322, Privatisation of a piece of the commons by Jan Godens, 15th century.

95 AAT, IV, Fund of Kalmthout-Essen-Huibergen, 325, Abolition of communal rights, 1623.
96 AAT, IV, Fund of Kalmthout-Essen-Huibergen, 326, Juridical advice for the abbey of Tongerlo concerning the communal use rights, 1624–8.
97 'Vonnis waer in het gebruyck der vruente tot Esschen ende Calmpthout gewesen wordt ten possesseren tot faveur vande gemeynte aldaer laetende den prelaet van Tongerloo in sijn geheel ter petitoir. 1628, 27 September'. AAT, Section IV, Fund of Kalmthout-Essen-Huibergen, 328–9, Sentence regarding communal use rights in favour of the community of Kalmthout-Essen, 1623–8.
98 Bastiaens and Deforce, 'Geschiedenis van de heide'.
99 Karel A.H.W. Leenders, *Verdwenen venen: Een onderzoek naar de ligging en exploitatie van thans verdwenen venen in het gebied tussen antwerpen, turnhout, geertruidenberg en willemstad, 1250–1750*, Gemeentekrediet, *Historische uitgaven* (Brussels: Pudoc, 1989).
100 Ibid.
101 AAT, II, 373, Rent register of Kalmthout, 1518.
102 AAT, II, 377, Nova census Kalmthout-Essen, 1518.
103 Leenders, *Verdwenen venen*.
104 Apart from the land that was registered as arable, pasture or meadow, the remaining wastelands were not all transformed into tenancies. As the village of Nieuwmoer possessed the same rights to the commons as the community members of Kalmthout, Essen and Huibergen, the remaining uncultivated patches of land, must have been restored as common wastelands.
105 De Kok, *Turnhout*.
106 This fitted into a more general policy of pushing for greater control over the region generally. For more information see Wim Blockmans, *Keizer karel v. De utopie van het keizerschap* (Leuven: Van Halewyck, 2001); H. De Schepper, 'Vorstelijke ambtenarij en bureaukratisering in regering en gewesten van 's konings nederlanden, 16de–17de eeuw', *Tijdschrift voor geschiedenis* 90 (1977); Maarten Van Dijck, 'Tussen droom en daad: De beperkte invloed van de centrale overheid op de rechtspraak in antwerpen en mechelen gedurende de 15de en 16de eeuw', *Justitie- en rechtsgeschiedenis: een nieuwe onderzoeksgeneratie* 3 (2008).
107 ARAB, Chambre des Comptes, 5212, Account of the domain of Turnhout, 1549.
108 Ibid.
109 Original text: 'goede begeerte vanden majesteyt vande coninginne van hongarien end evan bohemien regente, als vrouwe van turnhout van zekere quantiteyt van vroenten ten eynde die tot hoeven landt ende andere culturen gelabeurt te wordden'. ARAB, Chambre des Comptes, Administrative files, 'Cartons', 83/2, 37B.
110 'welcke voirseide hondert vierenveertich bunderen wy de voirseide vryheyden van Turnhout, ende Arendonck restitueren als vooren tot sulcker naturen als die te vooren waeren eer die voirseide vryheyden ons die gegeven ende gegunt hadden om die selve te gebruycken soe wel int gemeyne voeren ons als voeren onse gemeyne ondersaten beesten te beweyen, mayen ende gebruycken sonder ons ofte onse naecomelinghen enich besunder recht meer aen oft in te behouden, aen doen hanghen'. ARAB, Chambre des Comptes, Administrative files, 'Cartons', 83/2, 37B.
111 Clark, 'Common sense'.
112 Whyte, 'Contested pasts'.
113 ARAB, Chambre des Comptes, Administrative files, 'Cartons', 83/2, 37B.

5   The Road to Success

In the late medieval and pre-modern Campine, village communities were able first to create and then to maintain inclusive common pool institutions which were successful in both securing ecological resilience, and a fair distribution of benefits. They were also able to defend the common pool regime against pressures for privatisation and enclosure. How did they manage to be so successful against all odds? In this chapter we want to put forward three main characteristics of the Campine that stand out as reasons for the resilience and robustness of its CPIs: the existence of informal institutions, next to formalised CPIs; a capacity for strong collective action; and efficient conflict resolution mechanisms. We argue that these characteristics were extremely important in determining the history of the Campine commons: but we would not go so far as to maintain that they offer a universal model for all pre-modern commons.

Informal Institutions

Recently, the institutional approach pioneered by Douglas North has been dominant.[1] Institutions, and especially formalised institutions, are often perceived as stronger as and more resilient in the face of external pressures and shocks than informal institutions.[2] Formal institutions were recognised (or even founded) by local, regional or sovereign governments. They had the power to make by-laws to regulate the use rights of the community. Therefore, communities are investigated through the lens of normative sources of the common pool institutions. The by-laws and formal rules are often considered to be the most important part of common pool institutions.[3] However, too much weight is placed on the 'formal' aspects of the common pool institutions. Elinor Ostrom herself focussed exclusively on societies that did not introduce formal institutions and showed that not only were they able to survive for centuries, they could introduce remarkably similar regulations and maintain a sustainable environment.[4]

Moreover, until now, the view of formal CPIs lacks nuance. Communities could opt to formalise some aspects, while maintain important informal institutions and rules. In the case of the Campine, communities opted to formalise the foundation of the common pool institutions and use rights, but allowed the regulations to be more informal. The flexibility of non-formalised rules had a real value for peasant communities in pre-modern times. As was shown in Chapter 2, the Campine communities were granted use rights by either the formal charters of the Duke or oral agreements in the case of the villages outside the Duke's jurisdiction. They had sought formal recognition, since access to the commons and the right to manage their village and commons affairs was important. Nonetheless, the greatest power of communities in the Campine was their ability to circumvent formal institutions and create, mould and employ custom outside the formal framework whenever it suited them. These parallel, and in particular informal, institutions operated alongside the institutions presided over by the village government and more often than not ran against the rules and concepts introduced by the lord, bailiff and aldermen.

While formal charters and by-laws were powerful tools enabling communities to protect their communal activities and property in courts of law and against external opponents, they were rigid as well. Although Winchester and De Moor have shown that by-laws could and did change with circumstances, the majority of by-laws remained virtually unchanged for centuries.[5] Once a rule is written down, it is much more difficult to change it afterwards. Especially in the Low Countries, charters and privileges were important documents with an almost sacred character. The slightest change proposed by any interest group was often met with fierce resistance. This is well documented for the urban charters and by-laws.[6] Non-formalised institutions and unwritten rules left more breathing space and allowed communities to change their practices and strategies more quickly and without the conflicts that could arise from changing formal documents. Heather Falvey showed that in some instances peasant communities opted to refrain from introducing formal rules and relied mostly on custom.[7] Custom in itself was very powerful before around 1800, since Roman law was not dominant and claims of custom carried great weight, even in sovereign courts. Informal regulations were not invariably preferred by peasants alone.[8] Lords could prefer informal institutions as well. In Breckland, the same principle applied. The fold course system, allowing tenants and lessees to graze sheep in the seigniorial folds was fundamentally changed between the later Middle Ages and the end of the sixteenth century. Nevertheless, the formal framework of the common pool institutions was almost unaltered. The feudal lords monopolised all the folds, without formally excluding the peasants from the fold course.[9]

Some of the most important aspects of the commons were deliberately neither recorded nor formalised. The most important was the access regime itself. As we saw before, only references to the 'homines' of the village were registered and the exact access rules were never formally recorded. It was only thanks to accounting records that the identity of the community of users can be discovered. This informal access regime suited the interest of the Campine communities by giving access to all community members, even when the population grew and plots of land were divided among the children. Nevertheless, it left the door open to change the rules governing access when needed.

Another striking example of informal rules is the refusal of peasants herding cattle and sheep through the common wastelands to comply with the boundaries described and indicated by the village's charters and privileges. Boundaries, as a symbol of the jurisdiction of a lord, the village and a common pool institution's jurisdiction, were one of the most important issues in communal affairs. David Fletcher has stressed the internalising character of this issue, for an almost sacred aura was attached to village boundaries through the performance of processions around them.[10] Nevertheless, these strict and hierarchal boundaries, introduced and cherished by the village elites as a symbol of their jurisdiction, were repeatedly rejected by the peasants, who thought in terms of zones within which their grazing trails were situated, rather than strict limits. Despite numerous conflicts, renewed visitations, the setting of boundary markers and attempts to force the peasants to acknowledge them, their practices survived for centuries. Until the eighteenth century they defied formal boundaries through their own notion of space, which existed in parallel as well as in opposition to that of the village elites.[11] The Campine peasants insisted on their grazing practices themselves and claimed the right to define their grazing trails and routes. While having the landscape, the flocks and the ecological risks in mind, more flexible routes and changing tracks were preferred to rigid regulation.

Another informal practice was sanctioning. Ostrom defined sanctions, and especially graduated sanctions, as one of the most important design principles to prevent free riding and unsustainable policies.[12] Nevertheless, graduated sanctions were not a dominant feature of historical commons: It seems that successful common pool institutions relied more on social control and alternative forms of penalty than monetary fines.[13] In the Campine the same principles are found in the by-laws: graduated sanctions, monetary fines and alternative punishments. Formally appointed officials ('Vorsters') had to discover and apprehend trespassers, and report them to the village government. Afterwards the bailiff of the lord was responsible for sanctioning and had to collect the fines, although community members could receive a share for their information about trespassers.[14] Nevertheless, the Campine common pool institutions handled sanctioning in a more informal fashion that this would suggest. The complete lack of evidence for fines being levied or sentences in both aldermen's registers and the surviving bailiff's accounts suggests that informal sanctioning was the preferred way of handling conflicts.[15] According to Dinges, up to two-thirds of society preferred an informal to a formal setting to resolve a conflict in the early modern period.[16] Despite the obligation placed on all village officials to record fines and submit their records for audit by the ducal auditor's office, there are practically no conflicts or even fines to be found there throughout the fifteenth and sixteenth centuries. Apart from some records relating to the stealing and felling of trees (something that was vigorously controlled),[17] as well as criminal cases, these records remain silent about conflicts and resolutions regarding the commons. Although the possibility exists that separate registers for conflicts or trespassing existed and have been lost to us, it is more likely that local officials and community members did not want to settle their disputes 'on the record'.

Sanctioning therefore happened outside of the formal common pool institutions and mostly according to different rules. Fines and graduated sanctions were often replaced by compromises and alternative forms of punishment in less formal systems of dispute resolution.[18] The lack of graduated sanctions imposed by the formal common pool institutions is all the more remarkable since the Campine had inclusive commons and relatively unrestricted use rights. Strict and formal sanctions are therefore to be expected, but rather replaced by informal options. The fact that such informal institutions were a benefit rather than a disaster has much to do with the second source of strength, strong collective action and social cohesion.

Collective Action

Institutions, either formal or informal, will only work when they operate within a society that accepts the need for collective action and will adhere to communally-set rules. We do not want to argue that only one particular blueprint was the sole path to sustainability. Multiple options might be possible, but the Campine is an area in which collective action was able to create structures for the sustainable management of natural resources and the environment. Communal property and collective resources do not necessarily lead to solidarity and industrious maintenance. In regions where inequality grew and the faltering of formal or informal regulations developed, collective ties could unravel with detrimental effects. In the seventeenth-century Breckland, for example, socioeconomic polarisation and the dominance of manorial lessees made for antagonistic and opposed interest groups and polarised common pool institutions which were no longer able to cooperate efficiently. The management of the commons broke down, with a tragedy of the commons as a result.[19]

Collective action in the Campine was strong because the communities were cohesive and inclusive. It was based upon a non-polarised society, where all interest groups benefitted from the commons and engaged in collective action to maintain the common resources for future generations. The middle groups within society remained dominant. The rural elites were not growing in either number or political authority. In addition, the poorest groups within society were not excluded from political power: Indeed, it was still possible for poor individuals to become aldermen. The exclusion of the poor has, in certain contexts, been identified as detrimental to the environment as they would attempt to exploit the resources available to them to the maximum in order to survive.[20] This did not occur in the Campine where the inclusion of poor households in the CPI and the provision of basic relief by the Campine Holy Ghost tables served to limit free riding and degrading activities by them.[21] Strong and cohesive communities were more likely to support collective action which, in turn, prevented degradation.

As a result, the Campine peasant communities were strong enough to build, both literally and figuratively speaking, a region of resilience, what Franz Mauelshagen has called 'a landscape of coping'. A specific type of cultural landscape had to be created in order to manage risks and prevent degradation.[22] In the case of the Campine, this meant that the community had to prevent the lack of restrictions placed on animal herds placing the heathlands and pastures under pressures which might lead to the creation of disastrous sand drifts. They did this by making the entire community responsible for controlling the commons. Since no sections of the community were excluded and stints were not introduced, the whole community was responsible for securing conformity to the rules in order to prevent overexploitation and free riding. Collective and bottom-up systems introduced in the later Middle Ages survived until the end of the eighteenth century, as opposed to in, for example, coastal Flanders where dunes or pastures were leased by a small number of large-scale, and commercially orientated, tenant farmers who were at the same time the officials controlling the appropriators.[23] In the Campine the control and management of the commons was in the hand of all interest groups. Officials were appointed, but mostly control was performed via group pressure and social control.

The Campine communities did not rely solely on their appointed officers, stewards or bailiffs to control the commons. The complete village community was charged with watching out for and reporting any offences to the local officials or authorities. Although the 'vorsters' were required to 'go around the common wastelands and boundaries every 14 days together and with each other', it was impossible for them to control every communal activity or straying shepherd.[24] In return for their assistance, villagers would receive a portion of the fine.[25] In Arendonk the by-laws stipulated 'That everybody is allowed to report [a trespasser] and will receive half of the fine'. In this way, the entire village would watch out for cattle being illegally grazed on the common wastelands, report tree-felling on the fragile sand dunes, the damage caused by large flocks of sheep or other forms of illicit behaviour by neighbours.

In addition, villagers were renowned for their expertise when it came to cattle diseases. In a sheep-breeding region, such as the Campine, where sheep were grazed in communal herds on the common wastelands, sheep scab or other forms of animal plagues might be devastating. Therefore, 'good men' from the villages were appointed to make frequent inspections to check for infected animals. When precautionary measures had to be taken, their advice would be final.[26] In this way too, villages were subjected to their own internal discipline.

The village was collectively responsible for the maintenance of its commons. The prime concern in a sandy region was the prevention of soil degradation and emergence of sand drifts, an objective achieved by curbing grazing practices, prohibiting the cutting of sods beyond a certain level and restricting the felling of bushes and trees. In addition, the infrastructure of hedges and windbreaks needed to be maintained. The common wastelands were planted with trees and bushes. Practically every village required its inhabitants to help with the planting and maintenance of these plantations.[27] The villages of Retie, Kalmthout, Ravels, Geel and Arendonk all refer to small plantations or wooded areas, called 'heibossen' (heather forests), which were constructed on the wastelands in order to prevent or limit drifts.[28] From at least 1554, but probably from before that date, the community of Retie appointed two men who were responsible for the protection of the community against the sand and for planting trees.[29] In addition, once a year, all the inhabitants were required to perform communal tasks such as viewing hedges, clearing ditches and brooks, and maintaining the woodlands planted on the common heathland. The by-law of Ravels and Eel, for example, stated that 'the wood, needed to stop the sand, will have to be repaired by everyone on the punishment of 6 stuiver.[30] In addition, several villages had secured the right to plant trees on the commons, 10 feet away from their private land.[31] This, the 'pootrecht', secured their basic needs for timber, but equally functioned as a barrier against drifting sand. In this way, the greatest natural hazard of the Campine, drifting sand, was tamed and existing sand dunes were controlled and stabilised.

Conflict Resolution Mechanisms: Symbolic Action and Sovereign Courts

Continuous collective action was made possible because of the effectiveness of the Campine communities in resolving their conflicts, which otherwise might have prevented the exercise of communal responsibilities. Despite the common denominator or social equilibrium that was achieved, conflicts between and within interest groups, as well as between individuals, were frequent and reveal a reality that is far removed from the conception of the community as a harmonious entity, as portrayed by Blickle for example.[32] There were disputes over the management and use of the Campine commons between the different interest groups. Even the most basic design principles, such as inclusion and exclusion and the boundaries of commons, were subject to discussions. It has, however, also been generally accepted that conflicts were not mere arbitrary and pernicious acts resulting in violence and strife, but could be a form of negotiation and community building.[33] Peasants objected to lordly extractions and excessive dues and often refused to perform labour duties for the manorial lord. Unwanted and illegal enclosures might be ritually destroyed and criminal or immoral behaviour answered by a hue and cry, where the entire community was summoned to witness and perhaps even solve the problem.[34] The precondition for this community building process was the belief that conflicts could be solved efficiently and thoroughly.

The tensions regarding communal rights and common property could either paralyse Campine communities and prevent efficient collective action, or they could be resolved effectively in ways that strengthened the communal ties. Throughout the late medieval period, these conflicts or tensions were not able to disrupt the social cohesion in any fundamental way, nor was any one interest group able to pursue their interests at the cost of the other groups. The conflict resolution mechanisms were frequently invoked and because of their willingness to use litigation, the Campine peasants were able to protect their communal system.

Broadly, there were two kinds of conflicts that needed to be solved. The first included small quarrels and tensions arising out of day-to-day practices, the use rights of individual community members, illegal enclosures and free riding. The second dealt with more serious conflicts which threatened the continuance of the commons, such as privatisation attempts, exclusion mechanisms and external threats to abolish communal rights. Both types of dispute were efficiently handled by the peasant communities from the fifteenth century onwards because of their extensive knowledge of the judicial systems available to them and effective combination of both informal and formal conflict resolution mechanisms.

Local and small-scale conflicts were solved informally. Scholars investigating common pool institutions, as well as historians studying pre-modern communities, have emphasised the importance of alternative systems of conflict resolution.[35] Several scholars have stressed the fact that informal practices were exercised on a more extensive scale than formal procedures.[36] These semi-formal and informal alternatives to justice have increasingly been seen as the most efficient and preferred way of resolving conflicts.[37] Mediators—whether local neighbours, village dignitaries, officials and clergymen—were very important in the resolution of medieval and pre-modern conflicts.[38] A striking example is a conflict between the abbey of Tongerlo and the neighbouring lord of Bergen op Zoom over the right of pasture on the commons belonging to the seigniory of Kalmthout-Essen in 1440. A century after the original delineation of the commons, tensions began to rise regarding the exact location of two boundary markers on the heath. Both local villagers and the ruling elite of Putte claimed that they possessed the right to graze their animals on the piece of heathland in question. The Lord of Bergen op Zoom questioned these boundary markers. Initially, the officers of the seigniory and witnesses drawn from neighbouring villages were ordered by the court to attend at an inspection of the common boundaries where they declared which natural or man-made elements were the rightful boundary markers.[39] When that failed, the court appointed mediators who were required to perform a field inspection, hear witnesses and perambulate the boundary in a further attempt to secure a peaceful solution. We rarely see evidence of these practices, because they do not appear in court records. Only when attempts at mediation were unsuccessful was a final sentence was given by the court, in this case the sovereign Council of Brabant.[40]

When peaceful and orchestrated outcomes were impossible to achieve, more 'violent' or symbolic actions were used. Rural communities had their particular ways of squaring their accounts with trespassers who were illegally grazing or opposed interest groups regarding property and privileges. Enclosure issues were among the most dominant ones. Five cases can be found where fences, ditches or hedges constructed in order to enclose the fields were destroyed.[41] For example, Willem Hendrickxsoon van Brussel, inhabitant of Mierlo, brought a case before the sovereign court of Brabant in April 1554. According to him, his family had purchased a hay meadow called 'Molenbeemd' located in Helmond more than 70 years before, so long ago that nobody could remember it being any other way. Since he was the full owner, he had enclosed and 'liberated' the plot with ditches and hedges. Nonetheless, a group of people including Willem Diericxsmets, Jasper Vrancken, Jan Frans Peeterssoen, Ambrosius Jan Dreycker and their accomplices had violently destroyed the ditches and removed the hedges planted there with force, finally driving their cattle and sheep into the meadow.[42] Similar actions were carried out when rights of way were blocked. A certain Mathijs Verpoerten, inhabitant of Westerlo, claimed to have the right to cross the road and gate of the farmstead of Rombouts van Aken, steward of Mechelen. When he was refused passage by means of a closed gate, he forced his way through and carried four loads of wood through the gate. When van Aken locked the gate closed with a key, Verpoerten destroyed it and continued to pass through the gate.[43]

Ritualised fence-breaking and cattle-droving have been described in communities throughout pre-modern Europe. It can be considered to have been a dominant practice and justified manner of showing discontent. Christopher Dyer has described the destruction of fences during thirteenth-century enclosure riots as common practice in England, an accepted way to react against (alleged) illegal enclosure.[44] Similarly, Miriam Müller has described cases of arson or insubordination as one of a number of well-defined steps in the process of the settlement of any conflict.[45] Although the Habsburg monarchs were increasingly sensitive towards acts of violence or insubordination by peasants during the sixteenth century,[46] the sentences of the Council of Brabant seem to support Müller's and Dyer's theses. Although violent action was used and private property destroyed, the court twice decided in the favour of the violators.[47]

In this way, peasants hindered piecemeal enclosures and stopped infractions that could hurt communal practices. In the end, none of the issues such as illegal enclosures escalated and festered. Apart from some symbolic conflicts, such as boundary disputes which could last for centuries, most were settled quickly. The late medieval Campine communities were therefore quite efficient in dealing with their conflicts on a local and informal level.

Although the extent of such actions is difficult to assess, it must have been the dominant way of dealing with day-to-day issues within the community.[48]

However, as they relied on social consensus, shared norms and rules, and the willingness of both parties to accept these forms of ritualised conduct, a significant number of conflicts could not be settled in this manner.[49] Whenever different communities, parties with very unequal power, or political elites (especially the ruling elites themselves) were involved, it became less likely that a resolution could be achieved with local mediators and ritualised actions. In addition, the more important questions, such as the survival of communal rights, were simply too complex to solve in rural aldermen's benches and via informal mechanisms.

Despite the moral objections to litigation, more challenging issues and external threats were therefore resolved through recourse to the formal court system.[50] In the Campine area several judicial levels existed: the village aldermen's bench, rural appellate courts, urban aldermen's benches and the regional, and sovereign, court, the Council of Brabant. Thanks to overlapping jurisdictions and competing courts, Campine peasants were able to appeal to the court which would provide the most efficient, or rather, favourable juridical sentence for their particular case. Peasants did go to local aldermen's benches and urban courts in first instance, and asked for an appeal or advice, but major issues concerning the survival of the commons or the basic design principles of the common pool institutions appeared surprisingly often before the Council. An unknown number of suits were commenced in the Council but never proceeded beyond a complaint, but some reached the conclusion of a sentence and it is these that we know about. Therefore, our focus here lies on the Campine peasants in the sovereign Council of Brabant, rather than the urban and local courts.[51]

The development of royal institutions such as sovereign courts fitted into—and even enhanced—a legal revolution that was developing in sixteenth-century Europe. In local tribunals peasants had little chance of defending their interests against their seigniorial lords or other powerful elites. By contrast, the royal courts had a reputation for independence and even showed a readiness to curb the powers of the feudal lords. In turn, this encouraged the peasants to bring their pleas before them.[52] Van Dijck has claimed that the costs relating to taking a grievance to court were too great for the middling groups of society and poor households, forcing them to rely on violence and alternative forms of justice.[53] It appears, on the contrary, that Campine peasants developed other ways in order to participate in court.

The greatest weapon of the weak, or the 'action resources' as Ratner has called them, was their ability to adapt themselves to the system.[54] Instead of individually defending one's interests, peasants formed collectives. Social networks were, according to Ratner, the most important attributes one could have at one's disposal during a conflict.[55] The most important social network of the Campine peasant was that of the village community. As a village community, they received the right to skip the subaltern courts and immediately proceed to plead before the sovereign court.[56] Calling themselves the 'ingezetenen ende gemeyne geburen' or 'inhabitants and common neighbours', they pleaded as a single interest group in order to defend their communal privileges and property. This did not necessarily mean every inhabitant was involved or even supported the cause, but a substantial part or core of the community put themselves forward as representatives of the community, therefore laying claim to a communal identity.

When it came to defending common rights, actions brought in the name of the village community immediately enlarged their bargaining power. In a third of the court cases concerning common rights and communal privileges in the Council of Brabant brought by Campine plaintiffs and defendants, one or other litigant presented themselves as such communities.[57] Although, at certain times, different interest groups within the village community might sue each other, they would also form a coalition and present themselves to the outside world as a harmonious entity against external threats. References to individual smallholders are rarely found in the sentence registers. If peasants were able to join forces and act as communities, form interest groups or team up with other interest groups, they could fully participate in the judicial system, but financial or cultural barriers did exist.[58] Although peasants were able to find their way to court and be accepted as litigants in the Council of Brabant, develop a judicial strategy, construct a legal discourse and defend their interests before schooled jurors and elite officials, they were not often able to do so as single individuals. Consequently, only when an individual found support among his neighbours or was able to form an interest community with like-minded spirits, was it possible to bring a suit to a conclusion.[59]

But why opt for the Council of Brabant to resolve conflicts over commons? In disputes over the issue of access to commons between two communities, both were aware that a resolution was impossible to achieve in a village court. The sentence registers often state that the issue was brought before the highest court precisely because the conflict could not be settled locally.[60] Moreover, in disputes concerning roads, fences, property, access rights, common land and jurisdictions, aldermen or lordly representatives such as the bailiff were always involved as parties and so it was logical that the opposing parties tended to ask for an appeal to a different court rather than allow local officials to judge a case to which they were a party. In addition, urban courts had their own logic and interests that did not really favour Campine village communities. The city of 's Hertogenbosch, for example, often initiated attempts to force its rural surroundings into a dependent relationship with it. The citizens of towns were often involved in enclosure cases in neighbouring hamlets.[61] As a result, the court of 's Hertogenbosch would be considered to be biased against the peasantry in that part of the Campine which fell within its jurisdiction.

Peasants, however, did not only choose the Council of Brabant out of mistrust of the lower courts but because it was seen as a beacon of ducal power and justice that looked favourably upon peasants' interests. The image of the Burgundian dukes as the alternative to corrupt bailiffs and aldermen is seen clearly in a popular tale of the fifteenth century. Here a bailiff had stolen a cow from a poor household that had refused to sell it to him. To complain about this matter, the poor farmer went to Count Willem III and pleaded for justice. The Count ordered that the farmer be compensated and declared that the bailiff's punishment would be severe, because by his actions he had abused the duke's authority. In the end, the bailiff was sent to the executioner. A powerful image of the just ruler was therefore created.[62] It was precisely the image of the Duke of Brabant as a just ruler, concerned to curb the powers of the subaltern courts and punish the misdemeanours of his office, that was the main reason why Campine peasants and communities took their case to the highest, most expensive and furthest court.

The Dukes were the most obvious source of justice for the Campine peasantry. The Burgundian administration did not always favour peasant communities or particular claims, such as the maintenance of common rights, but neither did they do the opposite. Fence disputes, for example, show that the Duke was not necessarily opposed to the violent destruction of fences as a response to unlawful enclosures. Furthermore, claims that meadows had to be open after harvest often received the support of the court. The ducal administration often had a supportive attitude towards common property, custom and common use rights.[63] The real outcome, however, depended largely on the case itself and very specific circumstances as no correlation between certain arguments and sentences can be found. The ducal court protected both communal as well as private claims against 'illegal' transgressions.[64] As a result the Dukes of Brabant were the best, although not perfect, allies of the Campine communities.

Notes

1 North, *Institutions*.
2 Laborda Peman and De Moor, 'A tale of two commons'.
3 Winchester, 'Statute and local custom'; Van Weeren and De Moor, 'Controlling the commoners'; John M. Anderies, Marco A. Janssen, and Elinor Ostrom, 'A framework to analyze the robustness of social-ecological systems from an institutional perspective', *Ecology and Society* 9, no. 1 (2004).
4 Ostrom, *Governing the commons*.
5 Winchester, 'Statute and local custom'; Angus Winchester, *Harvest of the Hills: Rural life in northern England and the Scottish borders, 1400–1700* (Edinburgh: Edinburgh University Press, 2000); Van Weeren and De Moor, 'Controlling the commoners'.
6 R. Van Uytven and W. Blockmans, 'Constitutions and their application in the Netherlands during the middle ages', *Belgisch tijdschrift voor filologie en geschiedenis* 47, no. 2 (1969); Wim Blockmans, *Metropolen aan de noordzee: De geschiedenis van nederland, 1100–1560* (Amsterdam: Bakker, 2010).
7 Heather Falvey, 'The articulation, transmission and preservation of custom in the forest community of Duffield (Derbyshire)', in *Custom, improvement and the landscape*, ed. Hoyle (Farnham: Ashgate, 2011).
8 Thompson, *Customs in common*; Müller, 'Conflict'; Hoyle (ed.), *Custom*.

9 Bailey, 'Sand into gold'; Allison, 'Sheep-corn husbandry'; Allison, 'Flock management'; Whyte, 'Contested pasts'.
10 David Fletcher, 'The parish boundary: A social phenomenon in Hanoverian England', *Rural History* 14, no. 2 (2003).
11 De Keyzer, Jongepier, and Soens, 'Consuming maps'.
12 Ostrom, *Governing the commons*.
13 Van Weeren and De Moor, 'Controlling the commoners'.
14 See database: by-laws.
15 The aldermen's registers and bailiff accounts that were analysed are: RAA, OGA Gierle, 349–50, registers of the bench of aldermen, 1512–58; RAA, OGA Rijkevorsel, 145–80, Registers of the bench of aldermen, 1465–1609; ARAB, Chambre des Comptes, 12977, Account of the bailiff of Zandhoven, 1626–1770; ARAB, Chambre des Comptes, 12951–12952, Account of the bailiff of Herentals, 1412–1577; RAA, OGA Herenthout, 160, 'vorster account', 1653.
16 Martin Dinges, 'The uses of justice as a form of social control in early modern Europe', in *Social control in Europe, 1500–1800*, eds Herman Roodenburg and Pieter Spierenburg (Ohio: Ohio State University Press, 2004).
17 Trees growing on the common wastelands and streets were the property of the lord and could therefore not be felled by community members. Because timber was an important seigniorial property, infractions were severely punished.
18 Benoît Garnot, 'Justice, infrajustice, parajustice et extra justice dans la France d'ancien régime', *Crime, histoire & sociétés* 4, no. 1 (2000).
19 Postgate, 'Historical geography'.
20 W. Neil Adger, 'Social and ecological resilience: Are they related?', *Progress in Human Geography* 24, no. 3 (2000).
21 Eline Van Onacker and Hadewijch Masure, 'Unity in diversity. Rural poor relief in the sixteenth-century southern Low Countries', *TSEG* 12, no. 4 (2015); Chapter 3 above.
22 Mauelshagen, 'Flood disasters'.
23 Augustyn, *Zeespiegelrijzing*.
24 'alle 14 dagen tezamen en met elkaar in de heide en rond de palen van Ekeren te gaan'. Gielens, 'Keuren van ekeren'.
25 'iedereen mag klagen en de breuk voor de helft hebben'. Prims, 'Keuren'.
26 See database: by-laws.
27 Ibid.
28 Helsen, 'Het dorpskeurboek van retie'; Ernalsteen, 'Keuren van gheel'; Koyen, 'Keuren van ravels'; Gerard Meeusen, 'Keuren van esschen, calmpthout en huybergen', *Oudheid en Kunst*, 23 (1932); P. J. Verhoeven, 'Keuren van calmpthout', *Oudheid en Kunst*, 00 (1907); Prims, 'Keuren'.
29 The oldest version of Retie's by-laws dates back to 1554, but oral regulations predated this, the earliest written document. Helsen, 'Het dorpskeurboek van Retie'.
30 'Het hout ook voor indien het nodig mocht wezen om het zand te stoppen, zal iedereen komen en repareren op alle mogelijke manieren, op de straf van 6 stuivers'. Koyen, 'Keuren van Ravels'.
31 See for example: RAA, OGA Rijkevorsel, 12, Charter granting the right to plant trees, 1609.
32 Blickle, *Kommunalismus*.
33 Peter Arnade, 'Crowds, banners, and the marketplace: Symbols of defiance and defeat during the Ghent war of 1452–3', *Journal of Medieval and Renaissance Studies* 24, no. 3 (1994); Wim Blockmans, 'Revolutionaire mechanismen in vlaanderen van de 13de tot de 16de eeuw', *Tijdschrift voor sociale wetenschappen* 19, no. 2 (1974); Jan Dumolyn, ' "Criers and shouters": The discourse on radical urban rebels in late medieval Flanders', *Journal of Social History* 42, no. 1 (2008); Christopher Dyer, 'Conflict in the landscape: The enclosure

movement in England, 1220–1349', *Landscape History* 28 (2006); Richard Goddard, John Langdon, and Miriam Müller (eds), *Survival and discord in medieval society: Essays in honour of Christopher Dyer* (Turnhout: Brepols, 2010); Jelle Haemers, 'A moody community? Emotion and ritual in late medieval urban revolts', *Urban History* 5 (2005); C. Holmes, 'Drainers and fenmen: The problem of popular political consciousness in the seventeenth century', in *Order and disorder in early modern England*, eds Anthony Fletcher and John Stevenson (Cambridge: Cambridge University Press, 1987); Henry Landsberger (ed.), *Rural protest: Peasant movements and social change* (London: MacMillan, 1974); Briony A. K. McDonagh, 'Subverting the ground: Private property and public protest in the sixteenth-century Yorkshire Wolds', *Agricultural History Review* 57, no. 2 (2009).

34 Dyer, 'Conflict in the landscape'; Müller, 'Conflict'; Müller, 'Social control'.
35 Nicole Castan, 'The arbitration of disputes under the "ancien regime"', in *Disputes and settlements: Law and human relations in the West*, ed. John Bossy (Cambridge: Cambridge University Press, 2003); P. L. Larson, *Conflict and compromise in the late medieval countryside: Lords and peasants in Durham, 1349–1400* (London: Routledge, 2006); Craig Muldrew, 'The culture of reconciliation: Community and the settlement of economic disputes in early modern England', *Historical Journal* 39, no. 4 (1996); William M.E.A. Adams, 'Managing tragedies: Understanding conflict over common pool resources', *Science* 302 (2003); Pascal C. Sanginga, Rick N. Kamugisha, and Andrienne M. Martin, 'The dynamics of social capital and conflict management in multiple resource regimes: A case of the southwestern highlands of Uganda', *Ecology and Society* 12, no. 1 (2007); Garnot, 'Justice, infrajustice'; Müller, 'Conflict'; Dinges, 'Uses of justice'.
36 Griet Vermeesch, 'Explaining the "legal revolution" and the "great litigation decline". Processes of social change and changing litigation patterns in early modern Europe' (unpublished paper); Hervé Piant, *Une justice ordinaire: Justice civile et criminelle dans la prévôté royale de vaucouleurs sous l'ancien régime* (Rennes: Presses Universitaires de Rennes, 2006); Bossy (ed.), *Disputes and settlements*; Anne Bonzon, 'Les curés médiateurs sociaux dans la France du xviie siècle', *Revue d'histoire de l'Eglise de France* 97, no. 238 (2011); Muldrew, 'Culture of reconciliation'; Garnot, 'Justice, infrajustice'.
37 Müller, 'Conflict'; Müller, 'Social control'; Dinges, 'Uses of justice'; Garnot, 'Justice, infrajustice'.
38 Piant, *Une justice ordinaire*, 204; Bonzon, 'Les curés médiateurs sociaux'; Castan, 'Arbitration of disputes'; Larson, *Conflict and compromise*.
39 AAT, Section IV, Bundle Kalmthout-Essen-Huibergen, 101–04, Court records concerning boundary dispute between the abbey of Tongerlo and the Lord of Bergen op Zoom, 1439–40.
40 De Keyzer, Jongepier, and Soens, 'Consuming Maps'.
41 RAB, VB, 578, 38 (1531) Putte; 579, 132 (1532) Helmond; 588, 177 (1541) Vilvoorde; 595, 121 (1545) Putte; 602, 51 (1554) Helmond.
42 RAB, VB, 602, 51 (1554) Helmond.
43 RAB, VB, 595, 121 (1545) Putte.
44 Dyer, 'Conflict in the landscape'; Jean R. Birrell, 'Common right in the medieval forest: Disputes and conflicts in the thirteenth century', *Past and Present* 117 (1987).
45 Müller, 'Conflict in the landscape'; Müller, 'Arson'.
46 Peter Blickle, 'The criminalization of peasant resistance in the Holy Roman Empire: Toward a history of the emergence of high treason in Germany', *Journal of Modern History* 58 (1986).
47 RAB, VB, 579, 132 (1532) Helmond; RAB, VB, 588, 177 (1541) Vilvoorde.

48 Müller, 'Conflict'.
49 Garnot, 'Justice, infrajustice'.
50 Stein, *De hertog en zijn staten*.
51 For a further discussion of peasant access to courts in the late medieval period in the Low Countries, see De Keyzer, 'Access versus influence'.
52 Richard L. Kagan, *Lawsuits and litigants in Castile, 1500–1700* (Chapel Hill: The University of North Carolina Press, 1981), 99; Piant, *Une justice ordinaire*, 212–24; Marie-Charlotte Le Bailly, 'Langetermijntrends in de rechtspraak bij de gewestelijke hoven van justitie in de noordelijke nederlanden van ca. 1450 tot ca. 1800', *Pro Memoria* 13 (2011); Dinges, 'Uses of justice'; Stein, *De hertog en zijn staten*.
53 Maarten Van Dijck, 'Towards an economic interpretation of justice? Conflict settlement, social control and civil society in urban Brabant and Mechelen during the late middle ages and the early modern period', in *Serving the urban community: The rise of public facilities in the Low Countries*, eds Manon van der Heijden, Elise van Nederveen Meerkerk and Griet Vermeersch (Amsterdam: Aksant, 2009).
54 Blake D. Ratner et al., 'Resource conflict, collective action, and resilience: An analytical framework', *International Journal of the Commons* 7 (2013); James Scott, *Weapons of the weak: Everyday forms of peasant resistance* (New Haven: Yale University Press, 1985).
55 Ratner et al., 'Resource conflict'.
56 J. Monballyu, 'De gerechtelijke bevoegdheid van de raad van vlaanderen in vergelijking met de andere "wetten" (1515–1621)', in *Hoven en banken in noord en zuid*, eds B.C.M. Jacobs and P. L. Nève (Assen: Van Gorcum & Comp., 1994).
57 A total of 412 sentences and charters were examined covering a wide range of conflicts originating in and around the Campine. The sentences from the French-speaking part of the Duchy were not taken into account, nor were the conflicts from the most southern part of the Duchy. Southern Brabant and what is now Walloon Brabant were, after all, fundamentally different social agrosystems and might distort the picture if included in the analysis. Of these 412 cases, 204 were analysed more thoroughly, since the other cases contained only a summarised sentence without further information. See database: Juridical records.
58 Van Dijck, 'Towards an economic interpretation'.
59 For a more detailed discussion on peasant access and agency in courts, see De Keyzer, 'Access versus influence'.
60 RAB, VB, 585, 1 (1531) Meldert; RAB, VB, 564, 6 (1508) Putte; RAB, VB, 586, 104 (1538) Wijnegem; RAB, VB, 595, 134 (1546) Oirschot.
61 J. Coopmans, 'De onderlinge rechtsverhoudingen van 's-hertogenbosch en het platteland voor 1629', *Bijdragen tot de geschiedenis* 58, no. 1–2 (1975); Jacobs, *Justitie en politie*; M. M. P. Van Asseldonk, *De meierij van 's-hertogenbosch: De evolutie van plaatselijk bestuur, bestuurlijke indeling en dorpsgrenzen, circa 1200–1832* (Oosterhout: Leonard, 2001); Hein Vera, 'Rechten op woeste gronden in de meierij van den bosch', *Post Factum: Jaarboek voor geschiedenis en Volkskunde*, no. 1 (2009).
62 Stein, *De hertog en zijn staten*.
63 On the matter of custom in general see: Michael Goldman, ' "Customs in common": The epistemic world of the commons scholars', *Theory and Society* 26, no. 1 (1997); Hoyle (ed.), *Custom*; King, 'Legal change'; Thompson, *Customs in common*; Winchester, 'Statute and local custom'.
64 See database: Sentence registers.

6 Conclusion

'Freedom in the commons brings ruin to all'.[1] Garrett Hardin's conclusion has spurred academic debate. Although he attracted a large group of supporters, Hardin's views triggered a reaction, with many commentators stating that freedom in the commons was a myth. The Nobel Prize Laureate Elinor Ostrom set the tone of the debate from the nineties onwards. She argued strongly that commons do not inevitably have to lead towards a tragedy. On the contrary, she showed that communal regimes were able to maintain sustainable policies for centuries. One of the reasons for the commons' success was the absence of freedom. Communal resources after all differ from public goods by a distinction between entitled users and outsiders without communal rights. Although it is difficult for communal resources to exclude appropriators, it is not impossible. Common pool resources are always managed by common pool institutions that adhere to eight design principles. Two of these prevent freedom or free riding in the commons. The first states that a strict delimitation of the community of users and of the common pool resources needs to be implemented. The second refers to congruence between the natural environment and rules of appropriation in order to prevent an ecological disaster.[2]

As a result the debate has turned and commons are no longer associated with freedom, but rather with strictly demarcated communities of users. Scholars are now emphasising the exclusive character of common pool institutions. When resources are scarce or fragile, limiting the community of users and preventing the acceptance of new members are deemed the most important strategies to prevent overexploitation and unsustainable policies.[3] Northwestern Europe in particular, with high population pressure, urbanisation levels and limited communal resources, has been portrayed as the scene for more restrictive and exclusive common pool institutions. Historians have showed that from the later Middle Ages onwards, when population was rising, markets were developing faster and urbanisation levels increasing, common pool institutions reacted by introducing more exclusive measures in order to prevent increased pressure on natural resources.[4] As a result, not only outsiders, but also subgroups within the village communities, were excluded. These were often the poorest, landless labourers, new settlers or even children of entitled users who did not inherit a share in the commons.[5]

This book has shown that exclusivity is not a precondition for successful commons. Even within the core region of the late medieval Low Countries, where the market incentives and pressures on the landscape were the highest in Europe, a region existed where exclusivity was averted and the commons were enjoyed by the entire population. Outsiders were excluded from obtaining access to the commons, preventing an open access regime. Nevertheless, all community members or inhabitants of the rural villages were allowed to use the commons and 98 per cent did use them on a yearly basis during the later Middle Ages and pre-modern times. Even in a growth scenario, where increasingly large flocks of sheep were grazed on the commons, the population increased and urban centres such as Antwerp achieved a metropolis status, the Campine commons did not introduce more exclusive or restrictive rules. Even stinting or the numerical limitation of animals on the common wastelands was not resorted to in the Campine.

These remarkably inclusive commons did not lead to a tragedy, rather the contrary. They were truly successful commons. Until now, the success of commons has often been implicitly assumed, so long as no tragedy of the commons occurred or the common pool institutions endured. Commons were considered successful if they could survive for more than two centuries, or if they achieved a sustainable management.[6] Sustainability has suffered from the same conceptual vagueness as success and longevity is no proof of effective institutions. Ineffective institutions can last for centuries, as long as they serve the interests of the dominant interest groups of society. Therefore, this book has offered a new and stricter definition of what counts as a successful common. We argue that commons are only successful when they achieve three important characteristics. First, they must maintain ecological resilience which we define as the capacity of a system to absorb disturbance and re-organise while undergoing change so as to retain essentially the same structure, function, identity and feedbacks.[7] Second, they have to be able to fend off alternative modes of appropriation and protect their common property regime. Third, their benefits should be distributed equitably. With this definition, a framework to test the success of commons is provided, in order to move beyond an ad hoc evaluation of every common pool institution in its own terms.

In the light of this definition, the inclusive Campine common pool institutions were successful. First of all, they were able to prevent overexploitation and achieve ecological resilience. The sandy subsoil of the coversand belt, of which the Campine area was a tiny part, was easily overexploited and degraded, as the first settlements around the ninth and tenth century had discovered. The common pool institutions that developed from the thirteenth century were, however, capable of turning the tide, stabilising the landscape, and maintaining an ecologically diverse and resilient landscape, which lasted until the eighteenth century. Second, the benefits of the commons were distributed fairly. The Campine opted not to distribute fixed stints or shares to each household. Equitable rather than equal access was preferred. The benefits were distributed unevenly but tailored to the needs of all interest groups. Third, large-scale privatisations and enclosure movements were prevented throughout the pre-modern era. Although the abbey of Tongerlo, as one of the most wealthy and powerful landlords, and some of the rural elites were able to privatise and enclose parts of land from the sixteenth century onwards, this barely affected the common property regime of the Campine area. The combination of full-time common wastelands (consisting of 60–90 per cent of the total surface area) and seasonal common meadows survived until the large-scale, forced privatisations, imposed by first Maria Theresa and then the liberal Belgian government from the eighteenth century onwards.

These inclusive Campine communities were successful because of a particular social and institutional constellation. First of all, they tailored a specific institutional framework. The Campine communities opted to formalise their communal rights by securing formal charters and privileges but they refrained from all too strict and written regulations. Although written by-laws started to appear from the fifteenth century, there was a preference for managing the commons flexibly through unwritten rules. This allowed them to respond to new challenges and circumstances. These informal practices were effective because of the second characteristic: an egalitarian and inclusive society that allowed for efficient collective action. Compared to the surrounding regions, the Campine communities were remarkably egalitarian and included even the poorest members of the community in their common pool institutions. These strong communal ties offered the opportunity to rely on collective action and social control, rather than sanctions and formal top-down institutions, in order to implement rules and maintain the commons. The entire community was responsible for the management and maintenance of the commons, which discouraged free riding, overexploitation and unsustainable use of the commons. This *inclusivity* allowed the same goals to be secured as might be achieved elsewhere by social *exclusivity*. When collective management was threatened by conflicts and strife within the communities or by external challenges, the Campine communities used both informal and formal conflict resolution mechanisms to resolve the issues. Smaller tensions about the communal rights, local practices and trespassing were resolved thanks to mediators or the use of symbolic action within the communities themselves. More serious conflicts regarding the foundations of the common pool institutions and communal rights had to be taken to court. The Campine rural communities resorted to litigation when they needed to and were successfully able to use the courts, the Council of Brabant in particular, to protect their common rights and property. Inclusive commons and sustainability did not have to be a paradox. The Campine was able to design its society in such a way that free riding and overexploitation was prevented in as effective way as happened in the most successful exclusive communities.

We concede that more research is needed to get deeper insights into what made common pool institutions successful. More comparative research into inclusive common pool institutions is required to test the impact of different social and institutional frameworks on the level of success of inclusive commons. In addition, more comparisons between exclusive and inclusive institutions are required to test which strategies were the most effective in tackling challenges such as free riding and overexploitation. The experience of the Campine commons provides a yardstick against which other commons, and other forms of Common Pool Institutions, might in the future be benchmarked, both to test the uniqueness of arrangements here, but also to see how far the premises which underpinned the Campine commons are found elsewhere.

Notes

1 Hardin, 'Tragedy of the commons'.
2 Ostrom, *Governing the commons*.
3 Mckean, *People and forests*.
4 De Moor, Shaw-Taylor, and Warde (eds), *Management of common lands*; Casari, 'Gender-biased inheritance systems'; *Transhumance et estivage en occident*, ed. Laffont; Winchester and Straughton, 'Stints and sustainability'.
5 Whyte, 'Contested pasts'; Allison, 'Sheep-corn husbandry'; Poulsen, 'Landesausbau und umwelt in schleswig, 1450–1550j'; Shaw-Taylor, 'Management of common land'.
6 Van Weeren and De Moor, 'Controlling the commoners'. Shaw-Taylor, 'Management of common land'; Van Zanden, 'Paradox of the marks'; Casari and Plott, 'Decentralized management of common property resources'; Winchester, 'Common land in upland Britain'; Winchester and Straughton, 'Stints and sustainability'.
7 Folke, 'Resilience', 259.

Bibliography

Sources Included in Databases

(a) By-laws Database

Unpublished Sources

AAT, Bundel By-laws, Veerle and Oevel, Copy.
AAT, Bundel Tongerlo I: Rules for the village of Tongerlo, Copy.
RAA, OGA Gierle, 44, By-law.
RAA, OGA Herenthout, 3, By-law.
RAA, OGA Hoogstraten, 638, By-law.
RAA, OGA Rijkevorsel, 8, By-law.
Rijksarchief Antwerpen (RAA), Oud Gemeente-Archief (OGA) Tielen, 28.

Published Sources

De Longé, G., 'Coutumes de Santhoven, de Turnhout et de Rumpet', in G. De Longé (ed.), *Coutumes du pays et duché de Brabant: Quartier d'Anvers* (Brussel, 1870–1878).

De Longé, G., *Coutumes d'Herenthals, de Casterlé, de Moll, Balen et Deschel, de Gheel, de Hoogstraten, De Befferen Et De Putte, Et Feodales Du Pays De Malines, Recueil Des Anciennes Coutumes de la Belgique* (Brussel, 1878).

De Molder, T., 'Keuren van Oostmalle', *Oudheid en Kunst* 26, no. 1 (1935), pp. 3–15.

Erens, A., *De oorkonden der abdij Tongerloo*, 4 vols (Tongerlo, 1948).

Ernalsteen, J., 'Brecht: De keuren van 1601', *Oudheid en Kunst* 16, no. 2 (1925), pp. 25–32.

———, 'Keuren van Gheel', *Oudheid en Kunst* 26, no. 2 (1935), pp. 19–66.

Gielens, A., 'Keuren van Ekeren', *Oudheid en Kunst* 30, no. 1 (1939), pp. 167–83.

Helsen, I., 'Het dorpskeurboek van Retie', *Bijdragen tot de geschiedenis* 1, no. 1 (1949), pp. 85–107.

Koyen, M., 'Keuren van Ravels', *Oudheid en Kunst* 41, no. 2 (1958), pp. 3–19.

Lauwerys, J., 'Keuren van Westerloo', *Oudheid en Kunst* 28, no. 4 (1937), pp. 95–120.

Meeusen, G., 'Keuren van Esschen, Calmpthout en Huybergen', *Oudheid en Kunst* 23 (1932), pp. 112–24.

Michielsen, J., 'Keuren van Brecht', *Oudheid en Kunst* (1907), pp. 71–81.

Peeters, K. C., 'De Wuustwezelsche dorpskeuren (XVe–XVIIe Eeuw)', *Verslagen en mededelingen van de koninklijke Vlaamsche academie voor taal en letterkunde* (1932), pp. 595–709.

——, 'De Wuustwezelsche dorpskeuren (XVe–XVIIe Eeuw)', *Wesalia, Tijdschrift voor plaatselijke Geschiedenis en Folklore* 8, no. 1–2 (1933), pp. 2–48.

Peeters, R., 'De keuren van Turnhout (1550)', *Taxandria* 29, no. 1–4 (1957), pp. 61–122.

Prims, F., 'Keuren der vreyheyt van Arendonk', in H. Draye (ed.), *Feestbundel H. J. Van De Wijer, den jubilaris aangeboden ter gelegenheid van zijn vijfentwintigjarig hoogleeraarschap aan de R. K. universiteit te Leuven 1919–1943* (Leuven, 1944).

Van Gorp, J., 'De aartbrief van Terloo', *Bijdragen tot de geschiedenis* 18 (1927), pp. 437–54.

Van Olmen, E. H. A., 'De keuren van Vorselaar', *Taxandria* 7 (1910), pp. 35–49.

Verbist, F., *Costuymen van de hoofdrechtbank van Zandhoven, Uitgave 1664. Keuren en breuken, Uitgave 1665* (Zandhoven, 2007).

Verellen, J. R., 'De keuren van Herentals (1410–1567)', *Taxandria* XVI, no. 1 (1950), pp. 20–107.

Verhoeven, P. J., 'Keuren van Calmpthout', *Oudheid en Kunst* (1907), pp. 45–6.

(b) Juridical Records Database

Erens, A., *De oorkonden der abdij Tongerloo*, 4 vols (Tongerlo, 1948).

N° 67, 1213, Arnold Van Wezemaal vs Abbey of Tongerlo

N° 70, 1215, Winric Van Alphen (Knight) vs Abbey of Tongerlo

N° 93, 1226, Abbey of Tongerlo vs Michiel van Ranst

N° 239, 1284, Abbey of Tongerlo vs Walter Haweli and his brothers

N° 272, 1292, Duke of Brabant vs Abbey of Tongerlo

N° 337, 18 August 1301, Knight Daniel vs Abbey of Tongerlo

N° 348, 19 July 1303, Duke of Brabant vs Abbey of Tongerlo

N° 391, 8 March 1308, Steward of Brabant vs Abbey of Tongerlo

N° 404, 26 August 1308, Steven van Waalwijk vs Mathias van Hapert and Abbey of Tongerlo

N° 418, 13 December 1309, Jan de Sned, Jan Thomaszoon vs Hendric Bac

N° 421, 1 June 1310, Jan and Hendrik de Hase of Oevel vs Arnold Trenchelare of Morkhove

N° 441, 12 December 1311, Duke of Brabant vs Hospital of Turnhout

N° 515, 31 October 1316, Walter van Hamme vs Abbey of Tongerlo

N° 628, 9 January 1324, Steward of Brabant vs Abbey of Tongerlo

N° 743, 21 September 1331, Lord of Duffel and Geel vs Wouter van Uutschule

N° 744, 21 October 1331, Abbey of Tongerlo vs Chapter of Kamerijk

N° 755, 9 March 1332, Steward of Breda vs Jacop Zuetrix

N° 775, 30 May 1334, Duke of Brabant vs Village of Middelbeers

N° 795, 18 October 1335, Steward of Brabant vs Abbey of Tongerlo

N° 800, 2 March 1336, Duke of Brabant vs Abbey of Tongerlo

N° 921, 27 July 1348, Hendrick Boykens vs Abbey of Tongerlo

N° 979, 30 July 1352, Abbey of Tongerlo vs Hermits of Huibergen

N° 1009, 4 July 1354, Abbey of Tongerlo vs Lord of Wezemaal

N° 1077, 31 July 1358, Lord of Bergen op Zoom vs Abbey of Tongerlo

N° 1078, 1 September 1358, Lord of Bergen op Zoom vs Abbey of Tongerlo
N° 1079, 1 September, 1358, Ibid.
N° 1103, 14 April 1360, Hermits of Huibergen vs Abbey of Tongerlo
N° 1116, 14 June 1361, Abbey of Tongerlo vs Lord of Duffel and Geel

Abbey Archives of Tongerlo (AAT), Charters

N° 668, 1352, Abbey of Tongerlo vs Cloister of Huibergen
N° 720, 1358, Lord of Bergen op Zoom vs Abbey of Tongerlo
N° 18, 14th.century, Duke of Brabant vs property owners of Kalmthout
N° 19, 14th century, Abbey of Tongerlo vs Lord of Wezemaal
N° unknown, 27 June 1395, Lord of Duffel and Geel vs Abbey of Tongerlo
N° 29, 23 January 1420, Duke of Brabant vs Village of Ravels and Poppel
N° 31, 17 June 1420, Duke of Brabant vs Village of Ravels and Turnhout
N° 37, 11 November 1427, Lord of Wezemaal vs City of Geel and Oosterlo
N° 39, 15 April 1429, Lord of Noorderwijk vs Tanners of Herentals
N° 41, 42, 3 May 1429, Jan Godensz vs Bailiff and village of Kalmthout-Essen
N° 43, 24 April 1431, Village of Zammel vs Abbey of Tongerlo
N° 44, 5 May 1434, Jan vander Aa vs Lord of Hoogstraten
N° 51, 15 November 1441, Duke of Brabant vs Lord of Bergen op Zoom
N° unknown, 6 July 1459, Abbey of Tongerlo vs Village of Ravels
N° 67, 29 September 1463, Aart and Jan de Straeper vs Abbey of Tongerlo
N° 68, 4 October 1464, Abbey of Tongerlo vs Village of Brecht
N° 70, 15 December 1468, Abbey of Tongerlo vs Village of Oerle
Verkooren, A., *Inventaire des chartes et cartulaires des duchés de Brabant et de Limbourg et des Pays d'Outre-Meuse. Premier partie. Chartes originales et vidimées.* 1154–1338 (1910).

VOLUME 1

N° 81, 23 June 1236, Duke of Brabant vs Suburbs of Lier
N° 98, April 1247, Duke of Brabant Village of Herenthout
N° 202, 4 December 1300, Duke of Brabant vs Village of Oisterwijk
N° 208, 24 June 1303, Duke of Brabant vs City of Herentals
N° 227, 5 August 1310, Duke of Brabant vs Village of Vechel
N° 231, 21 August 1311, Duke of Brabant vs Hospital of Turnhout
N° 235, 27 September 1312, Duke of Brabant vs Inhabitants of Lotharingen, Brabant and Limburg

VOLUME 2

N° 18, 9.November 1321, City of Walhorn vs Suburbs of Walhorn
N° 26, 7.May 1326, Duke of Brabant vs Village of Liempde
N° 34, 24 September 1331, Duke of Brabant vs Village of Bergeik and Westerhoven
N° 54, 9 December 1337, Duke of Brabant vs Village of Liempde
N° 56, 22 July 1338, Duke of Brabant vs City of Turnhout
N° 66, 18 June 1344, Duke of Brabant vs City of 's Hertogenbosch
N° 79, 22 May 1351, Duke of Brabant vs Inhabitants of Lotharingen, Brabant and Limburg

N° 130, 4 February 1358, Duke of Brabant vs City of Lier
N° 203, 3 June 1378, Steward of Brabant vs Village of Kasterlee
N° 219, 24 August 1383, Duke of Brabant vs Aldermen and jurors of Oisterwijk

VOLUME 3

19 March 1436, Lord of Petersheim, Oirschot and Beke vs Thieric Dijcke of Maastricht
5 July 1436, Duke of Brabant vs City of Tilburg and Goerle
5 July 1436, Duke of Brabant vs City of Tilburg and Goerle
5 September 1436, Bailiff of Hilvarenbeek vs Village of Hilvarenbeek
5. of September 1436, Duke of Brabant vs City of Tilburg and Goerle
1436, Duke of Brabant vs Village of Kerk-Oerle
1438, Duke of Brabant vs Master de Dynther
1439, Limburg vs City of Aken
15 November 1441, Lord of Bergen op Zoom vs Abbey of Tongerlo
4 March 1446, Villages of Brabant vs Villages of Loon
22 April 1446, Village of Vessel vs Jean Boydens Marie
25 May 1446, Village of Vechel vs Village of Erpe
16 June 1449, Duke of Brabant vs City of Oisterwijk
20 September 1451, Duke of Brabant vs Inhabitants of Brabant
22 August 1458, Steward of Brabant vs Village of Wilmarsdonk and Oorderen
10 May 1462, Duke of Brabant vs Villages of Brabant
2 July 1462, Duke of Brabant vs Aldermen and jurors of Herentals
26 January 1463, Aldermen of Gref vs Steward of Brabant
21 April of 1464, Duke of Brabant vs Villages of Brabant

(c) Sentence Registers Database

Sentence Registers of the Council of Brabant: Rijksarchief Brussel (RAB), Conseil de Brabant, Archives of the Registry, General Sentence Registers

Book 564, N° 18, September 1494, Noorderwijk, Village of Noorderwijk vs Village of Biest
Book 549, N° 11, August 1495, Netersel, Village of Netersel vs Aldermen and village of Beke
Book 547, N° 35, 15 November 1495, Mierde, City of Turnhout and Arendonk vs Village of Mierde
Book 554, N° 58, 1498, Halen, Village of Halen vs Aldermen and Burgomasters of Halen
Book 557, N° 45, September 1498, Grootbeemd, Village of Oirschot vs Aldermen, jurors and village of Grootbeemd
Book 553, N° 63, November 1498, Vechel, Village of Vechel vs Village of Schijndel
Book 553, N° 47, June 1499, Lieshout, Village of Beke and Aerle vs Aldermen and village of Lieshout
Book 551, N° 57, July 1499, Geetbets, Reynier De Smet vs Jan van Halle
Book 553, N° 10, end of 15th. century, Zommeren, Abbey of Postel vs Village of Zommeren
Book 553, 13, December 1499, unknown, Holy Ghost table vs Henrick van Deurne

Book 553, N° 66, end of 15th.century, Oirschot, Vorster of Oirschot vs Bailiff of 's Hertogenbosch

Book 554, N° 51, End 15th. century, Leuven, Francken Loenkens vs Bailiff and Vorster Abbey of Leuven

Book 553, N° 57, End 15. century, Oirschot, Village of Grootbeemd vs Aldermen jurors and eight good men of Oirschot

Book 562, N° 38, March 1502, Richelle, Village of Richelle vs Our Lady's church of Aken

Book 555, N° 13, March 1502, Noorderwijk Peter vander Beke vs Claes Folbiers and Jan de Voldere

Book 562, N° 66, October 1504, Herentals, Burghers of Herentals vs Village of Mol, Dessel and Balen

Book 556, N° 85, September 1505, Putte, Jan De Bruyne vs Jan Wouters

Book 563, N° 49, 1507, Bakel, Lord of Bakel vs Village of Bakel

Book 557, N° 63, 1507, Mechelen, Janne vander Zenne vs Holy Ghost table of Saint Peter's of Mechelen

Book 564, N° 6, January 1508, Putte, Widow Jan van Voorspoel vs Jan Horeman

Book 558, N° 40, 1508, Deurne, Village of Deurne vs Damiele Melis Mauwerssoon

Book 559, N° 1, June 1509, Tilburg, Willems Wouwen inhabitant of Beke vs Bailiff and City of Tilburg

Book 565, N° 9, 1509, Turnhout, Peter Stynen vs Peter Pynaerts

Book 561, N° 67, July 1510, Vorst, Cloister of Vorst vs Bailiff Jan de Knibbere

Book 560, N° 33, November 1510, Kontich (Nl), Jan Papenelt vs Lord JAnne van-den Aa (knight)

Book 561, N° 16, 1510, Vroenhoven, Peeters vanden Berghen vs Village of Vroenhoven

Book 562, N° 75, 1511, Asse, Steward of Lord of Asse vs Church masters of Asse

Book 563, N° 76, 1512, Koersel, Jan Liebens and Jan Hillen vs Village of Koersel

Book 564, N° 53, March 1513, Oplinter, Village of Oplinter vs Aldermen and good men of Oplinter

Book 564, N° 35, June 1514, Werbeke, Village of Werbeke vs Peeteren Suys, Janne Arnts and fellows inhabitants of Retie

Book 565, N° 81, December 1516, Eppegem, Village of Houtham vs Bailiff of Eppegem

Book 576, N° 3, November 1522, Leende, Village of Leende vs Lord Maximiliaen van Horne

Book 576, N° 229, July 1524, Gaasbeek, Arnt van Hoechtem and fellows inhabitants of Leende vs Attorney General of Brabant, Bailiff and Lord van Horne of Gaasbeek

Book 586, N° 3, July 1525, Onze-Lieve-Vrouwe-Waver, Lucassen Cop vs Verberct

Book 581, N° 48, April 1526, Stiphout, Church masters of Saint John's 's Hertogen-bosch vs Village and property owners of Strijpe, Aerlebeke and Stiphout

Book 583, N° 12, January 1527, Heverlee, Cloister vander Banck vs Verone Priors

Book 580, N° 87, September 1527, Rixtel, Jan Wouterssoon van Dommelen vs Church masters of Rixtel

Book 576, N° 175, August 1529, Oplinter, Ottens van Malborch vs Bertelmeens de Hertoge

Book 577, N° 216, February 1530, Kortenaken, Guardian children Janne Vos vs Willem van Papenwerck

Book 579, N° 104, August 1530, Wuustwezel, Lady Maximiliaen vander Noot vs Village of Wuustwezel

Book 578, N° 38, May 1531, Putte, Cornelis Vervoert vs Jan Zeven

Book 585, N° 1, October 1531, Meldert, Village of Meldert and Hechelgem vs Abbey of Affligem

Book 578, N° 286, November 1531, Huldenberg, Lady of Houthem and Huldenberg vs Gielis vander Banwetten and fellows

Book 581, N° 33, November 1531, Wechelderzande, Wouters Versant vs Aert Stevens

Book 582, N° 117, March 1532, Wezembeek, Widow Pieter vanden Bossche vs Henrick Scheers

Book 581, N° 123, May 1532, Itegem, Unknown vs Mertens Lauwaerts Jan van Rotselaer and fellows

Book 581, N° 35, May 1532, Massenhove, Cloister of Saint Claes Bergen vs Gabriel van Dornicke

Book 579, N° 139, June 1532, Hersele, Abbey of Saint Geertruyde vs unknown

Book 586, N° 125, July 1532, Vechel, Henricke Beyens burgher of 's Hertogenbosch vs Aldermen, jurors and land surveyor of Vechel

Book 579, N° 132, December 1532, Helmond, Arnts Mominck vs Willem Thonis

Book 582, N° 41, March 1533, Unknown, Widow Clements Poels vs Claes Scampioen

Book 586, N° 94, July 1533, Schijndel, Janne Palm Burgher of 's Hertogenbosch vs Village of Schijndel

Book 580, N° 71, October 1533, Sterksel, Abbey of Averbode vs Village of Zoeveren

Book 583, N° 105, March 1534, Kasterlee, Jan Broothaze vs Jan Van Kets

Book 581, N° 11, March 1534, Meldert, Master Cornelis van Lathem and fellows vs Lord of Duras and Willem van Loeffelt

Book 581, N° 19, June 1534, Retie, Janne van Bergelen vs Lijsbeth Busscherts

Book 585, N° 198, June 1535, Stiphout, Village of Stiphout vs Church masters Saint John's of 's Hertogenbosch

Book 582, N° 253, June 1535, Rijsbergen, Widow Pieter van Ostaden vs Jan Wymeren

Book 583, N° 274, September 1535, Kerkkasteel, Village of Kerkkasteel vs Diercken Zweerts, Vuytgaerde, Widow Lambrechts Leenen, Diericken Steemans with his wife and children, Willem van Ermen, Arnde Arnts Papensoene van Ghestele, Janne Beerts, Katerine widow of Hermans Hollanders

Book 585, N° 21, October 1536, Assche, Roesbeke vs Nuffele

Book 600, N° 19, November 1536, Helmond, Lord of Helmond vs Village, burgomasters, aldermen and deans of Helmond

Book 591, N° 292, November 1536, Oirschot, Aldermen, jurors and city of Oirschot vs Village of Woensel

Book 584, N° 225, February 1537, Oisterwijk, Wouter vanden Venne and JAnne de Spijkere vs Janne Andriessoene Matheeus, JAns Andriessoene, Joahanna Blocx, Wouteren van Heusden, Jacoppe Blocx

Book 584, N° 164, April 1537, Oisterwijk, Aert van Uden vs Adriaen vanden Houte

Book 586, N° 19, May 1537, Olmen, Jacop Lemmens vs Arnden Lummelen

Book 586, N° 104, February 1538, Wijnegem, Church masters of Wijnegem vs Aldermen of Deurne

Book 599, N° 14, September 1538, Beerse, Janne Gheerden vanden Eynde burghers of Antwerp vs Adriaen Berchmans, Janne Willemaerts, Michielen vanden Hove, Sebastiaen Thems

Book 591, N° 7, November 1538, Herentals, Poor relief of Saint Peter's in MEchelen, Janne van Liefvelt, Janne van Beringen and fellows vs Aldermen of Herentals

Book 585, N° 169, November 1538, Rixtel, Village of Gemert vs Village of Beke, Aerle and Rixtel

Book 587, N° 3, February 1539, Chammont, Jans van Buret vs Pylet

Book 593, N° 218, November 1539, Ellich, Cloister of Cabbeke vs Jan Jacopssone and fellows

Book 594, N° 134, May 1540, Isschot, Village of Grootheze vs Village of Isschot

Book 589, N° 30, August 1540, Dongen, Lord of Venloon vs Prince of Orange, Steward of Oisterhout and Village of Dongen

Book 594, N° 152, December 1540, Anderlecht, Claesen Nagels and fellows of Anderlecht vs Aldermen of Brussels, Michiel Bech, Gheerden op den Bosch

Book 590, N° 87, Rixtel, Village of Aerle, Beke and Rixtel vs Village of Gemert

Book 593, N° 214, May 1541, Mierlo, Joes Snoecx vs Priest Jan de Costere and fellows

Book 593, N° 30, May 1541, Isschot, Henricx de Proest, Jans Huysmans and Gielis van Ysschot of Isschot vs Village of Grootheeze

Book 594, N° 98, August 1541, Veerle, Widow Johanne vander Straten vs Marien vander Thommen and tenant Janne Colijns

Book 590, N° 15, August 1541, Rixtel, Village of Aerle, Beke, Rixtel and Helmond vs Lord Wynande van Breyel Knight, Land commander van Baillien, vander Biesen of the German order of Our Lady of Jerusalem

Book 588, N° 177, November 1541, Vilvoorde, Peter van Lyere vs Tomas Chenue

Book 589, N° 48, December 1542, Unknown, Abbey of Saint Bernaerts vs Hubrecht de Ketelere, Adriaen Gestelere and fellows

Book 597, N° 251, June 1543, Meldert, Beys vs Vande Velde

Book 591, N° 46, June 1544, Dielegem, Warande master of Brabant and Abbey of Dielegem vs Steven vanden Steene

Book 593, N° 219, December 1544, Unknown, Marcelis Claessens vs Henrick Hoze

Book 602, N° 71, April 1545, Aken, Burgomaster, aldermen and council of Aken vs Bailiff aldermen and Village of Mothsem

Book 594, N° 28, April 1545, Diest, Henricks Roggen vs Jan van Boeckel and Jan Baecken

Book 595, N° 121, June 1545, Putte, Zoetmont vs Mathijs Verpoert

Book 595, N° 103, July 1545, Unknown, Janne van Floeshem, Janne de Bijl, Janne Roelants and fellows vs Clare Mathijs

Book 597, N° 26, August 1545, Aarschot, Aldermen, Church masters, Holy Ghost masters and Village of Landorp vs Abbey of Saint Geertruyde

Book 596, N° 323, August 1545, Pedeland, Widow Claes Wouterssoen vs Adriaen Wouters

Book 591, N° 113, 1545, Aken, Burgomaster, aldermen and council of Aken vs Burgomaster, bailiff, aldermen and village of Mothsem

Book 595, N° 67, July 1546, Aarschot, Abbey of Sint Truiden vs Lord Schoenhoven

Book 595, N° 63, October 1546, Valkenborg, Widow Matheeus Gruysen vs Jan Savelants and fellows

Book 597, N° 27, December 1546, Schaarbeek, Village of Schaarbeek vs Jacop Broman and Steward of abbey of Heilem

Book 595, N° 134, December 1546, Oirschot, Janne Aertsen, Henricke Hoppenbrouwers and fellows, aldermen, jurors and village of Oirschot vs Aldermen of 's Hertogenbosch

Book 598, N° 7, March 1547, Oisterwijk, Jurors and village of Haren and Belveren vs Bailiff burgomasters, aldermen, jurors and city of Oisterwijk

Book 598, N° 331, March 1547, Kumtich, Cornelis Lambierts vs Jan Fricx, Jan vander Gheeten, Mathijs van Coolhem and fellows

Book 595, N° 91, August 1547, Schoten, Deans of Our Lady of Antwerp vs Gregorius de Alva

Book 598, N° 13, October 1547, Schoten, Melchior Charles vs Abbey of Villers, Vincent van Zeverdonck and fellows

Book 596, N° 143, November 1547, Mierlo, Katerinen Snoecx vs Lenaerden Staelssen, Ruth Henrick Ruttenssoen

Book 597, N° 64, July 1548, Diest, Henrick Torrekens inhabitant of Diest vs Trudo Skeysers

Book 597, N° 284, October 1548, Wommelgem, Laureys Wrage vs Bailiff Wommelgem

Book 596, N° 111, August 1548, Oisterwijk, Village of Kerkeind vs City of Oisterwijk

Book 596, N° 112, August 1548, Oisterwijk, Burgomaster, aldermen, propriators and city of Oisterwijk vs Attorney General of Brabant, Mathijsen Ducge, Henricke Goidtscauwen and fellows inhabitants of Kerkeind

Book 595, N° 58, October 1548, Berlecom, Widow Claes Janssoen vs Dierick Goyaertssoene of Merevenne

Book 597, N° 284, October 1548, Wommelgem, Laureys Wrage vs Bailiff of Wommelgem

Book 597, N° 8, March 1549, Zeelst, Jans van Boert vs Willem Verwouts

Book 602, N° 225, August 1549, Wijnegem, Jans vanden Werve vs Franchois Gielis

Book 598, N° 68, September 1549, Oisterwijk, Joessen Wouterssen vs Mathijsen Wijns and Janne Claes

Book 599, N° 37, May 1550, Oisterwijk, Joosse Wouterssone, Wouter Janssoon, Jan Jans Crommenzoon vs Jurors Heynsen village near Gestel

Book 602, N° 76, October 1550, Breda, Cornelis Ablijn, Jan de Hertog vs Count of Nassau

Book 602, N° 247, Loenhout, Gheerts Vorsselmans vs Gors Putcuyps and fellows

Book 602, N° 51, April 1554, Helmond, Willem Henrickxsoon of Brussel inhabitant of Mierlo vs Willem Diericxsmets, Jaspar Vrancken, Jan Frans Peeterssoen, Ambrosius Jan Dreycker and fellows

Other Primary Sources by Archive

Archive of the Abbey of Tongerlo

Section I, Charters, 1133–1580

SECTION II, REGISTERS

206, Lease accounts of the abbey of Tongerlo, 1504–1513

292, Tenant farm descriptions of the abbey of Tongerlo, 1510–1653

293, Tenant farm descriptions of the abbey of Tongerlo, 1239–1600

332, General rent registers, 1362–1374

334, General rent registers, 1430–1434

335, General rent registers, 1435–1453

337, General rent registers, 1463
341, Rent registers of Tongerlo and its surroundings, 1529–1565
342, Rent registers of Tongerlo and its surroundings,1566–1621
373, Rent register of Kalmthout, 1518
377, Nova census Kalmthout-Essen, 1518
401, Rent register Ravels, Nova census, 1538
688, Lamb tithes in Alphen and environment, 1514
689, Register van het dorp Alphen voor de 100·ᵉ penning, 1559–1578
806, Lamb tithes in Nispen and Essen, 16th and 17th centuries

SECTION IV

Bundle Kalmthout-Essen-Huibergen, 101–104, Court records concerning boundary dispute between the abbey of Tongerlo and the Lord of Bergen op Zoom,
1439–1440
Fund of Kalmthout-Essen-Huibergen, 322, Privatisation of a piece of the commons
by Jan Godens, 15 century
Fund of Kalmthout-Essen-Huibergen, 324, Privatisation of a piece of the commons
by Hubrecht de But, 1544
Fund of Kalmthout-Essen-Huibergen, 325, Abolishment of communal rights, 1623
Fund of Kalmthout-Essen-Huibergen, 326, Juridical advice for the abbey of Tongerlo
concerning the communal use rights, 1624–1628
Fund of Kalmthout-Essen-Huibergen, 328–329, Sentence regarding communal use
rights in favour of the community of Kalmthout-Essen, 1623–1628

National Archives of Belgium, Brussels (ARAB)

Chambre des Comptes, Accounts of the domains, 12951–52, Account of the bailiff
of Herentals, 1412–1577
Chambre des Comptes, Accounts of the domains, 12977, Account of the bailiff of
Zandhoven, 1626–1770
Chambre des Comptes, Accounts of the domains, 4955–66, Accounts of the domain
of Herentals, 1424–1478
Chambre des Comptes, Accounts of the domains, 5212, Account of the domain of
Turnhout, 1549
Chambre des Comptes, Accounts of the domains, 5213/1–8 Accounts of the domain
of Turnhout 1550–1557
Chambre des Comptes, Administrative files, "Cartons", 83/2, 37B
Chambre des Comptes, Cartularies, MS diverse 5E, fº 219–220, cities, freedoms,
villages, ecclesiastical institutions and individuals

State Archives in Antwerp (RAA)

Ancien Regime archives (OGA)
OGA, Brecht, 2540A, Animal counts, 1605
OGA, Gierle, 344, Pieces concerning the 10th and 20th penny taks (penningcohier),
1554
OGA Gierle, 349–350, Registers of the bench of aldermen, 1512–58

OGA Herenthout, 160, "vorster account", 1653
OGA Loenhout, 3823, Land book, 1602
OGA Rijkevorsel, 12, Charter granting the right to plant trees, 1609
OGA Rijkevorsel, 145–180, Registers of the bench of aldermen, 1465–1609
OGA Rijkevorsel, 3141–3149, Animal counts, 1608
OGA Tongerlo, 896, Pieces concerning the 10th and 20th penny taks (panningco-hier), 1569
OGA Zandhoven, 148, 'Heideboek (common pool institution account), 1559–81

State Archives in Brussels (Anderlecht) (RAB)

Conseil de Brabant, Archives of the Registry, General Sentence Registers, 1498–1517, 1529–1555, 1574–1580

City Archive of Antwerp (SAA)

Ancien Regime archives of the city of Antwerp, other governments, Local governments and seigniories, Belgium, Duchy of Brabant, 5 Condition of the villages in the margraviate of Antwerp in 1593

City Archive of Turnhout (SAT)

973–1025, registers of the bench of aldermen, 1444–1600

Secondary sources

Printed

Adams, William M., Brockington, D., Dyson, J. and Vira, B., 'Managing tragedies: Understanding conflict over common pool resources', *Science* 302 (2003), pp. 1915–16.
Adger, W. Neil, 'Social and ecological resilience: Are they related?', *Progress in Human Geography* 24, no. 3 (2000), pp. 347–64.
Adriaensen, Leo, 'De plaats van oisterwijk in het kempense lakenlandschap', *THB* 41 (2001), pp. 27–48.
———, 'Een zestiende-eeuws vluchtelingenprobleem', *Brabants heem* 53, no. 4 (2001), pp. 196–205.
Agrawal, Arun, *Environmentality: Technologies of government and the making of subjects* (Durham, 2005).
Agrawal, Arun and Gibson, Clark C., 'Enchantment and disenchantment: The role of community in natural resource conservation', *World Development* 27, no. 4 (1999), pp. 629–49.
Allen, Robert C., *Enclosure and the yeoman: Agricultural development of the south Midlands, 1450–1850* (Oxford, 1992).
Allison, K. J., 'The sheep-corn husbandry of Norfolk in the sixteenth and seventeenth centuries', *Agricultural History Review* 5, no. 1 (1957), pp. 12–30.
———, 'Flock management in the sixteenth and seventeenth centuries', *Economic History Review* 11, no. 1 (1958), pp. 98–112.

Anderies, John M., Janssen, Marco A. and Ostrom, Elinor, 'A framework to analyze the robustness of social-ecological systems from an institutional perspective',
Ecology and Society 9, no. 1 (2004).

Arnade, Peter, 'Crowds, banners, and the marketplace: Symbols of defiance and
defeat during the Ghent war of 1452–3', *Journal of Medieval and Renaissance
Studies* 24, no. 3 (1994), pp. 471–97.

Arts, Nico, Huijbers, Antionette, Leenders, K. A. H. W., Schotten, Jacob, Stoepker,
Henk, Theuws, Frans and Verhoeven, Arno, 'De middeleeuwen en vroegmoderne tijd in zuid-nederland', *Nationale onderzoeksagenda Archeologie* 22 (2007)
pp. 1–89.

Augustyn, Beatrijs, *Zeespiegelrijzing, transgressiefasen en stormvloeden in maritiem
vlaanderen tot het einde van de xvide eeuw* (Brussels, 1992).

Avonds, Piet, 'De brabants-hollandse grens tijdens de late middeleeuwen', *Regionaal-
historisch tijdschrift* 14, no. 3–4 (1982), pp. 128–32.

——, *Brabant tijdens de regering van hertog jan iii (1312–56): De grote politieke
crisissen* (Verhandlingen van de Koninklijke Vlaamse Aademie voor Wetenschappen. Letteren en Schone Kunsten van België 46, Brussels: Paleis der Academiën,
1984).

Bailey, Mark, *A marginal economy? East Anglian Breckland in the later middle ages*
(Cambridge, 1989).

——, 'Sand into gold: The evolution of the fold-course system in west Suffolk,
1200–1600', *Agricultural History Review* 38 (1990), pp. 40–57.

Ballarini, M., Wallinga, J., Murray, A. S., van Heteren, S., Oost, A. P., Bos, A. J. J.
and van Eijk, C. W. E., 'Optical dating of young coastal dunes on a decadal time
scale', *Quaternary Science Reviews* 22, no. 10–13 (2003), pp. 1011–17.

Bankoff, Greg, 'Cultures of disaster, cultures of coping: hazard as a frequent life
experience in the Philippines', in C. Mauch and C. Pfister (eds), *Natural disasters,
cultural responses: Case studies toward a global environmental history* (Lanham,
2009).

——, 'The "English lowlands" and the North Sea basin system: A history of
shared risk', *Environment and History* 19 (2013), pp. 3–37.

Bastiaens, Jan, Brinkkemper, Otto, Deforce, Koen and Maes, Bert, *Inheemse bomen
en struiken in nederland en vlaanderen herkenning, verspreiding, geschiedenis en
gebruik* (Amsterdam, 2007).

Bastiaens, Jan and Deforce, Koen, 'Geschiedenis van de heide. Eerst natuur en dan
cultuur of andersom?', *Natuur.focus* 4, no. 2 (2005), pp. 40–4.

Bastiaens, Jan and Van Mourik, J. M., 'Bodemsporen van beddenbouw in het
zuidelijk deel van het plaggenlandbouwareaal. Getuigen van 17de-eeuwse landbouw intensivering in de blegische provincies antwerpen en limburg en de nederlandse provincie noord-brabant', *Historisch geografisch tijdschrift* 3 (1994),
pp. 81–90.

Bastiaens, Jan and Verbruggen, C., 'Fysische en socio-economische achtergronden
van het plaggenlandbouwsysteem in de antwerpse kempen', *Tijdschrift voor ecologische geschiedenis* 1, no. 1 (1996), pp. 26–32.

Bastiaensen, Jean, 'Landbouwstatistiek uit de 14de eeuw', *De Spycker* 47 (1990),
pp. 34–49.

Bateman, Mark D. and Godby, Steven P., 'Late-holocene inland dune activity in the
UK: A case study from Breckland, East Anglia', *The Holocene* 14, no. 4 (2004),
pp. 579–88.

Beerten, K., Deforce, K. and Mallants, D., 'Landscape evolution and changes in soil hydraulic properties at the decadal, centennial and millennial scale: A case study from the Campine area, northern Belgium', *Catena* 95 (2012), pp. 73–84.

Berents, D. A., 'Taak van schout en schepen', *Maandblad Oud Utrecht* 45, no. 8 (1972).

Birrell, Jean R., 'Common right in the medieval forest: Disputes and conflicts in the thirteenth century', *Past and Present* 117 (1987), pp. 22–49.

Birtles, Sara, 'Common land, poor relief and enclosure: The use of manorial resources in fulfilling parish obligations, 1601–1834', *Past and Present* 165 (1999), pp. 74–106.

Blickle, Peter, 'The criminalization of peasant resistance in the Holy Roman Empire: Toward a history of the emergence of high treason in Germany', *Journal of Modern History* 58 (1986), pp. 88–97.

———, *Kommunalismus: Skizzen einer gesellschaftlichen organisationsform* (München, 2000).

Blockmans, Wim, 'Revolutionaire mechanismen in vlaanderen van de 13de tot de 16de eeuw', *Tijdschrift voor sociale wetenschappen* 19, no. 2 (1974), pp. 123–40.

———, 'The social and economic effects of plague in the low countries, 1349–1500', *Belgisch tijdschrift voor filologie en geschiedenis* 58 (1980), pp. 835–63.

———, *Keizer karel v. De utopie van het keizerschap* (Leuven, 2001).

———, *Metropolen aan de noordzee: De geschiedenis van nederland, 1100–1560* (Amsterdam, 2010).

Blockmans, Wim, Mertens, Jos and Verhulst, A., 'Les communautés rurales d'ancien regime en flandre: Caracteristiques et essai d'interpretation comparative', *Les Communautés rurales. Recueils de la Société Jean Bodin* 44 (1987), pp. 223–48.

Blockmans, Wim P., Pieters, G., Prevenier, Walter and Van Schaïk, R. W. M., 'Tussen crisis en welvaart: Sociale veranderingen 1300–1500', in D. P. Blok et al. (eds), *Algemene geschiedenis der nederlanden* 4 (Haarlem, 1980), pp. 42–86.

Blok, Dirk Peter (ed.), *Algemene geschiedenis der nederlanden*, vols 2, 3, 4 (Haarlem, 1977–83).

Blume, H-P. and Leinweber, P., 'Plaggen soils: Landscape history, properties and classification', *Plant Nutrition and Soil Science* 167 (2004), pp. 319–27.

Bonzon, Anne, 'Les curés médiateurs sociaux. Genèse et diffusion d'un modele dans la france du xviie siècle', *Revue d'histoire de l'Eglise de France* 97, no. 238 (2011), pp. 35–56.

Boone, Marc, 'Les métiers dans les villes flamandes au bas moyen âge (xive–xvie siècles): Images normatives, réalités socio-politiques et économiques', in P. Lambrechts and J.-P. Sosson (eds), *Les métiers au moyen âge: Aspects économiques et sociaux* (Louvain-La-Neuve, 1994), pp. 1–22.

Bossy, John (ed.), *Disputes and settlements: Law and human relations in the West* (Cambridge, 1983).

Bousse, A., 'De verhoudingen tussen antwerpen en het platteland', *Bijdragen tot de geschiedenis* 58, no. 1–2 (1975), pp. 139–48.

Brakensiek, Stefan, 'The management of common land in north-western Germany', in De Moor, Shaw-Taylor and Warde (eds), *Management of common land in north west Europe*.

———, 'Les biens communaux en allemagne. Attaques, disparition et survivance (1750–1900)', in M. Demélas and N. Vivier (eds), *Les propriétés collectives face aux attaques libérales, 1750–1900* (Rennes, 2003).

Campbell, Bruce M. S., 'The regional uniqueness of English field systems? Some evidence from eastern Norfolk', *Agricultural History Review* 29 (1981), pp. 16–28.

Casari, Marco and Plott, Charles R., 'Decentralized management of common property resources: Experiments with a centuries-old institution', *Journal of Economic Behavior & Organization* 51, no. 2 (2003), pp. 217–47.

Castan, Nicole, 'The arbitration of disputes under the "ancien regime"', in Bossy (ed.), *Disputes and settlements*.

Clark, Gregory, 'Commons sense: Common property rights, efficiency and institutional change', *Journal of Economic History* 58, no. 1 (1998), pp. 73–102.

Congost, Rosa and Santos, Rui, 'Working out the frame: From formal institutions to the social contexts of property', in R. Congost and R. Santos (eds), *Contexts of property: The social embeddedness of property rights to land in Europe in historical perspective* (Turnhout, 2010), pp. 15–38.

Coopmans, J., 'De onderlinge rechtsverhoudingen van 's-hertogenbosch en het platteland voor 1629', *Bijdragen tot de geschiedenis* 58, no. 1–2 (1975), pp. 73–112.

Curtis, Daniel R., 'Tine de Moor's "Silent Revolution": Reconsidering her theoretical framework for explaining the emergence of institutions for collective management of resources', *International Journal of the Commons* 7, no. 1 (2013), pp. 209–29.

——, *Coping with crisis: The resilience and vulnerability of pre-industrial settlements* (Farnham, 2014).

Cuvelier, J., *Les dénombrements de foyers en brabant (xiv–xvi siècle)*, 3 vols (Brussel, 1912).

Dejongh, G., 'De ontginningspolitiek van de overheid in de zuidelijke nederlanden, 1750–1830: Een maat voor niets?', *Tijdschrift van het Gemeentekrediet* (1999), p. 31.

De Keyzer, Maïka, 'The impact of different distributions of power on access rights to the common waste lands: The Campine, Brecklands and Geest compared', *Journal of Institutional Economics* 9, no. 4 (2013), pp. 517–42.

——, 'Access versus influence: Peasants in court in the late medieval Low Countries', in M. Müller (ed.), *Handbook of rural life* (London, 2018).

De Keyzer, Maïka, Jongepier, Iason and Soens, Tim, 'Consuming maps and producing space: Explaining regional variations in the reception and agency of cartography in the Low Countries during the medieval and early modern periods', *Continuity and Change* 29, no. 2 (2014), pp. 209–40.

De Keyzer, Maïka and van Onacker, Eline, 'Beyond the flock: Sheep farming, wool sales and social differentiation in a late medieval peasant society: The Campine in the low countries', *Agricultural History Review* 64, no. 2 (2016), pp. 157–80.

Dekkers, P. J. V., 'Brandend zand. Hoe de hertog van brabant zijn heerschappij op de kempense zandgronden verwierf ten koste van de lokale en regionale adel', *Noordbrabants historisch jaarboek* 12 (1995), pp. 10–40.

De Kok, Harry, *Turnhout: Groei van een stad* (Turnhout, 1983).

——, 'De aard van zes dorpen: Beerse, vosselaar, lille, wechelderzande, gierle en vlimmeren. Een casusonderzoek van een kempense gemene heide', *Post Factum. Jaarboek voor geschiedenis en Volkskunde* no. 1 (2009), pp. 277–86.

De Longé, Guillaume, 'Coutumes de santhoven, de turnhout et de rumpet', in G. De Longé (ed.), *Coutumes du pays et duché de brabant: Quartier d'anvers* (Recueil des anciennes coutumes de la belgique, Brussels, 1877).

——, *Coutumes d'herenthals, de casterlé, de moll, balen et deschel, de gheel, de hoogstraten, de befferen et de putte, et feodales du pays de malines* (Recueil des anciennes coutumes de la belgique, Brussels, 1878).

De Molder, Th., 'Keuren van oostmalle', *Oudheid en Kunst* 26, no. 1 (1935), pp. 3–15.

De Moor, Martina, Shaw-Taylor, Leigh and Warde, Paul (eds), *The management of common land in north west Europe, c.1500–1850* (Turnhout, 2002).

——, 'Comparing the historical commons of north west Europe: An introduction', in De Moor, Shaw-Taylor and Warde (eds), *Management of common land*.

De Moor, Tine, 'The silent revolution: A new perspective on the emergence of commons, guilds, and other forms of corporate collective action in Western Europe', *International Review of Social History* 52, suppl. 16 (2008), pp. 179–212.

——, 'Avoiding tragedies: A Flemish common and its commoners under the pressure of social and economic change during the eighteenth century', *Economic History Review* 62, no. 1 (2009), pp. 1–22.

——, 'Participating is more important than winning: The impact of socioeconomic change on commoners' participation in eighteenth- and nineteenth-century Flanders', *Continuity and Change* 25, no. 3 (2010), pp. 405–33.

Derese, Cilia, Vandenberghe, Dimitri, Eggermont, Nele, Bastiaens, Jan, Annaert, Rica and Van den haute, Peter, 'A medieval settlement caught in the sand: Optical dating of sand-drifting at Pulle (N Belgium)', *Quaternary Geochronology* 5 (2010), pp. 336–41.

De Ridder, Paul, *Hertog jan i van brabant (1267–1294)* (Antwerp, 1978).

De Schepper, H., 'Vorstelijke ambtenarij en bureaukratisering in regering en gewesten van 's konings nederlanden, 16de–17de eeuw', *Tijdschrift voor geschiedenis* 90 (1977), pp. 358–77.

De Vries, Jan, *The Dutch rural economy in the golden age, 1500–1700* (New Haven, 1974).

De Wachter, Astrid, 'De opname van de kempen in het hertogdom brabant (elfde tot dertiende-veertiende eeuw). Een politiek-geografische probleemstelling', *Tijdschrift van de Belgische vereniging voor aarderijkskundige studies* 1 (1999), pp. 111–39.

Dinges, Martin, 'The uses of justice as a form of social control in early modern Europe', in H. Roodenburg and P. Spierenburg (eds), *Social control in Europe: 1500–1800* (Ohio, 2004), pp. 159–74.

Droesen, W. J., *De gemeentegronden in noord-brabant en limburg en hunne ontginning: Eene geschied- en landhuishoudkundige studie* (Roermond, 1927).

Dumolyn, Jan, 'Criers and shouters: The discourse on radical urban rebels in late medieval Flanders', *Journal of Social History* 42, no. 1 (2008), pp. 111–32.

Dyer, Christopher, 'The English medieval village community and its decline', *Journal of British Studies* 33, no. 4 (1994).

——, *Everyday life in medieval England* (London, 2000).

——, 'The political life of the fifteenth-century', in L. Clark and C. Carpenter (eds), *Political culture in late medieval Britain* (Woodbridge, 2004), pp. 135–57.

——, 'Conflict in the landscape: The enclosure movement in England, 1220–1349', *Landscape History* 28 (2006), pp. 21–33.

Enklaar, Diederik Theodorus, Gemeene gronden in noord-brabant in de middeleeuwen (Utrecht, 1941).

Ensminger, Jean, *Making a market: The institutional transformation of an African society* (Cambridge, 1996).

Erens, A., *De oorkonden der abdij tongerloo*, 4 vols (Tongerlo, 1948).

Ernalsteen, J., 'Keuren van gheel', *Oudheid en Kunst* 26, no. 2 (1935), pp. 19–66.

Falvey, Heather, 'Voices and faces in the rioting crowd: Identifying seventeenth-century enclosure rioters', *Local Historian* 39, no. 2 (2009), pp. 137–51.

———, 'The articulation, transmission and preservation of custom in the forest community of Duffield (Derbyshire)', in Hoyle (ed.), *Custom, improvement and the landscape*, pp. 65–100.

Fanta, Josef and Siepel, Henk (eds), *Inland drift sand landscapes* (Zeist, 2010).

Ferraris, Josef Johan, *De grote atlas van de ferraris. De eerste atlas van belgië. Kabinetskaart van de oostenrijkse nederlanden en het prinsbisdom luik* (Tielt, 2009).

Fletcher, David, 'The parish boundary: A social phenomenon in Hanoverian England', *Rural History* 14, no. 2 (2003), pp. 177–96.

Folke, Carl, 'Resilience: The emergence of a perspective for social-ecological systems analyses', *Global Environmental Change* 16, no. 3 (2006), pp. 253–67.

Garnot, Benoît, 'Justice, infrajustice, parajustice et extra justice dans la france d'ancien régime', *Crime, histoire & sociétés* 4, no. 1 (2000), pp. 103–20.

Gielens, A., 'Keuren van ekeren', *Oudheid en Kunst* 30, no. 1 (1939), pp. 167–83.

Gijsbers, Wilhelmina Maria, *Kapitale ossen: De internationale handel in slachtvee in noordwest-europa (1300–1750)* (Hilversum, 1999).

Goddard, Richard, Langdon, John and Müller, Miriam (eds), *Survival and discord in medieval society: Essays in honour of Christopher Dyer* (Turnhout, 2010).

Goldman, Michael, ' "Customs in common": The epistemic world of the commons scholars', *Theory and Society* 26, no. 1 (1997), pp. 1–37.

Gunderson, Lance H., 'Ecological resilience in theory and application', *Annual Review of Ecology and Systematics* 31 (2000), pp. 425–39.

Haemers, Jelle, 'A moody community? Emotion and ritual in late medieval urban revolts', *Urban History* 5, pp. 63–81.

Haller, Tobias (ed.), *Disputing the floodplains: Institutional change and the politics of resource management in African wetlands* (Leiden, 2010).

Haller, Tobias, Acciaioli, Greg and Rist, Stephan, 'Constitutionality: Conditions for crafting local ownership of institution-building processes', *Society and Natural Resources* 28, no. 9 (2015), pp. 1–20.

Haller, Tobias and Chabwela, Harry N., 'Managing common pool resources in the Kafue flats, Zambia: From common property to open access and privatisation', *Development Southern Africa* 26, no. 4 (2009), pp. 555–67.

Hammond, J. L. and Barbara, Hammond, *The village labourer, 1760–1832* (First pub. 1911; Stroud, 1995).

Hardin, Garrett, 'The tragedy of the commons', *Science* 162, no. 3859 (1968), pp. 1243–8.

Heerman, Cedric, 'Het abdijdomein van de abdij van tongerlo in de 15de-16de eeuw (met speciale aandacht voor de pachthoeves van de abdij)', *Taxandria, Jaarboek van de Koninklijke geschied- en oudheidkundige kring van de Antwerpse Kempen* (2006), pp. 121–224.

Heidinga, H. A., 'The birth of a desert: The kootwijkerzand', in J. Fanta and H. Siepel (eds), *Inland drift sand landscapes* (Zeist, 2010).

Helsen, I., 'Het dorpskeurboek van retie', *Bijdragen tot de geschiedenis* 1, no. 1 (1949), pp. 85–107.

Hiddink, Henk, *Opgravingen op het rosveld bij nederweert 1: Landschap en bewoning in de ijzertijd, romeinse tijd en middeleeuwen* (Zuidnederlandse archeologische rapporten, Amsterdam, 2005).

Hilton, Rodney, *Bond men made free: Medieval peasant movements and the English rising of 1381* (London, 1973).

Hipkin, Stephen, ' "Sitting on his penny rent": Conflict and right of common in Faversham Blean, 1595–1610', *Rural history* 11, no. 1 (2000), pp. 1–35.

Hodgson, R. I., 'The progress of enclosure in county Durham, 1550–1870', in H. S. A. Fox and R. A. Butlin (eds), *Change in the countryside: Essays on rural England, 1500–1900* (London, 1979), pp. 83–102.

Holmes, C., 'Drainers and fenmen: The problem of popular political consciousness in the seventeenth century', in A. Fletcher and John Stevenson (eds), *Order and disorder in early modern England* (Cambridge, 1987).

Hoppenbrouwers, Peter, 'De middeleeuwse oorsprong van de dorpsgemeenschap in het noorden van het hertogdom brabant', *Noordbrabants historisch jaarboek* 17–18 (2000–1), pp. 45–90.

——, 'The use and management of commons in the Netherlands: An overview', in De Moor, Shaw-taylor and Warde (eds), *Management of common land*, pp. 87–109.

Hoyle, R. W. (ed.), *Custom, improvement and the landscape in early modern Britain* (Farnham, 2011).

Humphries, Jane, 'Enclosures, common rights, and women: The proletarization of families in the late eighteenth and early nineteenth centuries', *Journal of Economic History* 50, no. 1 (1990), pp. 17–42.

Hurenkamp, Menno, Tonkens, Evelien and Duyvendak, Jan Willem, *Wat burgers bezielt: Een onderzoek naar burgerinitiatieven* (The Hague, 2006).

Jacobs, B. C. M., *Justitie en politie in 's-hertogenbosch voor 1629: De bestuursorganisatie van een brabantse stad* (Assen, 1986).

Kagan, Richard L., *Lawsuits and litigants in Castile, 1500–1700* (Chapel Hill, 1981).

King, Peter, 'Legal change, customary right and social conflict in late eighteenth-century England: The origins of the great gleaning case of 1788', *Law and History Review* 10 (1992), pp. 1–31.

Kos, Anton, *Van meenten tot marken. Een onderzoek naar de oorsprong en ontwikkeling van de gooise marken en de gebruiksrechten op de gemene gronden van de gooise markegenoten (1280–1568)* (Hilversum, 2010).

Koster, Eduard, 'Aeolian environments', in E. Koster (ed.), *The physical geography of western Europe* (Oxford, 2007), pp. 139–60.

——, 'Origin and development of late holocene drift sands: Geomorphology and sediment attributes', in Fanta and Siepel (eds), *Inland drift sand landscapes*.

Koyen, Milo, 'Keuren van ravels', *Oudheid en Kunst* 41, no. 2 (1958), pp. 3–19.

Laborda Pemán, Miguel and De Moor, Tine, 'A tale of two commons. Some preliminary hypotheses on the long-term development of the commons in Western and Eastern Europe, 11th-19th centuries', *International Journal of the Commons* 7, no. 1 (2013), pp. 7–33.

Laffont, P-Y. (ed.), *Transhumance et estivage en occident: Des origines aux enjeux actuels* (Toulouse, 2006).

Lana Berasain, José Miguel, 'From equilibrium to equity. The survival of the commons in the Ebro basin: Navarra from the 15th to the 20th centuries', *International Journal of the Commons* 2, no. 2 (2008), pp. 162–91.

Landsberger, Henry (ed.), *Rural protest: Peasant movements and social change* (London, 1974).

Larson, P. L., *Conflict and compromise in the late medieval countryside: Lords and peasants in Durham, 1349–1400* (London, 2006).

Lauwerys, J., 'Keuren van westerloo', *Oudheid en Kunst* 28, no. 4 (1937), pp. 95–120.

Le Bailly, Marie-Charlotte, 'Langetermijntrends in de rechtspraak bij de gewestelijke hoven van justitie in de noordelijke nederlanden van ca. 1450 tot ca. 1800', *Pro Memoria* 13 (2011), pp. 30–67.

Leenders, Karel A. H. W., *Verdwenen venen: Een onderzoek naar de ligging en exploitatie van thans verdwenen venen in het gebied tussen antwerpen, turnhout, geertruidenberg en willemstad 1250–1750* (Historische uitgaven, 80, Brussels, 1989).

———, *Van turnhoutervoorde tot strienemonde. Ontginnings- en nederzettingsgeschiedenis van het noordwesten van het maas-schelde-demergebied (400–1350)* (Zutphen, 1996).

———, 'Van wolvenput naar de ellendige berk. Het landschap van de kempense wildernis 1200–2000', *Post Factum. Jaarboek voor geschiedenis en Volkskunde* 1 (2009), pp. 246–66.

Lemmens, K., 'Rekenmunt en courant geld', *Jaarboek van het Europees genootschap voor munt- en penningkunde* (1998), pp. 19–52.

Limberger, Michael, *Sixteenth-century Antwerp and its rural surroundings: Social and economic changes in the hinterland of a commercial metropolis (ca. 1450–1570)* (Studies in European Urban History, 14, Turnhout, 2008).

Lindemans, Paul, *Geschiedenis van de landbouw in belgië*, I, 2 vols (Antwerp, 1952).

Lübken, Uwe and Mauch, Christof, 'Uncertain environments: Natural hazards, risk and insurance in historical perspective', *Environment and History* 17 (2011), pp. 1–12.

Mauelshagen, Franz, 'Flood disasters and political culture at the German North Sea coast: A long-term historical perspective', *Historical Social Research* 32, no. 3 (2007), pp. 133–44.

McCarthy, Nancy, Kamara, Abdul B. and Kirk, Michael, 'Co-operation in risky environments: Evidence from southern Ethiopia', *Journal of African Economies* 12, no. 2 (2003), pp. 236–70.

McDonagh, Briony A. K. 'Subverting the ground: Private property and public protest in the sixteenth-century Yorkshire Wolds', *Agricultural History Review* 57, no. 2 (2009), pp. 191–207.

McKean, Margaret A., *People and forests: Communities, institutions, and governance* (Cambridge, MA, 2000).

Meeusen, Gerard, 'Keuren van esschen, calmpthout en huybergen', *Oudheid en Kunst* 23 (1932), pp. 112–24.

Michielsen, J., 'Keuren van brecht', *Oudheid en Kunst* (1907), pp. 71–81.

Monballyu, J., 'De gerechtelijke bevoegdheid van de raad van vlaanderen in vergelijking met de andere "wetten" (1515–1621)', in B. C. M. Jacobs and P. L. Nève (eds), *Hoven en banken in noord en zuid* (Assen, 1994).

Moriceau, Jean-Marc, *Histoire et géographie de l'élevage français: Du moyen âge à la révolution* (Paris, 2005).

Muldrew, Craig, 'The culture of reconciliation: Community and the settlement of economic disputes in early modern England', *Historical Journal* 39, no. 4 (1996), pp. 915–42.

Müller, Miriam, 'Conflict, strife and cooperation: Aspects of the late medieval family and household', in I. Davies, M. Müller and S. R. Jones (eds), *Marriage, love and family ties in the middle ages* (Turnhout, 2003).

———, 'Social control and the hue and cry in two fourteenth-century villages', *Journal of Medieval History* 31, no. 1 (2005), pp. 29–53.

———, 'Arson, communities and social conflict in later medieval England', *Viator* 43, no. 2 (2012), pp. 193–208.

Neeson, J. M., *Commoners: Common right, enclosure and social change in England, 1700–1820* (Cambridge, 1993).

Netting, R. and McGuire, R., 'Leveling peasants? The maintenance of equality in a Swiss alpine community', *American Ethnologist* 9 (1982), pp. 273–74.

Neveux, Hugues, *Les grains du cambresis (fin du xive, début du xvii siècles): vie et declin d'une structure economique* (Lille, 1974).

Newman, Edward I., 'Medieval sheep-corn farming: How much grain yield could each sheep support', *Agricultural History Review* 50, no. 2 (2002), pp. 164–80.

North, Douglas, *Institutions, institutional change and economic performance* (Cambridge, 1990).

Ogilvie, Sheilagh, ' "Whatever is, is right"? Economic institutions in pre-industrial Europe', *Economic History Review* 60, no. 4 (2007), pp. 649–84.

Ostrom, Elinor, *Governing the commons: The evolution of institutions for collective action* (Cambridge, 1997).

Overton, Mark and Campbell, Bruce M. S., 'Norfolk livestock farming, 1250–1740: A comparative study of manorial accounts and probate inventories', *Journal of Historical Geography* 18, no. 4 (1992), pp. 377–96.

Paepen, Nico, 'De aard van de zes dorpen 1332–1822: Casusonderzoek naar de kempense gemene heide (deel 1)', *Taxandria, Jaarboek van de Koninklijke geschied- en oudheidkundige kring van de Antwerpse Kempen* LXXVI (2004), pp. 5–78.

Pascua, Esther, 'Communautés de propriétaires et ressources naturelles à saragosse lors du passage du moyen âge à l'époque moderne', in Laffont (ed.), *Transhumance et estivage en occident*, pp. 137–50.

Peeters, K. C., 'De wuustwezelsche dorpskeuren (xve—xviie eeuw)' (*Verslagen en mededelingen van de koninklijke Vlaamsche academie voor taal en letterkunde*, 1932), pp. 595–709.

———, 'De wuustwezelsche dorpskeuren (xve–xviie eeuw)', *Wesalia, Tijdschrift voor plaatselijke Geschiedenis en Folklore* 8, no. 1–2 (1933), pp. 2–48.

Piant, Hervé, *Une justice ordinaire: Justice civile et criminelle dans la prévôté royale de vaucouleurs sous l'ancien régime* (Rennes, 2006).

Pierik, Harm Jan, van Lanen, Rowin J., Gouw-Bouman, Marjolein T. I. J., Groenewoudt, Bert J., Wallinga, Jakob and Hoek, Wim Z. 'Controls on late Holocene inland aeolian drift-sand dynamics in the Netherlands', *The Holocene* (in press).

Poulsen, Bjørn, 'Landesausbau und umwelt in schleswig 1450–1550j', in M. Jakubowski-Tiessen and K.-J. Lorenzen-Schmidt (eds), *Dünger und dynamit. Beitrage zur umweltgeschichte schleswig holsteins und dänemarks* (Neumünster, 1999).

Prak, Maarten, *Gezeten burgers: De elite in een hollandse stad leiden 1700–1780* ('s Gravenhage, 1985).

Prims, Floris, 'Keuren der vreyheyt van arendonk', in H. Draye (ed.), *Feestbundel H. J. Van de wijer, den jubilaris aangeboden ter gelegenheid van zijn vijfentwintigjarig hoogleeraarschap aan de R. K. Universiteit te leuven 1919–1943* (Leuven, 1944).

Rasmussen, Carsten Porskrog, 'An English or a continental way? The great agrarian reforms in Denmark and Schleswig-Holstein in the late eighteenth century', in Congost and Santos (eds), *Contexts of property in Europe*.

———, 'Innovative feudalism. The development of dairy farming and *koppelwirtschaft* on manors in Schleswig-Holstein in the seventeenth and eighteenth centuries', *Agricultural History Review* 58, no. 2 (2010), pp. 172–90.

Ratner, Blake D., Meinzen-Dick, Ruth, May, Candace and Haglund, Eric, 'Resource conflict, collective action, and resilience: An analytical framework', *International Journal of the Commons* 7, no. 1 (2013), pp. 183–208.

Renes, Hans, 'Grainlands: The landscape of open fields in a European perspective', *Landscape History* 31, no. 2 (2010), pp. 37–59.

Rheinheimer, Martin, *Die dorfordnungen im herzogtum schleswig: Dorf und obrigkeit in der frühen neuzeit* (Stuttgart, 1999).

———, 'Umweltzerstörung und dörfliche rechtssetzung im herzogtum schleswig (1500–1800)', in M. Jakubowski-Tiessen and K.-J. Lorenzen-Schmidt (eds), *Dünger und dynamit. Beitrage zur umweltgeschichte schleswig-holsteins und dänemarks* (Neumünster, 1999).

Rodgers, Christopher P., Straughton, Eleanor A., Winchester, Angus J. L. and Pieraccini, Margherita, *Contested common land. Environmental governance past and present* (London, 2011).

Rogers, Graham, 'Custom and common right: Waste land enclosure and social change in west Lancashire', *Agricultural History Review* 41, no. 2 (1993).

Sabbe, E., 'De hoofdbank van zandhoven', *Tijdschrift voor geschiedenis en folklore* 7, no. 1–2 (1954), pp. 3–34.

Sanginga, Pascal C., Kamugisha, Rick N. and Martin, Andrienne M., 'The dynamics of social capital and conflict management in multiple resource regimes: A case of the southwestern highlands of Uganda', *Ecology and Society* 12, no. 1 (2007).

Scott, James, *Weapons of the weak: Everyday forms of peasant resistance* (New Haven, 1985).

Sevink, Jan, Koster, Eduard, van Geel, Bas and Wallinga, Jakob, 'Drift sands, lakes, and soils: The multiphase holocene history of the laarder wasmeren area near Hilversum, the Netherlands', *Netherlands Journal of Geosciences* 92, no. 4 (2013), pp. 243–66.

Shaw-Taylor, Leigh, 'Labourers, cows, common rights and parliamentary enclosure: The evidence of contemporary comment, c.1760–1810', *Past and Present* 171 (2001), pp. 95–126.

———, 'Parliamentary enclosure and the emergence of an English agricultural proletariat', *Journal of Economic History* 61, no. 3 (2001), pp. 640–62.

———, 'The management of common land in the lowlands of southern England circa 1500 to circa 1850', in De Moor, Shaw-Taylor and warde (eds), *Management of common land*.

Sheail, John, 'Documentary evidence of the changes in the use, management and appreciation of the grass-heaths of Breckland', *Journal of Biogeography* 6, no. 3 (1979), pp. 277–92.

Soens, Tim, *De spade in de dijk? Waterbeheer en rurale samenleving in de vlaamse kustvlakte (1280–1580)* (Ghent, 2009).

———, 'Threatened by the sea, condemned by man? Flood risk, environmental justice and environmental inequalities along the North Sea coast, 1200–1800', in G. Massard-Guilbaud and R. Rodger (eds), *Environmental and social justice in the city: Historical perspectives* (Cambridge, 2011).

———, 'Capitalisme, institutions et conflits hydrauliques autour de la mer du nord (xiiie–xviii siècles)', in P. Fournier (ed.), *Eaux et conflits dans l'europe médiévale et moderne: Actes des xxxiies journées internationales d'histoire de l'abbaye de flaran, 8 et 9 octobre 2010* (Toulouse, 2012).

Soens, Tim and Thoen, Erik, 'The origins of leasehold in the former county of Flanders', in B. Van Bavel and P. Schofield (eds), *The development of leasehold in northwestern Europe, c.1200–1600* (Turnhout, 2008), pp. 31–56.

Soldevila I Temporal, Xavier, 'L'élevage ovin et la transhumance en catalogne nord-occidentale (xiiie–xive siècles)', in Laffont (ed.), *Transhumance et estivage en occident*, pp. 109–18.

Soly, H., *Urbanisme en kapitalisme te antwerpen in de 16de eeuw: De stedebouwkundige en industriële ondernemingen van gilbert van schoonbeke* (Brussels, 1977).

Sommerville, A. A., Hansom, J. D., Housley, R. A. and Sanderson, D. C. W., 'Optically Stimulated Luminescence (OSL) dating of coastal aeolian sand accumulation in Sanday, Orkney Islands, Scotland', *The Holocene* 17, no. 5 (2007), pp. 627–37.

Sosson, Jean-Pierre, 'Les métiers, normes et réalité. L'exemple des anciens pays-bas méridionaux aux xive et xve siècles', in J. Hamesse and C. Muraille-Samaran (eds), *Le travail au moyen âge: Une approche interdisciplaire* (Louvain-La-Neuve, 1990).

Spek, Theo, *Het drentse esdorpenlandschap: Een historisch-geografische studie* (Utrecht, 2004).

Stabel, Peter, 'Guilds in late medieval Flanders: Myths and realities of guild life in an export-oriented environment', *Journal of Medieval History* 30 (2004), pp. 187–212.

Stein, Robert, *De hertog en zijn staten: De eenwording van de bourgondische nederlanden ca. 1380–ca. 1480* (Hilversum, 2014).

Steurs, Willy, 'Les franchises du duché de brabant au moyen age: Catalogue alphabetique et chronologique provisoire', *Handelingen van de Koninklijke commissie voor geschiedenis* 25 (1971–2), pp. 139–291.

———, *Naissance d'une région. Aux origines de la mairie de bois-le-duc, recherches sur le brabant septentrional aux 12e et 13e siècles* (Memoire de la classe des lettres, III, Brussels, 1993).

Tack, Guido, Ervynck, Anton and Van Bost, Gunther, *De monnik-manager, abt de loose in zijn abdij 't ename* (Leuven, 1999).

Tack, Guido, Van Den Brempt, Paul and Hermy, Martin, *Bossen van vlaanderen, een historische ecology* (Leuven, 1993).

Thijs, Alfons, 'Structural changes in the Antwerp industry from the fifteenth to the eighteenth century', in H. Van Der Wee (ed.), *The rise and decline of urban industries in Italy and in the Low Countries* (Leuven, 1988), pp. 207–12.

Thirsk, Joan (ed.), *The agrarian history of England and Wales*, IV, *1500–1640* (Cambridge, 1967).

Thoen, Erik, *Landbouwekonomie en bevolking in vlaanderen gedurende de late middeleeuwen en het begin van de moderne tijden* (Ghent, 1988).

———, *Rechten en plichten van plattelanders als instrumenten van machtspolitieke strijd tussen adel, stedelijke burgerij en grafelijk gezag in het laat-middeleeuwse Vlaanderen, buitenpoorterij en mortemain-rechten ten persoonlijken titel in de kasselrijen van Aalst en Oudenaarde, vooral toegepast op de periode rond 1400* in *Machtsstructuren in de plattelandsgemeenschappen in Belgie en aangrenzende gebieden (12 de–19de eeuw)* (Handelingen van het 13de internationaal colloquium Spa, 3–5 September 1986, Brussels, 1988).

———, 'A "commercial survival economy" in evolution. The Flemish countryside and the transition to capitalism (middle ages-19th century)', in P. Hoppenbrouwers and Jan Luiten Van Zanden (eds), *Peasants into farmers? The transformation of rural economy and society in the Low Countries (middle ages-19th century) in light of the Brenner debate* (Turnhout, 2001), pp. 102–57.

———, ' "Social agrosystems" as an economic concept to explain regional differences: An essay taking the former county of Flanders as an example (late middle ages-19th century)', in B. Van Bavel and P. Hoppenbrouwers (eds), *Landholding and land transfer in the North Sea area (late middle ages-19th century)* (Turnhout, 2004).

———, 'The rural history of Belgium in the Middle Ages and the *Ancien Régime*: Sources, results and future avenues for research', in E. Thoen and L. Van Molle (eds), *Rural history in the North Sea area: An overview of recent research (middle ages- twentieth century)* (Turnhout, 2006), pp. 177–216.

Thoen, Erik and De Vos, Isabelle, 'Pest in de zuidelijke nederlanden tijdens de middeleeuwen en de moderne tijden: Een status quaestionis over de ziekte in haar sociaal-economische context', *Academia Regia Belgica Medicinae. Dissertationes. Series Historica* 7 (1999), pp. 19–43.

Thoen, Erik and Soens, Tim, 'Land use and agricultural productivity in the North Sea area: Introduction', in E. Thoen and T. Soens (eds), *Struggling with the environment: Land use and productivity* (Turnhout, 2015).

Thoen, Erik and Vanhaute, Eric, 'The "Flemish husbandry" at the edge: the farming system on small holdings in the middle of the 19th century', in B. Van Bavel and E. Thoen (eds), *Land productivity and agro-systems in the North Sea area (Middle Ages-20th century): Elements for comparison* (Turnhout, 1999), pp. 271–96.

Thompson, E. P., *Customs in common* (London, 1991).

Van Asseldonk, M. M. P., *De meierij van 's-hertogenbosch: De evolutie van plaatselijk bestuur, bestuurlijke indeling en dorpsgrenzen, circa 1200–1832* (Oosterhout, 2001).

van Bavel, Bas, *Transitie en continuïteit: De bezitsverhoudingen en de plattelandseconomie in het westelijke gedeelte van het gelderse rivierengebied, ca. 1300–ca. 1570* (Hilversum, 1999).

———, *Manors and markets: Economy and society in the Low Countries, 500–1600* (Oxford, 2010).

van Bavel, Bas and Thoen, Erik, 'Rural history and the environment: A survey of the relationship between property rights, social structures and sustainability of land use', in B. Van Bavel and E. Thoen (eds), *Rural societies and environments at risk. Ecology, property rights and social organisation in fragile areas (middle ages-twentieth century)* (Turnhout, 2013).

——— (eds), *Land productivity and agro-systems in the North Sea area (middle ages-20th century): Elements for comparison* (Turnhout, 1999).

van Boven, M. W., 'De verhouding tussen de raad van brabant en de hoofdbanken inzake de appelrechtspraak in civiele zaken', in B. C. M. Jacobs and P. L. Nève (eds), *Hoven en banken in noord en zuid* (Assen, 1994).

Van Den Branden, Walter, 'De schout of officier van de landsheer te lille, wechelderzande en vlimmeren: Aspecten van het dorpsbestuur in het land van turnhout in het ancien régime, vooral in de zeventiende en achttiende eeuw', *Heemkundige kring Norbert de Vrijter Lille* (1989), pp. 57–99.

Van Der Haegen, Herman, 'Hoe de kempense gemeenschappen hun aard verkregen, gebruikten . . . En verloren. Een overzicht', *Post Factum. Jaarboek voor geschiedenis en Volkskunde*, no. 1 (2009), pp. 244–5.

Van Der Wee, Herman, *The growth of the Antwerp market and the European economy (14th–16th centuries)* (The Hague, 1963).

van der Westeringhe, W., 'Man-made soils in the Netherlands, especially in sandy areas ("plaggen soils")', in W. Goenman-van Waateringe and M. Robinson (eds), *Man-made soils* (Oxford: British Archaeological Reports, Int. Ser., 410, 1988).

Van Dijck, Maarten, 'Tussen droom en daad. De beperkte invloed van de centrale overheid op de rechtspraak in antwerpen en mechelen gedurende de 15de en 16de eeuw', *Justitie- en rechtsgeschiedenis: een nieuwe onderzoeksgeneratie* 3 (2008).

——, 'Towards an economic interpretation of justice? Conflict settlement, social control and civil society in urban Brabant and Mechelen during the late middle ages and the early modern period', in M. van der Heijden, E. van Nederveen Meerkerk and G. Vermeersch (eds), *Serving the urban community: The rise of public facilities in the Low Countries* (Amsterdam, 2009).

Vangheluwe, Daniel and Spek, Theo. 'De laatmiddeleeuwse transitie van landbouw en landschap in noord-brabantse kempen', *Historisch geografisch tijdschrift* 26, no. 1 (2008), pp. 1–23.

van Ginkel, Evert, Theunissen, Liesbeth and Meffert, Martin, *Onder heide en akkers. De archeologie van noord-brabant tot 1200* (Utrecht, 2009).

Van Gorp, J., 'De aartbrief van terloo', *Bijdragen tot de geschiedenis* 18 (1927), pp. 437–54.

Vanhaute, Erik, 'De mutatie van de bezitsstructuur in kalmthout en meerle, 1834–1910', *Bijdragen tot de geschiedenis* 71, no. 1 (1988), pp. 173–80.

——, *De invloed van de groei van het industrieel kapitalisme en van de centrale staat op een agrarisch grensgebied: De noorderkempen in de 19de eeuw (1750–1910)* (Brussels, 1990).

Van Looveren, E., 'De privatisering van de gemeentegronden in de provincie antwerpen: Vier case-studies', *Bijdragen tot de geschiedenis* 66, no. 1 (1983), pp. 189–216.

Van Olmen, E. H. A., 'De keuren van vorselaar', *Taxandria* 7 (1910), pp. 35–49.

van Onacker, Eline and Masure, Hadewijch, 'Unity in diversity: Rural poor relief in the sixteenth-century southern Low Countries', *TSEG* 12, no. 4 (2015), pp. 59–88.

Van Rompaey, J., 'Het compositierecht in vlaanderen van de veertiende tot de achttiende eeuw', *Tijdschrift voor rechtsgeschiedenis* 44 (1961), pp. 43–79.

Van Uytven, R., 'Landen en 's hertogenbosch: De hoofdvaart', in Th. E. A. Bosman, E. J. M. F. C, Broers, B. C. M. Jacobs, F. W. M. de Koning-Klaassen and O. E. Tellegen-Couperus (eds), *Brabandts recht is . . . Opstellen aangeboden aan prof. Mr. J.Pa. Coopmans ter gelegenheid van zijn afscheid als hoogleraar nederlandse rechtsgeschiedenis aan de katholieke universiteit brabant* (Assen, 1990).

Van Uytven, R. and Blockmans, W., 'Constitutions and their application in the Netherlands during the middle ages', *Belgisch tijdschrift voor filologie en geschiedenis* 47, no. 2 (1969), pp. 399–424.

Van Weeren, René and De Moor, Tine, 'Controlling the commoners: Methods to prevent, detect, and punish free-riding on Dutch commons in the early modern period', *Agricultural History Review* 62, no. 2 (2014), pp. 256–77.

Van Zanden, Jan Luiten, 'The paradox of the Marks. The exploitation of commons in the eastern Netherlands, 1250–1850', *Agricultural History Review* 47 (1999), pp. 125–44.

Vera, Hein, 'Rechten op woeste gronden in de meierij van den bosch', *Post Factum. Jaarboek voor geschiedenis en Volkskunde* no. 1 (2009), pp. 267–76.

Verbist, F., *Costuymen van de hoofdrechtbank van zandhoven, uitgave 1664: Keuren en breuken, uitgave 1665* (Zandhoven, 2007).

Verboven, Hilde, Verheyen, Kris and Hermy, Martin, *Bos en hei in het land van turnhout (15de–19de eeuw). Een bijdrage tot de historische ecologie* (Leuven, 2004).

Verellen, J. R., 'Lakennijverheid en lakenhandel van herentals in de 14e, 15e en 16e eeuw', *Taxandria* 27, no. 3–4 (1955), pp. 118–80.

Verhaert, Alde, Annaert, Rica, Langohr, Roger, Cooremans, Brigitte, Gelorini, Vanessa, Bastiaens, Jan, Deforce, Koen, Ervynck, Anton and Desender, Konjev, 'Een inheems-romeinse begraafplaats te klein-ravels', *Archeologie in Vlaanderen* 8 (2001–02), pp. 165–218.

Verhoeven, P. J., 'Keuren van calmpthout', *Oudheid en Kunst* 3 (1907), pp. 45–6.

Verkooren, Alphonse, *Inventaire des chartes et cartulaires des duchés de brabant et de limbourg et des pays d'outre-meuse, I* (Brussels, 1961).

Vermoesen, Reinoud and De bie, Annelies, 'Boeren en hun relaties op het vlaamse platteland (1750–1800)', *Tijdschrift voor geschiedenis* 121 (2008), pp. 430–45.

Vervaet, Lies, 'Het brugse sint-janshospitaal en zijn grote hoevepachters in de 15e en 16e eeuw: Wederkerigheid en continuïteit in functie van voedselzekerheid', *Revue Belge de Philologie et d'Histoire* 90, no. 4 (2012), pp. 1121–54.

Vivier, Nadine, *Proprieté collective et identité communale: Les biens communaux en france, 1750–1914* (Paris, 1998).

Warde, Paul, 'Common rights and common lands in south west Germany, 1500–1800', in De Moor, Shaw-Taylor and Warde (eds), *Management of common land*, pp. 195–224.

Whyte, Nicola, *Inhabiting the landscape: Place, custom and memory, 1500–1800* (Oxford, 2009).

———, 'Contested pasts: Custom, conflict and landscape change in west Norfolk, *c.*1550–1650', in Hoyle (ed.), *Custom, improvement and the landscape*, pp. 101–26.

Winchester, Angus, *Harvest of the hills. Rural life in northern England and the Scottish borders, 1400–1700* (Edinburgh, 2000).

———, 'Upland commons in northern England', in De Moor, Shaw-Taylor and Warde (eds), *Management of common land*, pp. 33–58.

———, 'Common land in upland Britain: Tragic unsustainability or utopian community resource?' in Franz Bosbach, Jens-Ivo Engels and Fiona Watson (eds), *Umwelt und geschichte in deutchland und grossbritannien: environment and history in Britain and Germany* (Munich, 2006).

———, 'Statute and local custom: Village byelaws and the governance of common land in medieval and early-modern England', in B. Van Bavel and E. Thoen (eds), *Rural societies and environments at risk. Ecology, property rights and social organisation in fragile areas (middle ages—twentieth century)* (Turnhout, 2008).

Winchester, Angus J. L. and Straughton, Eleanor A., 'Stints and sustainability: Managing stock levels on common land in England, *c.*1600–2006', *Agricultural History Review* 58, no. 1 (2010), pp. 30–48.

Wintle, Ann, 'Luminescence dating of quaternary sediments—introduction', *Boreas* 4 (2008), pp. 469–70.

Unpublished Theses

Castel, Ilona, 'Late holocene aeolian drift sands in Drenthe (the Netherlands)' (Unpublished thesis, University of Utrecht, 1991).

Dahlström, Anna, 'Pastures livestock number and grazing pressure 1620–1850: Ecological aspects of grazing history in south-central Sweden' (Unpublished thesis, Swedish University of Agricultural Sciences, 2006).

De Keyzer, Maïka, 'The common denominator: The survival of the commons in the late medieval Campine area' (Unpublished thesis, University of Antwerp, 2014).

De Meester, Jan, 'Gastvrij antwerpen? Arbeidsmigratie naar het 16de-eeuwse antwerpen' (Unpublished thesis, University of Antwerp, 2011).

De Moor, Tine, ' "Tot proffijt van de ghemeensaemheijt": Gebruik, gebruikers en beheer van gemene gronden in zandig vlaanderen, 18de en 19de eeuw' (Unpublished thesis, University of Ghent, 2003).

Dombrecht, Kristof, 'Plattelandsgemeenschappen, lokale elites en ongelijkheid in het brugse vrije (14de–16de eeuw)' (Unpublished thesis, University of Ghent, 2014).

Heerman, Cedric, 'Het abdijdomein van de abdij van tongerlo in de 15de–16de eeuw (met speciale aandacht voor de pachthoeves van de abdij)' (Unpublished thesis, University of Ghent, 2003).

Luypaers, Caroline, ' "Le goût pour les spectacles est tellement devenu à la mode . . ." Spektakelcultuur in het achttiende-eeuwse antwerpen' (Unpublished thesis, Catholic University of Leuven, 2001).

Postgate, Malcolm Robert, 'Historical geography of Breckland, 1600–1850' (Unpublished MA thesis, University of London, 1960).

Van Dijck, Guido, 'Het landbouwleven in de antwerpse kempen volgens de dorpskeuren (speciaal de hoofdbank van zandhoven)' (Unpublished thesis, Catholic University of Leuven, 1965).

Van Onacker, Eline, 'Leaders of the pack? Village elites and social structures in the fifteenth and sixteenth-century Campine area' (Unpublished thesis, University of Antwerp, 2014).

Venner, Gerardus Hubertus Antonius, 'De meinweg, onderzoek naar de rechten op gemene gronden in het voormalig gelders—guliks grensgebied circa 1400–1822' (Unpublished thesis, Universiteity of Nijmegen, 1985).

Vera, Hein, '. . . Dat men het goed van den ongeboornen niet mag verkoopen: Gemene gronden in de meierij van den bosch tussen hertog en hertgang 1000–2000' (Unpublished thesis, Radboud University, 2011).

Unpublished Papers and Conference Presentations

Broers, Anna, 'Drift sand activity phases in northwest Europe' (unpublished paper, 2014).

Casari, Marco, 'Gender-biased inheritance systems are evolutionary stable: A case study in northern Italy in the xii–xix century' (unpublished seminar paper, Utrecht, 2010).

Espín-Sánchez, José-Antonio, 'Let the punishment fit the crime: Self-governed communities in southeastern Spain' (unpublished conference paper, *Design and Dynamics of Institutions for Collective Action*, Utrecht, 2012).

Panjek, Aleksander, 'Reclamation of commons in an integrated rural economy: Pre-industrial western Slovenia (an Alpine area)' (unpublished paper given at World Economic History Congress, Stellenbosch, 2012).

Thoen, Erik and Soens, Tim, 'Elévage, prés et paturage dans le comté de flandre au moyen age et au début des temps modernes: Les liens avec l'économie rurale régionale' (Paper presented at the Prés et pâtures en Europe occidentale: 28e journées internationales d'histoire de l'abbaye de Flaran, 2008).

Van Uytven, Raymond, 'Brabantse en antwerpse centrale plaatsen (14de-19de eeuw)' (Paper presented at the Het stedelijk netwerk ik België in historisch perspectief, 1350–1850, 1990).

Vermeesch, Griet, 'Explaining the "legal revolution" and the "great litigation decline". Processes of social change and changing litigation patterns in early modern Europe' (unpublished paper).

Index